Rupert Everett was born  at Ampleforth College, he was ~~~~~~~~~~~~~~ ool of Speech and Drama in London, but soon made a name for himself at the avant-garde Glasgow Citizens Theatre. In 1984 he found international fame following his lead role in *Another Country*, and has since appeared in many successful films, including *Shakespeare in Love*, *An Ideal Husband*, *The Madness of King George III*, *The Importance of Being Earnest*, *Dance with a Stranger*, *Prêt-à-Porter* and *My Best Friend's Wedding*.

'Everett's superb second volume of autobiography stands head and shoulders above the season's celeb memoirs ... With nobody left in Tinseltown to please, Everett unleashes himself as a hilarious, unsparingly bitchy chronicler of celebrity hell ... irresistible'
Sunday Times Books of the Year

'Five years ago, he published *Red Carpets and Other Banana Skins*, a deliciously irreverent account of his adventures in La-La land, one of the best recent theatrical memoirs. Now he's done it again ... Everett's eye for hilarious detail turns any elegy into a riot'
Robert McCrum, *Observer* Books of the Year

'Almost every sentence is worth savouring with one great anecdote after another ... a no-holds-barred memoir with everything a fan of the genre could wish for: humour, honesty, self-deprecation, sharp observation and his friend, Madonna'
Independent Books of the Year

'A major work, in which he savages a number of people but nobody as badly as himself'
Simon Callow, *Sunday Express*

'There's some gorgeous stuff here ... Everett is fearless when gossiping about A-listers in a book because he wants nothing from them – indeed, he might even see their shunning as a side benefit. Whatever, his loss is our gain – because, yes, seer or sidekick, most of all he is just a very good writer indeed'
Julie Burchill, *Observer*

'A rare blend of wistful lament, comic observation and opinionated mischief'
Decca Aitkenhead, *Guardian*

'Page after page echoes with the hissing sound of giant egos deflating, as Everett's friends and enemies (it is sometimes hard to tell them apart) are lined up in the crosshairs of his wit'
Daily Telegraph, ★★★★★

'He is brilliant at taking the reader on captivating journeys through the loops of his memory ... his sentences glisten with intelligence and at the heart of this book are profound, stirring meditations on human growth and loss'
Express

'Irresistible ... a hugely entertaining and affecting book'
Irish Times

'[An] instant classic ... a complex mixture of impassioned nostalgia, self-criticism, risky candour and deadpan amusement. I have never read a theatre autobiography that made me laugh and smile so much in appreciative delight'
Nicholas de Jongh, *Independent*

'A winning combination of celebrity scandal, sentimental journey and shrewd self-awareness'
Vogue

Also by Rupert Everett

Fiction

HELLO DARLING, ARE YOU WORKING?

THE HAIRDRESSERS OF ST TROPEZ

Non-fiction

RED CARPETS AND OTHER BANANA SKINS

Vanished Years

RUPERT EVERETT

ABACUS

First published in Great Britain in 2012 by Little, Brown
Reprinted 2012 (four times)
This paperback edition published in 2013 by Abacus
Reprinted 2013 (three times), 2014

A CIP catalogue record for this book
is available from the British Library.

ISBN 978-0-349-00023-7

Typeset in Electra by M Rules
Printed and bound in Great Britain by
Clays Ltd, St Ives plc

Papers used by Abacus are from well-managed forests
and other responsible sources.

MIX
Paper from
responsible sources
FSC® C104740

Abacus
An imprint of
Little, Brown Book Group
100 Victoria Embankment
London EC4Y 0DY

An Hachette UK Company
www.hachette.co.uk

www.littlebrown.co.uk

For my father

Contents

PROLOGUE

CHAPTER ONE

A Short Story

I am sitting on a bench in a run-down park on the side of a hill over-looking the port of Ocho Rios in Jamaica. Far below, a giant cruise ship moves from the harbour out to sea. It is like a block of flats. Clockwork people wave from its decks in pretty colours. The blast of its horn bounces off the hills as it accelerates as fast as a car into the blue. In a matter of minutes this tub crammed with life – four thousand loved ones, shitting and pissing and complaining – is on the edge of the horizon. Soon it is a dot. Then nothing, engulfed in the flaming edge of dusk. It is quite romantic and slightly depressing – the perfect combination.

The noise of the town is a distant hum. Turtle-doves moan and flap in the trees and the shadows grow long over a derelict hotel, boarded up, pink and white, on the hill above me. Its terraces have been reclaimed by nature. In the old colonial days this used to be its garden. A waterfall cascades down a cliff into a series of pools filled with gigantic bleached goldfish that stare at you with vacant mulatto eyes from just beneath the surface, presided over by a vast banyan tree. Under its branches, butterflies flit in and out of the dim beams of the sinking sun. The occasional splosh is their death knell. A few gardeners move through the park, dressed in blue dungarees. They don't seem to be doing much, but Jamaica is a lazy place locked in slow motion.

Two women appear at the top of the hill and walk carefully down the path towards the pools and the tree. They are an odd couple. One is a sturdy brunette squeezed into a black mini dress. It barely covers her arse. She has a large nose and drooping eyes and speaks English with a Jamaican lilt. She could be black. She could be white. Actually she could be Jordanian. Her friend is like a baby sparrow that has fallen from its nest, slightly disorientated as she hops from step to step down the hazardous path in Uggs and a track-suit.

They are white, ageless and slightly chavvy. They look as if they might have been sleeping rough. Or perhaps they are from the cruise ships and have simply missed the boat and are now living in the bushes. Either way, they sit down and both light up cigarettes, which they suck at thoughtfully while contemplating the view and the next move.

'I got Demerol,' says the larger one finally.

'Doesn't work for me,' replies the little sparrow curtly. She has a gravelly Viennese accent with a Thames Estuary undertow. She is mildly bad tempered. 'What are we gonna do?'

'Drive to Montego Bay, I suppose. What else can we do?'

'All the way to Montego Bay for a fucking prescription? You gotta be kidding.'

'Barbiturates she said! You need a special form. A papal fucking dispensation.'

They have arrived at some kind of impasse, returning their attention to the view with two co-ordinated huffs, followed by another cigarette. One has the pack. The other has the lighter. It's a Busby Berkeley routine of hands and mouths, of leaning in and lighting up and leaning back, and they are suddenly – comically – engulfed in smoke.

'Steve has Percocet,' says the brunette drearily, a sudden thought, barely energised as the fog lifts.

'Percocet! Vicodin! Demerol! I told you. Morphine doesn't agree with me. I need codeine.' The little bird would be furious now if she had the energy. She is a strange creature, beautiful and graceful despite her moon boots. Her eyes are fierce and black for a moment but then she cocks her head to one side and chuckles. 'I haven't heard that word for years.'

'What word?'

'Barbiturates. It's quite *Valley of the Dolls*, isn't it?' She speaks like a child, trustingly, with no filter, and she reminds me of someone, but I can't think who.

I get up and walk towards them.

'I couldn't help overhearing what you were saying,' I say politely.

'My God,' snorts the nose, deeply put out. She hurls a protective sausage of an arm around the little bird's bony shoulder.

'But I happen to have some Tramadol near by, if you would like some.'

They stare at me aghast for a moment, and then the bird breaks into a dazzling smile. 'I'm afraid Tramadol doesn't suit me. As you probably heard, I am allergic to morphine.'

'It was just a thought.'

'Are you from one of the ships?' asks the little bird.

'Good lord, no.' It is my turn to be shocked.

'You staying at the inn?' accuses the nose.

'Yes, I am.'

'Did you get lost? No one from the inn comes up here.'

'I was searching for a house.'

They both look bewildered, and so I explain. It's a long pointless story and their attention dims with the day.

'It's called Honeycomb. I thought it was on this street.'

'Honeycomb?' sneers the nose. 'Who lives there?'

'No one. A friend's godparents lived there after the war. When I said I was coming, he showed me a postcard of it. It looked rather sweet. I thought it might be fun to see if it was still there.'

I have a crotchety friend in London called Bob. Over the years he has occasionally talked about his rather ghastly godparents called John and Joyce. They moved to Jamaica in the fifties and came home every summer on a boat, regaling Bob's mother with tales of Caribbean horror – how the local shopkeeper called Joyce an evil white bitch (she was, actually), how Noël Coward once came for drinks and then was overheard saying that if he ever saw them again he was moving to St Lucia. How Bob always thought that with enough sucking up they might leave the house to him. (No such luck.) John died, and Joyce sold up and moved to the South Coast of England. Death in Bournemouth. In our friendship they became a byword for everything that was stuck-up and conventional. 'It was a bit John and Joyce, dear,' Bob once said after a rather dreary performance of mine in a Jacobean tragedy, and the phrase stuck.

A few weeks ago, at lunch, I tell Bob that I am going to Ocho Rios, and he digs out letters and a picture of their pretty colonial bungalow called Honeycomb. We have a laugh and think no more about it. But arriving in Jamaica, desperately searching for a reasonable excuse not to start work on the book I am writing, I suddenly remember. Honeycomb! What a marvellous idea. Bob will love it if I manage to track it down. I ring him up and ask for directions. He is not particularly amused.

'God, you must be bored, dear.'

'Not bored. Desperate.'

So I have spent two fruitless days scouring the hills, high on ganja. Now I have arrived at the end of the road – literally – and the gates of this run-down park.

'This place is a tip since the cruise ships came,' says the little bird at the end of my tale.

'So it's probably been knocked down.'

'Unless it's that strip joint with the dwarf,' suggests the nose.

'God. Where's that?'

'You want to go?' asks the bird, brightening.

'Not really.'

'It doesn't really get started until after midnight.'

'Oh. I'm in bed by then.'

'Me too.'

Silence. The nose's cellphone rings and she begins a long conversation in patois.

'Do you want to have a walk around the garden?' suggests the bird.

'I'd love to.'

We potter slowly around the park, through its collapsed arbours and overgrown pathways. I feel as if I have known this woman in a past life. We chat pleasantly, tipsy with anonymity, revealing too much. She must be at least sixty but she acts like a little girl. Her face is deeply lined, but her eyes sparkle and her smile is radiant. She knows the names of all the trees, and picks their leaves, crushing them in her fingers.

'Smell this.'

'Delicious.'

'I can't think where that pimento tree went. It was here yesterday.' She is stooping – looking at the ground for clues.

'Over here!' shouts her friend from another part of the garden, laughing. 'She can't remember anything!'

'Oh yes. That's where it's gone.' The little bird hops over.

It is dusk and we are back at the edge of the park.

'I'm Anita, by the way,' says the bird.

'Rupert.'

'See you at the inn maybe. We swim there sometimes.'

And I get into my car and drive back to the hotel.

Later, I am sitting in the empty bar of the hotel nursing a second rum punch, staring vacantly at the view. The moon and the first stars are sliding up the dimming sky. The cocktail chatter, a tinkling piano and the distant slap of the waves against the beach are more cheap wine to my doused senses and something clicks in my head.

'Anita Pallenberg,' I say out loud. Someone is walking on my grave.

*

Flashback. A bus groans up a misty hill onto the North Yorkshire moors. It is a dismal Saturday afternoon in 1973. I am sitting at the back with three other boys from my school, Brock, Elliot and Wynton. We are out of bounds and are trying to blend in, but our plummy accents set us apart from the other travellers – grim Yorkshire housewives in heavy coats and scarves, sitting like giant chickens among their shopping bags. The outside world is shrouded in a thick mist, so that one can see only the road, the stone walls either side and the silhouettes of nearby trees in the milky space, until we come upon a village, first one cottage, then another and then a little high street of grey doll's houses looms at us through the haze. With stifled giggles and beating hearts we cower in our seats. We must not be discovered.

The bus grinds to a halt in front of the post office, and we hold our breath as two monks – teachers from our school – appear through the mist, majestic in their black winding sheets, arms folded inside, deep in conversation. Monks don't walk, they hover, and for a horrible moment it looks as though they are going to hover on to the bus, but at the last moment they turn into the pub. Christ's mission is thirsty work. The door slams shut and the bus strains back onto the open road. We boys sigh dramatically with relief. A snaggle-toothed lady in front of us turns round.

'Tha' were looky.' She winks a pouchy eye.

'Wasn't it?' agrees Wynton, somewhat frostily.

As we hit the open country we all light cigarettes and relax. Friendships are intense and uncomplicated when you are a child. They begin and end in a moment, but for the time being, me, Brock, Elliot and Wynton live in each other's pockets. We are an offbeat gang, living fully and without fear because the future is as misty as the view from the bus. We are fourteen years old, obsessed by sex and rebellion, and have discovered an exotic cinema in York, which enables us to indulge both of these delicious new pleasures at the same time. It's a run-down music hall with a circle and a balcony – scattered with a mélange of flashers, bonking couples and art-house freaks (such as there are in York), showing X-rated films and soft porn. The red velvet seats are spattered with cigarette burns and the whole place smells of that delicate blend of smoke, sweat and semen, with an added note of carbolic wafting from the toilets – the signature fragrance of the British provincial fleapit. In the alley running along one side of the theatre is a fire escape with a broken door.

Last week we watched a film called *Black Snake* starring our favourite wank material Anouska (née Hempel, now Lady Weinberg). Elliot claims to have come fourteen times under his anorak watching her. The rest of us are sceptical. However, we have just discovered orgasm and we practise achieving it religiously in our cubicles, day and night, kneeling before our stupas to Anouska and other Blessed Virgins. We have not yet learnt to be secretive about sex. Wanking is still innocent, a gentleman's pursuit. I am already conducting clandestine homosexual experiments in the classics room, but this is another me, coiled and complicated, and I have learnt to ignore him. He is completely effaced in the present company and I shall be wanking as hard as the others under my anorak during the famous sex scene in *Performance* – the most scandalous and amoral film of the decade, according to Fr Martin in the Art Room.

In York we skulk around the streets biding our time. Being out of bounds – particularly as far away as York – is living dangerously and we face 'rustication' if caught. We take every corner like an army manoeuvre, arriving at the swing doors into the alley at exactly the right moment. As the last show's audience dribbles out, we slip through the gate and run up the fire escape, heading straight for the loos where we hide until the next show starts. For about half an hour we whisper and giggle in our cubicles, dissecting the usual schoolboy issues, the holidays, the people who are pissing us off, looking at the usual pictures of hairy splayed vaginas and cocks shooting sperm. The cistern drips and the occasional man comes in to relieve himself, his footsteps scratching against the concrete floor. At the familiar sound of the Pearl & Dean anthem, we creep from the loo into the theatre. We do not sit together. It's a rule. If one of us is caught, we meet at the bus stop later.

The film begins. The voices echo through the darkness from the clapped-out sound system. The stalls are half full. Smoke curls up to the gods from a hundred glowing cigarettes smoked listlessly by ghostly faces intent on the action. The usherette weaves down the aisle with her torch, a busty silhouette in front of the huge screen. I get comfortable with my anorak and open my flies and a glorious feeling of freedom shimmers through my body.

How I love *Performance*. Coming from a solid background of *Reach for the Sky*, *The Sound of Music* and recently *All About Eve*, shunted between a Georgian rectory and a freezing dormitory, with its bells, times for meals, respect for one's elders, tame children's parties, hunting, stalking and stockbroking, confession and communion, it has never crossed my mind that people like Mick Jagger and Anita Pallenberg could possibly exist. When James Fox – dazzling as the hit man Chas – walks into their house in Notting Hill, my world stands still.

I completely forget about wanking.

The place itself amazes me. Within the familiar architectural confines of a decaying London mansion, the fuck pad of a down-at-heel Tangier queen has been conjured up, with a dash of Dracula thrown in. I have never seen a place like this. It is the magic island of an androgynous Prospero, decorated with Hammond organs and loudspeakers like upright coffins, afghan rugs and Moroccan cushions, lit by candles and Tiffany lamps.

Fifteen feet high, Anita – naked under a fur coat, with a Super-8 camera rather than a handbag – stalks into a darkened room with a heavily draped bed where two people sleep in one another's arms. Are they men or women? It is hard to tell. (Mick Jagger's teats look as tugged as a Jersey cow's.) Anita stumbles across the huge bed and straddles the sleeping beauties, tweaking a nipple here and licking a giant lip there, before dropping her coat to reveal a lithe boy's body. Roused and aroused, they all begin to fuck – still half asleep – their bodies merging into one another until you can't tell who's doing what to who. Mick pulls the covers over them. In the tent underneath the *partouze* rolls on. Anita rubs coke on her teeth with her finger and for a second she looks rabid and dangerous. They stroke and squeeze and mount one another, until Anita finally emerges from the sea of soiled sheets exhausted. It is the first full-on sex scene I have ever watched.

Looking across the stalls, I can see that the others are already hard at it, shuddering like washing machines on full spin, but I am in shock and have forgotten to start. These three androgynous beauties are what I want to be, how I want to live. Everything these characters do seems to be incredibly important, intensely real, not like conventional acting. I am spellbound by Mick's face, his gigantic flesh-eating lips, the rows of teeth, the enormous dog's tongue, made for licking things out, the eyes caked in kohl, glimmering with scag, not that I have the first idea what all these things are yet. I just know instinctively that they've got my name written on them. Anita is staggeringly beautiful and her smile lights up the screen in a new way. I don't know who I want to be more. Him or Her. They are characters from a fairy story. Anita gives a big magic mushroom to James, nuzzling his ear, and whispering in a breathless European lilt, well mannered, to the manor born but a big slut at the same time, 'Can't you stay one more day?'

I am in heaven. I don't know why. I don't even know what a magic mushroom is. I am completely gobsmacked. *Performance* is the closing door through which I bolt and now – quite suddenly – the whole of my world is a question mark. On the bus drive back to school nothing looks the same, not even Brock and Elliot and Wynton. They hated the film. Elliot only came once. Our friendships cool from this day on, and I am out of that cloister of black beetles and rugger buggers within six months.

The inn is a blue and white colonial hotel built into the hill above a small bay a couple of miles outside Ocho Rios. Its beautiful gardens slope down to the beach. There is a croquet lawn with an old roller parked next to it. The sea splashes gently onto the beach and amazing birds – herons, egrets and pink doves – fly from one side of the rocky cove to the other, breathtaking silhouettes against the sky spattered with fluffy clouds.

Mary is the manager of the hotel. She is a white Jamaican lady, extremely thin, dressed to the nines each night, a pirate queen in couture, with two spaniels at her feet. She runs the place as if it were her own home – a benign dictatorship where her rule of law extends to the guests who worship her. They are an eccentric group of upper-class English couples who flock to this time warp like birds to an oasis at sunset. Folded in among them are some old-school Americans, a reclusive model and her boyfriend, and, last week, the Archbishop of York in a kaftan. It is a delightful place, full of surprises, an old photograph come to life. Jackets are worn at night and a band plays oldie hits and comfortable reggae while the guests dine and dance cheek to cheek among the tables.

I never find Honeycomb. All trace of John and Joyce has been swept away. Instead I have strangely – uncannily – found myself. The chance encounter with Anita shines a new light on old times. Sloshed on a deckchair, looking out to sea, feeling rather dramatic, it occurs to me that in fact my childhood went down without a trace that afternoon in York. *Performance* was the iceberg. Within a year (it takes a long time to sink a middle-class Catholic upbringing) I had thrown myself into a life of excess on the seabed. Within three I had constructed a new world for myself – or underworld – in similar darkened rooms and dank basements, and if my budget extended only to lava lamps, beanbags and Indian prints from Barker's Bargain Basement, then those economies were largely written off by an excess of sexual ambiguity and mind-bending chemicals. The contract I later forged with show business – to disastrous effect and a risible blindness: the National Theatre was not a Nic Roeg film after all – was directly inspired by the image of these people: Mick, Anita and Michelle Breton, the third wheel of the act, living outside the law and writing their own constitution. 'Sister Morphine' was my theme tune, and I dreamt of being arrested as much as awarded.

Even now the impact of that crash with *Performance* echoes through my life. My flat is still Moroccan Baroque, and now Anita, the ultimate goddess of my youth, has risen from the sea in wellington boots and a tracksuit, as unrecognisable as the resurrected Jesus on the Sea of Tiberias. The penny has dropped too late. The days turn to weeks but I have no further visions although she has been constantly on my mind.

It is strange meeting famous people. One knows so much about them. Alone at dinner one night I suddenly remember that she shot a young man.

'No, darling,' says Bob on the telephone the next day. (Apart from being John and Joyce's godson, he is an expert on anything concerning the sixties.) 'He shot himself. It was *her* gun. She had taken a room in Claridge's and no one could get her out.'

'She sounds fabulous.'

'Deranged, actually.'

In his book Keith Richards describes a summer dawn – or dusk, I can't remember which – in the sixties: he and Anita in a sports car screeching round hairpin bends through clouds of orange blossom in the hills above the coast of Spain. Keith is steering. Anita is sucking him off. The car roars and brakes, grinding through its gears as Anita drives Keith to distraction. 'You don't know what a blow job is until you have had one from Anita Pallenberg,' he writes. With word of mouth like that, who needs a publicist?

It is the last afternoon. Tomorrow I am moving further along the island. It is nearly dusk, that moment on a beach when colours intensify. Anita is walking into the ocean in a red bikini. She splashes at the water, suddenly disappears and surfaces some distance off, standing again, looking out to sea, pushing the hair from her face with both hands. She is a young girl again. She sees me and waves.

'Where have you been?' I shout, accusingly.

'Here.'

'I'm leaving tomorrow for Firefly.'

'From Honeycomb to Firefly. What are you? An elf?'

She comes out of the water, tottering slightly as she is carried by a wave onto the beach. She sits down, dripping, suddenly ancient.

'I've had so much to do up at the house. Can't you stay one more day?'

The same line years later, a different *Performance*. Maybe I should write a short story. A travelling player with broadening hips and a femme fatale from the sixties marooned in a colonial hotel at the end of the world. Complete strangers. Destination unknown. She is wise and childlike. He is foolish and complicated. Both have a shadowy past. Her nerve endings have shrivelled and died in those shadows – hence the codeine. He has lost his nerve coming out of them.

'How's your book going?'

'It isn't. Actually I might start with a short story about you looking for the missing pimento tree in the park.'

Anita laughs. 'A very short story.'

The setting sun plays tricks. For a moment it shines directly at her, throwing razor-thin shadows along every line of her face. Suddenly she is the dark witch of legend, the evil beauty whose terrible deeds I have heard of for as long as I can remember. It's just for a moment. The world rolls over, the shadows deepen and her smile cuts through them as a good-looking waiter with a gold watch and a tight white shirt arrives with a coconut. He gives it to her and she is a child again. He is extremely flirtatious. I am impressed.

'You've still got it, Anita.'

I laugh as we watch his tight arse walk back up to the hotel, dragging a long shadow behind it across the lawn.

'Not bad for nearly seventy, eh?'

We chat on as the night draws in – old friends catching up after a lifetime, although in fact we have hardly met. Anita is a blonde Buddha, open and empty, affectionate and humorous. She expresses no rancour for the past, nor expectation for the future, beyond the desire never to winter in England again, if she can help it. She has survived with dignity, on her own terms. Once she was at the epicentre of an exploding universe. Now she is a solitary diamond flickering in the night sky. As the light falls from her face it seems to me that she is changing again, ebbing with it, almost invisible as life reduces to a single point in the darkness. The water behind her is blood red for a minute. The stars appear one by one as the last orange squiggle melts into the sea and we are silent as the same thought hits us both. It is extraordinary just to be here.

Anita is still my ideal. Tomorrow I will begin my book.

CHAPTER TWO

An Escort Called Joe

I am sitting at the bar. I am leaving early tomorrow. A man in pink trousers with a matching face introduces me to his wife. Next season I should really get a job playing the piano here. It would be the perfect end. We discuss various films I have or have not made. They are sweet and old-fashioned, extremely courteous.

'Bad show about *The Apprentice*,' he says expansively, as they get up to leave.

'What do you mean?' I can't think what he is talking about.

'Walking out like that. We were watching.'

'Oh. I see. Yes. Wasn't it awful.'

'It showed a complete lack of moral fibre.' His wife tries to pull him away.

'Come on, darling.'

'It couldn't have been *that* bad?' He beams ferociously.

'You had to be there.'

He sits down again. I groan inwardly.

'Do tell us about it. Dorothy adores Piers Morgan.'

*

I am sitting at a table in a sumptuous hotel suite with three men. I do not know them but we are straining every nerve to connect because we're a team, taking part in a reality TV show for charity. Circling us silently, like sharks, are three figures with cameras. Their lenses scrutinise us – weird glassy black holes that we try to ignore, dilating as one of us says something funny, coming in close so that our skins shiver. They feel like living creatures, these cameras, while their operators are possessed drones and our brains go into a performance overdrive for their sake. Cables are held by obedient vassals. They are fed with care through doors into other rooms where banks of winking computers have replaced beds and the action next door is compressed into TV screens standing one on top of another. Production assistants watch intensely, making notes on clipboards and whispering to each other. The air throbs with a vibration I have not sensed since leaving boarding school at the age of fifteen.

Why am I here? A complicated question that may take a little time and some soul searching to answer. There is a lady named Emma Freud. She is married to a man called Richard Curtis. He is the wunderkind of the British film business. Curtis, for anyone who doesn't know, is to Blair's Britain what Leni Riefenstahl was to Hitler's Germany, and *Notting Hill*, a film he wrote and produced, was the silver-screen face of Cool Britannia. A grim, lifeless romantic comedy about 'the special relationship' between Julia Roberts and Hugh Grant. But already I digress. Focus.

Richard Curtis's life is a movie (*Richard Actually*) and Emma is his perfectly cast cohort. Impeccably connected, she is the daughter of Clement Freud, the niece of Lucien and the great-granddaughter of Sigmund. Her brother is the official diabolical nuncio Matthew Freud, himself gastrologically aligned for power, married as he is to the daughter of Rupert Murdoch, our recently deposed puppet master, and all these people live very close to power. Emma knows all the backstairs routes that connect number ten with number eleven. (I know only routes between numbers one and two. And not

Downing Street.) These people have always avoided me, as I have them.

A few years earlier, Robbie Williams asked me to compère his swing concert at the Albert Hall, and sing with him the track we had recorded together. It sounded like fun. Richard Curtis was the director. It sounded even better. Richard was preparing *Love Actually* at the time. My brain went into overdrive. Maybe during the Robbie rehearsals I could grab the leading role from the jaws of Hugh Grant. Yes, I would be more amusing, more debonair, so deep that Richard would turn to Emma in bed one night and say: 'I think I've had enough of Hugh. Rupert will be my new muse.'

Well, at first it all went according to plan. I sat with Richard and Emma during rehearsals. There wasn't much directing to do. Robbie was a one-man band. He knew how to work a crowd, and at the Albert Hall concert he reached his zenith. We all just sat around, waiting for our turn to be sucked dry by his hoover-like magnetism. Richard wrote my part, and we had a little rehearsal. The show was a great success. The BBC got a record number of complaints, which is always the sign of a hit. After the show, Richard came into my dressing room.

'You were absolutely marvellous,' he said.

'Thanks, Richard,' I replied, pinching myself just to make sure I wasn't dreaming. Was it all going to work out as I had planned? 'I hope we see each other soon,' I ventured hopefully.

'Yes, that would be lovely. Here. Let me give you my number.'

Orgasm. Images of renewed Hollywood stardom burst across my brain like fireworks. 'And the winner is ... Rupert Everett for *Love Actually*.' I could hear the applause.

Unfortunately, a party of hags and swamp bitches had congregated in my dressing room and were all dangerously drunk. One of them, drunker than the rest, was the director John Maybury, a friend of mine from the dawn of time. He lurched towards us, his blue eyes glittering dangerously, and thrust his face in between Richard and me.

'This is my friend John Maybury,' I stammered, smelling trouble and alcohol on the same breath.

The room suddenly turned silent. I looked round. John's boyfriend Baillie was looking at me with a frightful grimace, arms outstretched. Everyone else – Princess Julia, Antony Price, Huge Crack, Les Childs and Connie, my PR – stood and gaped. It must feel like this on a beach momentarily drained of sea before the onslaught of a tsunami.

'Oh, hello, John,' said Richard, pleasantly. 'I did so enjoy *Love Is the Devil*.'

John thought for a moment and cracked a smile as huge as the Cheshire cat's. He had a big famous mouth in more ways than one.

'Why, thank you, Richard,' he replied. 'But look at your own achievements. You have single-handedly destroyed British cinema.'

'Aw my gawd!' muttered Princess Julia, but otherwise silence.

Richard's pupils dilated slightly, and the tip of his nose flushed. I broke into a sweat.

All I could see were eyes. John's were bloodshot fried eggs and Richard's were narrow and icy, like a ferret's. Mine were enormous and about to pop out of their sockets and roll across the floor. John took a generous gulp from his glass and waited for the ball to be lobbed back, with the same killer smile cutting his face (one of them) in half, but Richard just looked at his watch.

'Well, let's be in touch. All the best.' And he left the room.

Needless to say, I did not get a part in *Love Actually* or anything else actually, then or since.

So when Emma Freud called me and asked me to take part in a charity version of *The Apprentice*, I should have just said *no*. But I didn't. I never can.

'When is it?' I asked lamely.

'Not for a couple of months. There is a task,' explained Emma on the phone, 'and it's *made* for you. It'll be a doddle. Only four days' work.'

Four days in two months' time was a dot on the horizon, and I said yes. I didn't have a television and had never even seen *The Apprentice*, but I imagined it was something along the same lines as *The Avengers*, so I gurgled encouragingly back down the line and thought no more about it, hoping I'd get the Purdey role. I should have asked, what kind of task would be a doddle? What is a doddle in the Curtis–Freud world? But I put down the phone and thought no more about it.

The day before the show was due to begin, a lady telephoned and told me to pack enough clothes for four nights away.

'But I'm not going away,' I said.

'They want all the teams to stay together during the task.'

Teams?

'Oh well, I can't. I have to go home to my own bed.' Silence. God, I remember thinking, I've always hated Red Nose Day, and now this . . .

The next evening a car came with the same lady inside to collect me and take me to the secret venue where I was to meet with the rest of my team, and the other team, and, of course, Alan Sugar.

'Who on earth is Alan Sugar?' I laughed, intrigued.

'You don't know Alan Sugar?'

'No, I don't. Is he a singer?'

'No. He is the star of *The Apprentice*.'

'Aha,' I said knowingly.

It was just before Christmas. People tumbled about the streets in Santa hats, drunk from the office party. Soon we left the West End behind, then west London. Where the fuck were we going? Finally we arrived at a kind of disused warehouse, where there were a lot of other cars and vans, and more official-looking ladies bundled up against the cold, breathing smoke, waving clipboards and screaming red-carpet jangles into their walkie-talkies.

'Copy that. Go for Ginger. I have Mr Everett.'

I was taken into a dimly lit scene dock where twelve celebrities were gathered in the gloom. The walls were black and it felt like being in a gigantic aquarium. Cameramen circled the stars like sharks around bloody meat, pilot fish at their shoulders, expression-less lads holding mini lamps, which were shone on the weird pasty faces of our favourite dishes. There was a gnawing tension in the air as everyone tried to acclimatise themselves to the cameras. The women's team were huddled together, and I wished I was one of them. Susannah Constantine, Cheryl Cole and Jo Brand. They were acting normal, heightened, slightly hysterical, but to anyone in the know their eyes gave them away, momentarily swivelling round, looking for the familiar things: the bar, the PR, the way out. They carried suitcases and seemed to have barricaded themselves behind them against the onslaught of the male team who were circling with the cameramen, trying to get some juicy dialogue going for the show.

This team of men, this band of brothers, glistened with testosterone in the spotlights. It oozed from their every pore like sap and froze me to the marrow. Alastair Campbell, Piers Morgan and Ross Kemp had their suitcases in their hands as if they were getting on the school train. In fact the whole thing reminded me of school. Here were the same rugger buggers and bullies I had escaped all those years ago, wearing the same slouchy sixth-form clothes. I could think of one thing only. Escape.

Emma Freud sidled up to me, and I had to restrain myself from breaking her neck. A camera swept in with her.

'So you know the task?' she giggled. 'Everyone else does.'

'No. No one told me.' My eyes were about to pop out. I had to send a message to my eyelids.

'You're going to love it.'

'Am I? Are you sure?'

'Yes. It's made for you.'

Now Piers Morgan emerged from the depths towards me.

'You've got to call Madonna,' he boomed. 'What's her number?' He got his cellphone out ready to dial.

At the word Madonna, the camera lens dilated and looked at me questioningly.

'Madonna,' I blundered. 'I don't know if I have her number.'

'Course you do. Where's your phone?'

Piers was definitely not afraid of the camera. He had been itching to get in front of it for years. This may have been a charity event but it was also a diving board. He was going to bellyflop into the water and splash around until he got what he wanted. (*American Idol* followed by the Parkinson slot.)

'Come on!' he said.

'Well, she's not really talking to me at the moment,' I said, looking guiltily at the camera.

'Ah!' mimicked Piers unpleasantly. 'Where's your phone?'

I produced my battered old Nokia with the smashed screen, and waved it hopelessly.

'What am I going to tell her?'

'She's got to give us a lot of money.'

'She won't like that.' I started scrolling.

Piers looked at me. He was about to speak when our camera spied something more interesting across the room and shot away. The lights snapped off. The scene was over. Piers swam off.

I went over to talk to the girls.

'God, I wish I was on your team,' I said.

'I know. Poor you,' said Jo.

'Are we all meant to stay the night together?'

'Yes. In some hotel.'

'I didn't bring any things,' I whined. I was turning into clingy desperate me. Ugh.

The hospitality girls arranged us in a line and gave us each a cue to go into the next room where apparently Alan Sugar was waiting for us like the Wizard of Oz. One by one our names were called out and we mounted the scaffold.

'Have a fabulous time,' said Emma, blowing a kiss, as my name was called out.

Imagine my surprise when I saw Sid James sitting on one side of a large table.

'Isn't that ...?' I whispered to Piers.

'That's Alan Sugar,' Piers replied in a worshipful murmur.

Our two teams sat opposite him. Sid was flanked by Hattie Jacques and some other *Carry On* character. Both flunkeys regarded us severely.

Alan introduced himself to each of us, with that blunt insolence peculiar to all barrow-boy billionaires. I suppose this was all part of the fun. He laid into poor Jo Brand for being too fat. She couldn't have cared less, rummaged in her bag and extracted a giant bar of Fruit and Nut and threw it at him. It was water off a duck's back to Jo, but Ross Kemp was slightly more sensitive. Sid made some unpleasant remarks about Ross's recent divorce. They dripped with innuendo. It was all way above my head.

'What's this all about?' I whispered to Piers.

'Apparently Rebekah his wife found him in bed with someone. The police had to be called in to pull them apart.'

'What? Ross and the someone? Had they got stuck?'

'No. Ross and Rebekah, you idiot.'

Rebekah, incidentally, was the editor-in-chief of the *Sun* newspaper. It was a juicy scandal. After a few minutes of Sid's grilling Ross went purple.

This rough-diamond aggression was Alan Sugar's trademark, and he worked it to the hilt. It was a strangely Vaudeville performance, and weird too, because in contrast to the blunt insults that came from his mouth, he had the sad hangdog eyes of a St Bernard under a troubled brow. He was quite vain, and a little girl popped up from under the table to adjust the hair that was like beige haircord and powder down the klaxon nose. He was a postmodern clown, tragic and angry, and *The Apprentice* was this year's Big Top. His delivery was sheer Sid James. They could have been twins.

In fact, I am not at all sure, to this day, that the whole Lord Sugar phenomenon is not one great big heist. Maybe the whole *Carry On* team have been made Labour peers without us knowing it. Barbara, Duchess of Windsor. Anyway, whether he was Alan or Sid, he was pretty unpleasant to everyone, and if that wasn't enough for one day, he then explained the task. We were to organise a giant funfair for one thousand celebrities that was to take place in three days. We had to raise a certain amount of money, and each group had to set up sideshows, bars and hot-dog stands, parking, security, publicity, everything.

My heart sank. It was the week before Christmas! The one week in the whole year when everybody has plans for every minute of every day. *Nobody* is sitting around during the week before Christmas doing nothing, and *if* they are, then the last thing they want to do is go to yet another Red Nose Day event in the freezing cold where they have to lay out a whole lot more cash than they have already spent, satiating their starving chicks on the Christmas orgy. It seemed ludicrous.

I looked for signs of fatigue among the other contestants but their smiles were glued on, except for Ross Kemp who was fuming.

'Any questions?' growled Sid James. No one answered. 'Then good luck. Enjoy yourselves.'

We were dismissed and taken to a bar to get to know each other. I sat on a couch in the corner with a glass of wine and wished I was dead. This was a nightmare.

Actually it was a dream come true. Ever since I can remember, I have had a recurring dream about being sent back to boarding school. Sometimes I am packing my trunk. At others I am arriving in my dormitory, or going in to school prayers. Everybody whispers as I walk by, because I am not a child in these dreams. I am the person I am on the day of the dream, so usually I am a famous movie star. Sometimes I am going to a première in my school cap and shorts. I can't take them off because I might be spanked. (Wet dream.) Sometimes I am late for a performance in the theatre in London because I am brushing my teeth at a row of sinks, ludicrous in dressing gown and slippers, in a crowd of tiny boys. (Anxiety dream.) Or sometimes I am on the skids and am sent back to school by my agent. (Realistic dream.) No matter how much I try to explain that I shouldn't be there, that I have to leave, no one listens. They look right through me because they can see only a small boy acting up.

'But Mummy, I'm famous now.'

'I know, darling. Isn't that super?'

How can I go and live in a dormitory with other boys?

'You're boring me now, darling! Pull yourself together. You'll love it when you get there.'

Dreams do come true. This was the first day of school. There were the big boys, with their untucked shirts and terrifying testosterone levels, the friendly matrons and misses, sympathetic but distant, and finally, appearing out of nowhere, everyone's hero, our very own scoutmaster, Mr Curtis.

'Gather round, everyone!' he said.

'Hooray!' we all roared. We jostled in, eager scouts and cubs. Richard was rather like a big blond schoolboy, a white rat. He had that confidence one loves in the school's most popular prefect.

'Sir. Sir. Sir.'

We all put up our hands in worship, hoping for a nod, a wink, a wank even.

'Now you all know the form,' he continued, arms akimbo. Only his toggle was missing. 'It's going to be tough. But a lot of fun, I think. I believe you're going to the hotel now, and the sooner you all get started the better. There's a lot of work to do. Any questions?'

'Yes. I have one,' drawled Jo Brand. 'Couldn't we just click our fingers like they did in Los Angeles?'

Polite giggles. Mr Curtis threw back his head and laughed.

'No, Jo, we can't!' he said.

I wanted to ask when dinner was, but didn't dare.

'Well, good luck everyone. Have a smashing time.'

Everyone picked up their suitcases, signed their release forms and braced themselves for the next circle of the inferno.

I was bundled into a car with Alastair Campbell. It was already nine o'clock. Alastair and I were squeezed onto the back seat while two camera sharks and their pilot fish squatted at our feet, pointing their various tools in our direction. There was obviously going to be no off-camera time. We were both rigid with performance as we scrolled through our phones, pretending to look for people to call and ask for money.

'I don't know anyone,' I moaned.

'Of course you do,' encouraged Alastair, looking over my phone. 'Who's Joe Escort?'

I took a moment to think. The camera's black hole rounded on me enquiringly, dilating into a close-up.

'Um. An escort called Joe?'

'Any money?' replied Alastair without missing a beat.

'Tons probably. Cash too.'

We drifted off into our own thoughts. I tried to think of some ingenious way to escape, because I knew I could not spend four days with these people and their cameras in our faces 24/7. I had arrived at my charity Waterloo. Here I was, sitting in a car with the man who sexed up the dossier that took us to war in Iraq. Actually he was rather nice in person, but so was Hitler. Alastair was discreet and world weary, like a retired gym teacher. He seemed big, badly dressed and sexy, and his sad eyes looked medicated. Maybe taking us to war had exhausted him. Being too close to power had eaten a chunk out of him. At any rate he wasn't going to headbang anyone on this gig, although he did have a big knobbly nose that was made for aggression or at least cunnilingus. It was going to get bigger as he got older. But the old Blair thug was no longer there. Not even a whisper. Thank God. Hopefully the camera was not reading my thoughts because my shark looked briefly from his eyepiece and winked. He seemed exhausted too.

We finally arrived at some West End hotel in a suite that reminded me of Tutankhamen's tomb. The bedrooms had been stripped of furniture and crammed with all the apparatus of reality. Behind their closed doors, directors and assistants huddled over banks of screens, whispering instructions on walkie-talkies, while in the large sitting room Piers and Ross were warming up, lobbing chit-chat back and forth. Thank God for the painkillers I had stolen from my mother's bathroom. A couple of Tramadol and a large vodka in the bar on the way up, and the flooding panic began to subside. Sort of. I sat down. A little round make-up lady scuttled from a cupboard to powder me down and then ran back in, slamming the door behind her. Cables coiled across the floors, dragged by unseen forces round the furniture and under doors. Piers paced the room talking at length to Philip Green, another bright light on the charity scene, while Alastair Campbell called Tony Blair's office. Maybe I should phone the escort called Joe and liven things up a bit. I began to feel sick.

'Tony's going to try and come down,' said Alastair. Cameras U-turned and screeched to a halt at our various faces to catch the ecstatic reaction.

'Wicked,' said Ross, making a thumbs-up sign. (Big hands, incidentally.)

I have never been a very 'interior' actor, but I learnt fast. Vomit was about to explode from my mouth (Tramadol OD, vodka and Tony) but I managed to make it look as though I were simply blowing my cheeks out in orgasmic disbelief. Meanwhile I swallowed hard and raised my eyebrows. Luckily I could that month. When I got the puke back down to my stomach, I added a little knowing giggle. I must have been purple under the powder because the make-up lady elbowed aside the camera that was three inches from my nose and shoved hers right up close.

'Look at you,' she whispered, placing a Kleenex over my face.

'Just leave it there,' I said.

'What, dear?'

'Nothing.'

This make-up lady was a giant lazy bee, buzzing around the table with her little bag of tricks, bumping into a camera, bouncing back, and hovering over her blooms as she patted and primped and sprayed us down before zooming at a sedate pace back to her hive.

We were each given a writing pad and a pencil, and sat around the table to start our first meeting.

'When you want. In your own time,' shouted a voice through a door, which then slammed, and we were off.

'OK,' ordered Piers. 'Let's get organised.'

How much longer could I look constantly intrigued without having a stroke, I wondered. My camera looked at me accusingly. 'Do something!' it seemed to be saying, so I scribbled frantic doodles on the pad.

'Philip Green is providing *all* the champagne!' bellowed Piers. I wrote that down, just in case I forgot. I'm sure they'll all be thrilled to pieces down at the sweatshop in Bangladesh. Maybe Lucifer could bring the nibbles.

'Now. What about the hamburger stand?' asked Alastair.

'Ah yes. We need to make ten thousand quid on it if we're going to beat the girls,' replied Piers.

'That's not going to be easy,' said Ross. 'Ten thousand pounds' worth of hamburgers! That's a thousand hamburgers.'

'And stars don't eat, remember,' I ventured.

Suddenly I saw a chink of light.

'What about if I leave the show, and come back and buy one hamburger for ten thousand pounds?'

Everybody and their lenses turned to me.

'What?' said Alastair, thrusting slightly. He glanced at Piers, who raised his eyebrows in disbelief.

'Yes. I was thinking. It could be quite good. Why don't I leave? And then you don't even need to buy the burgers. Or cook them, for that matter.'

'You're not serious,' said Piers. It was a statement, not a question.

'Deadly. It could be a solution. I really don't think I'm cut out for all this.'

'For God's sake, pull yourself together,' boomed Piers.

'OK,' I replied meekly.

'You can do it if you pay a hundred thousand,' was his generous last thought on the subject.

'No, I don't have that kind of money.'

'Then stop whining and get on with it.'

'OK. Right.'

Piers then went upstairs to try to sell me to the girls' team, but unfortunately they weren't buying.

I went to the loo, so that the others could have the bitch about me I could tell they needed. As I came out I passed a small door. It was ajar. I peeked through. Outside was a service staircase. I felt like the character from *Midnight Express*. I looked around. There was no one in sight. I slipped through and shut the door behind me. I leant against it, my heart racing so hard, my vision throbbed. Did I dare? What would everyone say? Someone walked past talking loudly. Probably Philip Green had arrived with the champagne. Fuck it.

I ran down that staircase three at a time. I crashed against the emergency door. An alarm screamed inside the building, and I ran across the road. I have rarely felt so exhilarated in my life. I sprinted all the way to Piccadilly, crossed the street and nearly crashed into Richard Curtis getting out of a taxi. I swerved into the Ritz. It was a narrow escape. In the Ritz everything was going on as usual. I collected myself, looked back to make sure the scoutmaster wasn't following and about to blow his whistle at any moment. What a stroke of luck that I was wearing a suit. There seemed to be only one thing for it. I straightened my tie, did up my jacket, smiled at the receptionist, and breezed down that beautiful long corridor, with its cream walls and gilt mirrors, its sconces with their wonky little lampshades, past the Palm Court, where a fat bald man played the violin accompanied by a grim spiritualist on the piano, and straight into the restaurant.

'Do you have a table for one, by any chance?' I asked the maître d'.

'Of course, Mr Everett. This way, please.'

He led me through the half-empty room to a table in the window. I sat down and stroked the crisp pink linen. I was in heaven. The restaurant at the Ritz was one of the most beautiful dining rooms in the world. At night it had a soft pink glow and a slightly religious atmosphere. Conversation was hushed, delicate, and broken only by the sound of corks being drawn from bottles. Candles fluttered in the breeze from the waiters' tailcoats, and ghosts of a thousand dinners could be heard under those ceilings of pink and blue skies if you listened very carefully. Outside, Green Park stretched down towards the Palace. Lamps shone in necklaces laced through the bare winter trees.

I called my agent.

'Michael. I left. You've got to tell Richard. Say I'm sorry. I couldn't take it.'

'What happened? Why are you whispering?'

'I'm very upset. It was just hideous. I can't talk.'

I had a delicious dinner and then went home.

I never slept so well in my life as I did that night. When I woke up it felt like the first morning of the school holidays. I went out with my bike to get the papers and have a leisurely breakfast, but on my front doorstep was the lady who had collected me the night before.

'What are you doing here?' I asked, without stopping, panic suddenly exploding through me again.

'They want you to come back,' she said.

'No. I can't.'

I got on my bike. Another lady appeared. Christ, maybe they were going to abduct me. The second lady grabbed my handlebars.

'Look. I'm sorry. I'm very late. I am not coming back. Ever.'

'They just want you to do a scene on London Bridge, with the others, of you leaving.'

'Sorry.'

I took her hand from the bar and set off as fast as I could round the corner and didn't stop until I reached King's Cross. I went into the station. Now I knew what it felt like to be a spy on the run. I was seeing *Apprentice* folk everywhere. What should I do? How could I escape?

'The train leaving from platform five is the eight-eighteen for Ely and King's Lynn.'

There is a God. I ran towards platform five and jumped on the train. Within five minutes the guard had blown his whistle and the train was straining laboriously into action. I looked out of the window as the station receded, half expecting to see the two lady producers burst onto the platform, but the guard turned and ambled back towards the barrier and I settled down in my seat, sighing with relief. I would get off at King's Lynn and cycle all the way to Burnham Market. My grandmother lived there. I hadn't seen her for at least ten years. I could hide out until the storm blew over.

There was another man in the first-class compartment. He was older and dressed rather lavishly for an English train journey in a bottle-green corduroy suit, with a brightly patterned silk handkerchief gushing from his breast pocket. His face was obscured by an extravagant black fedora. Two fleshy lips – framed by stubble, hanging slightly – were all that could be seen under its rim. After about three minutes I nearly screamed. It was Clement Freud, Emma's father. My life was turning into *The Lady Vanishes*. Any minute now I would disappear without trace.

We chatted cautiously during the journey and he left the train at Ely. I laughed all the way to King's Lynn, but was still looking nervously over my shoulder as I arrived exhausted at Burnham Market after twenty miles on my bicycle. Thank God Norfolk is flat.

CHAPTER THREE

My Grandmother at Brancaster Staithe

Snapshot. A tall freak in a tracksuit rides a bike down a bumpy track towards a farmhouse on the edge of a vast marsh. It is the late afternoon of a brilliant December day. The tide has turned and the sea is threading her way back, like blood coursing through veins, into the winding estuaries and creeks, overflowing their banks until, quite suddenly, the land has been reclaimed by the ocean. It is biblical. The only noise is the bike's jangle, the freak's breath, gusts of wind and the lonely screech of the sandpiper high above. The huge billowing sun spills pink on the low cloud, gold on the disappearing marsh, silver on the incoming tide, and a weird out-of-body experience on the freak.

In middle age the tide turns and the genes drag one back to the beaches of one's youth. All the parading and playing, lying and cheating, heartbreak and disappointment have been nothing more than a strong spring tide that drags one out into life, sometimes too far. In the deep relentless roll of the ocean, dreams and illusions dissolve as slowly one succumbs to the irresistible pull of the current, back towards the long-forgotten edges of memory and the Norfolk marshes where I was born.

Nothing has changed. There's the windmill at Burnham Norton and the round flint tower of Deepdale Church. The gables of 'the Old Rec', the house where I was born, peek over the poplar wood my grandfather planted after the flood of '51. This view is the frame to my whole life. The rest will be a reaction. And yet, standing here now, it feels as remote as an old painting, black with varnish, under a dim picture lamp, seen for the first time in years, by chance, in an unfamiliar place.

A strange noise fills the air and suddenly from behind the setting sun thousands of migrating geese appear. They swarm against the horizon, banking and diving, finding their bearings, before hurtling over the marsh in formations like giant ripples on a clear sea. Their honking chorus precedes them on the wind, ghostly and prehistoric. Wave after wave, these strange creatures come, long necks stretched towards the unknown goal, wings black against the sky, ploughing through the sound and light in a picture of such intense beauty that my brain empties, like a full bath, or a flushing loo. It's the most extraordinary feeling and for a moment I'm in a new dimension. A new address. Gone is the B-list, first-world fraud of north Norfolk, Cool Britannia, EU. G8. For a moment I am just a little clam with squeaky hinges, winking from the ocean floor.

I am not on drugs.

This feeling of tiny vastness lasts only a moment because a muffled shot thuds from somewhere far out in the marsh and an unlucky dot crumples from the flock and spirals majestically to the ground, as the rest, thousands upon thousands of them, bank high and head out to sea. God is in the world. He's a man with a gun.

The sea wall is a long triangular bank that divides the low Norfolk farmland from the marsh, and holds the high spring tides at bay like a bath. It curves away towards the horizon and the dunes of Brancaster beach two miles away. Little figures with dogs are dotted across it. Sometimes you can hear their voices close, chucked in your face by the wind. Sometimes, if you listen very carefully, you can hear voices from the distant past.

'Roo! Don't run like that with your shrimping net. You'll fall over.'

And there I suddenly am, half a century ago, that treasured shrimping net in my hand and nothing in my head but a glorious tingling expanse, as wide as the marsh, as deep as the ocean before it, and as high as the sky above, crossed only by the occasional thought, flapping like a bird out to sea and leaving no trace. I am trotting ahead of three matriarchal generations of my family: my mother first, her sister close behind; my grandmother; and further back, deep in conversation, Great-Granny M and Second Cousin Sylvia. The men are sailing round to meet us at Bird Island, which you can get to on foot when the tide is low.

How they love me, these women. If I close my eyes now, I can still feel it. But love comes with peculiar gifts and these three queens infused all the jagged facets of Empire in their lavender embrace: an empire viewed through chinks in the purdah wall. Great-Granny M brought its best part, a kind of faded romance. She travelled by boat to India in 1907 to marry a man she hardly knew, with whom she had tremendous altercations 'but marvellous reconciliations'. Possibly she was too bohemian, coming from a large jolly family in Northumberland, for the officers' mess in Peshawar. However, one of those marvellous reconciliations produced my grandfather, who was born there in 1908, but the altercator was struck down by a mystery illness. By 1910, Great-Granny M was back in England and already a widow. Both she and Cousin Sylvia were consigned by penury to a life touring the north of Italy, or staying for extended periods in the draughty houses of their wealthier connections.

This kind of existence was seen to be bordering on vagrancy in Edwardian England where a forwarding address at American Express in Genoa was seen as a failing rather than a falling on hard times. But hundreds of small sepia photographs left me by Cousin Sylvia reveal an enchanted life in Bordighera and Portofino, while the First World War raged across northern France. Young girls in white, arms around each other's waists, Great-Granny M and her sister laughing in their floppy hats, crumbling villas swamped in ivy, outdoor productions of Shakespeare, and tables under trees laid for lunch. The pictures turn to colour after the Second World War, but in fact their world turned black and white, and Great-Granny M ended her days in a bedsitting room in Exeter – but all this 'failure' gave her a human quality, which, quite frankly, the rest of my family lacked. While they were busy fitting in, she pottered about with bird's nest hair and enormous, low-hanging jugs tucked under her arms like an Ealing Comedy medium. She was inquisitive and perceptive. One day she heard me banging on a piano and insisted that I 'was playing a tune'. The rest is history!

Granny, on the other hand, was Empire under siege, small, neat and viceregal. Duty came before everything with Granny and she was ready to go down with the sinking ship if necessary, sensibly attired with a hairstyle that never once changed in seventy years. It was her job to make sure that Grandpa's world was organised according to his plan and their home, the Old Rec, was operated with naval precision. Even if the British Empire was crumbling, the sun never set on it at the Old Rec.

Granny was quite frosty and formidable in her dealings with the outside world, but secretly I think she was a romantic. Her bedroom was pink, with two little pink beds for her and Grandpa, and her drawing room was a marvellous emerald green, in a house that was otherwise more or less a gentleman's residence, where rationing and war hung in the air and the family VCs nestled by Granny's heavily varnished Ruysdaels on the verdigris walls. She had a pretty face with sparkling eyes and I worshipped her. With us she let down her defences and effortlessly entered the simple world of childhood. When our parents were away we would be sent to stay with her, and at night she would read us stories until my grandfather's voice could be heard booming from the hall, calling for her to join him.

'You'd better go, Granny,' my brother would say with sympathy.

At the head of the line came my mother and the collapse of

Empire. Her generation buried its head in the sand, grasped desperately at the values of the past and nursed the hangover of rationing;
debbing and standing up when grown-ups came in and calling everybody sir, as the two-hundred-year party wound down and a cold crisp
dawn came up on the welfare state.

My mother met my father in Malta, where he was stationed after
the war and where Grandpa was a captain in the navy. It was a fairy-
tale backdrop to a military *Romeo and Juliet*. The fleet was in Valletta
harbour. A band played a song called 'Sugarbush' in a nightclub
every evening where the fishing fleet – sisters and daughters of soldiers and sailors – trawled for a husband, presumably entranced by
the rather uncomfortable life of an army wife. (The Queen was a
naval officer's wife at the time, living in Malta, and has since claimed
it to be the happiest time of her life.)

My father lived in a honey-coloured house in the walled city of
Medina, with a balcony full of geraniums. He was rigidly conventional, ambitious, suave and without any semblance of a 'connection'
that might inspire Granny and Grandpa to part with their eldest
child. However, my mother was headstrong, extremely pretty, and
had already thrown down the gauntlet to poor Granny by becoming
a Catholic as a teenager. She and Aunt Katherine had been sent to a
boarding school run by nuns in Sussex called Les Oiseaux. The
Birds. It was wartime. Granny left the two girls on the first day of
term in their new converted stately home and walked off down the
long tree-lined drive, seven miles to the nearest station, to catch a
series of trains back to Northumberland.

My poor mother got a brief and blinding crush on a nun called
Mother Emanuel (the Sapphic gene was to lie dormant for another
generation), but it was soon artfully transferred to Baby Jesus and con-
version to the incomprehensible religion was only a matter of time.
Mummy was no intellectual, but she enjoyed singing along to the
Latin Mass, and like many British Catholics was absolutely horrified
much later when the liturgy was translated into English, and she could
see for herself what a lot of old twaddle the whole thing was. She

ingeniously consoled herself by substituting the pill for the communion host, and everlasting life for birth control. But I get ahead of myself.

Sailing round Skolt Head as I am skipping down the sea wall with these women are the three men who completed the construction of my interior world. Grandpa, Uncle David and Daddy. These people are going to try to teach me to sail.

At the helm of his treasured sailing boat, the *Wayfarer*, sat Grandpa. He had been aboard the *Ark Royal* when the Germans torpedoed it. Probably he had supervised the abandoning of the ship in the same way he presided over the dining room table at the Old Rec. Practical, humorous and rather withering, he loved Granny and golf, Polly his parrot and sailing, but not much else. He had been brought up and worshipped by large women: Great-Granny M and her enormous sister Aunt Lottie. If he had found Great-Granny M's love smothering, he had pruned Granny's passion into a pretty box hedge behind which he stood in his dealings with the outside world.

He found his children quite irritating, and his grandchildren were definitely to be seen and not heard. Occasionally one of us said something he found amusing and, immensely gratified, we vainly tried to repeat the joke, at which point his interest snapped off like an electric light.

Neither did my father particularly convince him in those early days. Daddy left the army at the beginning of the sixties and pursued his dreams in the City, in a stiff collar and a top hat, making a fortune along the way, indulging in the gin-and-Jag existence of the permissive world that my grandfather found frankly appalling. But time is the great healer, and by the time he died, in the same room in which I was born, Grandpa and Daddy had long ago forgotten their ancient reservations.

Now I am sitting in a car with my grandmother in the middle of the marsh, watching another swarm of geese fly above us across the pink and white sky. She is ninety-six. I am forty-eight. She is five feet. I am seven feet. We are in a small car.

She no longer lives at the Old Rec. It was sold after Grandpa died two years ago. Now she lives alone in a small house near by, and I have come to visit. We are more or less strangers. The wind rattles the windows, the sea creeps and gurgles up the track towards the car, and we are bathed in the unearthly glow of another glorious sunset. Granny is ageless in it, translucent, a child's face impossibly lined. Her eyes glow at the explosion of nature hurtling through the sky above, at the planet rolling slowly over, at the evening star and the moon flying up, dragging the North Sea towards us, in a blanket of fog for the night. A veil of mist already curls around the church at Deepdale, tucking Grandpa into his grave for the night (hospital corners) and creeping over the wall and up the lawn towards the derelict Old Rec.

Sitting still in all this movement, the two of us, side by side, just the handbrake between us and a gulf of time. Somewhere in our eyes the early intimacy flickers, like a ripple at the bottom of a deep well, but we both know that too much has happened for us ever to be able to find our way back to it. However, Granny is philosophical, to say the least; too old, possibly, to care that much about the hiccoughs of youth, or the scars inflicted on ancient battlegrounds. She tells marvellous stories, as the light fades theatrically around us: of Lancasters flying over a marsh covered in tin foil on their way to bomb Dresden, of the anxiety of never knowing where Grandpa was during the war, and then of always knowing where he was after it was over. The noises of horses' hooves when straw was laid on the streets of London during a winter freeze, and the summer day she met Grandpa on the beach at Cromer. She expresses herself in a forgotten idiom, delightful to my ears, conjuring up the lost world of all my household gods, Mitford, Greene and Waugh.

'You were such a solitary child,' Granny says dreamily. 'Very quiet. You always played alone. You hated birthday parties. Now I read in *Hello!* that you're the life and soul of every party. What happened?'

'Life,' I reply. 'Life changes one.'

She looks at me with a faint smile, and shrewd eyes. I know what she's thinking. Life, including two wars, never changed anyone else in her family.

We sit in silence for a moment. I suddenly feel vulnerable, small, in the certain world of my forebears.

'Maybe I'm having a mid-term crisis, Granny,' I say.

'Goodness. Aren't you a bit young?'

'Fifty, nearly!'

'So you are! I sometimes wonder if Grandpa had one when he left the Admiralty.'

It is nearly dark and the shooting begins far out on the marsh.

'Ducks are not very nice to their relations,' she says. 'Has the season begun?'

PART ONE

CHAPTER FOUR

The Loading Zone

When I left you, dear reader, in 2001 at the end of my last book, I was escaping America, boarding a plane for São Paulo. I was forty-two years old. My brief career as a Hollywood siren had spluttered to a standstill, but a carefree holiday on Ipanema beach was also brought to a shuddering halt by a phone call from my lawyer in LA – Barry Hirsch – to say that the *National Enquirer* (an American scandal magazine) had photos of me having sex in a toilet in Miami and were going to print them in a week.

'A toilet!' said I, trying to summon up a bit of gravitas, but my voice cracked and it came out like Lady Bracknell. Electricity shimmered across my body and minuscule beads of sweat oozed from my nerve endings, dripping down the hairs on my arms, which stood waving with electricity in the air-conditioning. It was during moments like this that cancer cells, shot with adrenalin, divided and ruled. The kind of moment that every celebrity dreads, but at the same time taunts. Caught on camera smoking crack. Oops. There goes my skincare line! I looked out of my window twenty floors up and a terrible feeling of despair settled on me.

Sugar Loaf Mountain glimmered through the haze. A cable car laboured towards its peak, a silhouette against the pink sky. It was nearly dusk and lights were already winking to life across the bay, but it was virtual, untouchable from up here. All the noise and bustle of the crowded beach below was a dumb show, a million bronzed insects in coloured shorts crashing into the silent waves. The only noise was the unearthly breath of recycled air, my own heartbeat and the compressed voice of Barry flying into the room on dark vibrations from Century City.

'I have to ask you a very awkward question,' said Barry.

'If you must.'

'Yes. I must. Did you have sex in – where was it, Tracy – the Loading Zone?'

Barry enunciated these last two words with courtroom deliberation, clearly horrified by their implication, and I shuddered with embarrassment for us both, but him mostly. (I can't think why, though. He was also Richard Gere's lawyer, after all, so our conversation couldn't have been any more awkward than the one he must have had one morning with the great Botty-sattva himself, enquiring whether that gentleman had ever had intimate relations with a gerbil.)

'Well? They say they have film,' he continued. 'Did you have sex in the Loading Zone?'

'Not on camera,' I replied carefully.

'What does that mean?'

One must always come clean with one's lawyer. I remembered that from an old *Ironside* episode. So I told him everything I knew.

The Loading Zone was a dive in Miami Beach. It no longer exists. It was a big, black, barely lit hangar with a bar in the middle and a ghoulish fishtank in one corner. It was one of those hit-or-miss places where extraordinary encounters sometimes happened but usually didn't. And that's what I loved about it. The only time it was ever full was for the monthly sex party, which was usually raided by the police. The City of Miami Beach was hell-bent on shunting the gay world out of South Beach towards the ghettoes of Fort Lauderdale. (First the Jews. Now us. But that's another story.) Any minute now the Loading Zone would be closed down but for the time being there it was, a black hole at the end of that wonky universe of go-go bars and cocktail lounges, and at some point during a night out one's little spaceship felt its magnetic pull and was dragged blinking towards it, little by little, planet by planet, until suddenly one was sucked inside. In the low visibility of its atmosphere the bar itself was an island in a patch of light, the barmen stripped to the waist, while a handful of freaks usually flitted through the shadows beyond. The grumpy fish observed the proceedings with big open mouths from the tank where a treasure chest blew bubbles from the seabed. It all felt rather exotic.

I usually went there with my friend David and we could sit for hours and the world stood still. We were both blind as bats and everyone looked good enough to eat, until we went in for the kill and soon came flying back like boomerangs.

'That backpack turned out to be a hunchback.'

There were two barmen. One, Luis, from Panama, an illegal, was really handsome, with a glass eye that twinkled in the gloom, and the other was a big old slut from Argentina with work papers and gigantic overtugged nipples. Well, to make a short story long, one night during a cold front I was the only person there and – yes – I started making out with the Panama Canal. Just to keep warm really. After a little while things got a bit more serious and so he sweetly suggested that we adjoin to the nearby store cupboard, which we did, leaving the bar in the hands of the Argentinean slut.

'Was there a surveillance camera in that storeroom?' quizzed Barry.

'I don't know, Barry. I wasn't really looking.' I was getting tetchy.

'You do realise that if this comes out, your deal with NBC will fall apart?' said Barry.

My heart was ready to explode. The NBC deal. Oh, no. That was my last stand. My Chappaquiddick. (Was that where Custer was cornered or where Teddy Kennedy's secretary was drowned? Check facts.)

After I got off the phone with Barry – my world caving in – I called David in Miami. There seemed to be a party going on and David was playing to the gallery. I explained the situation and he relayed it to the group of layabouts around his pool.

'If there's any film of me having sex we need to get it.'

'Then we can put it out ourselves and you can be the new Paris Hilton.'

'I don't have her legs. With me it would backfire.'

'Ryan is here and says maybe you got caught on their penis cam.' I could hear muffled shrieks from around the pool.

'David. This is serious.'

'So is Ryan. They installed cameras in the urinals and your dick comes up on screen in the bar while you're pissing.'

'Or whatever!' screamed a familiar voice. More laughter.

'What's Gingi doing there? I thought she was in prison.'

'She's out. Good behaviour-can-you-believe-it?'

There was an impenetrable mood of sloshed frivolity in Miami and there was no use trying to lance it with shafts of gloom from the outside world. That's why people were there. It was going to be tough master-minding a sting or whatever one called it – a pincer movement – to bring these video-dealing queens to justice. I was Charlie, going round and round on a leather wing armchair in some glamorous undisclosed location while David was my Farrah-Force-It-Major-Blind-Nelly.

A couple of days later he called with an update. 'You'll never guess what I wore to go there.' He giggled.

'What?'

'A deerstalker! Someone left it in our house. Genius, *non*?'

David was on a new mystery medication and could never be seri-ous. It was getting quite irritating. Having been in a terrible mood for the last twelve years, he had suddenly become a jolly Buddha and would crack a joke as soon as you said 'hello'.

'Wouldn't a pair of glasses be more appropriate?'

'Boys don't make passes at girls wearing glasses and I needed all the leads I could get.'

'Well?'

'Yes. A reporter has been sniffing around the bar. Several times. He said he knew you went there and that apparently you had committed lewd acts in public. That's not really fair, I said. After all, some of your films aren't that bad.'

'Were there any cameras?'

'He offered money to the barmen. The Panama Canal said no way, but the Argentinean slut said yes. He thought he could get famous. By the way, you didn't tell me you had him too.'

'Not on camera.'

'You're screaming'

'You would be screaming too if your whole career was about to go down the drain.'

'OK. Keep your hair on! Anyway PC persuaded AS not to talk, and the penis cam has been broken for two years – typical Miami – so it looks like you're safe. Incidentally, the reporter is the same one that busted Britney Spears for doing coke in the loo of the Delano. So in one sense you've really made it.'

'Who is this journalist?'

'A dwarf living in Kendall. I got his address – 433 West 110th Street.'

'We should go there and break his legs.'

I reported all this to Barry who immediately dispatched a thousand-page letter to the *Enquirer*, saying that if they published the story they would have to pay me the money I would lose from NBC, which could run into millions of dollars, and anyway there was no film. So the story was never printed, but I was completely drained. On the other hand at least the NBC deal was still in place.

A year or so later David and I stalked the Kendall dwarf to his clapped-out bungalow in the Everglades. It was a hot sticky afternoon in a tumbledown street carved into the edge of the swamp. Weeds grew out of the cracked sidewalk and biblical swarms of mosquitoes hovered in clouds ready to attack.

We found the dwarf's residence and rang the bell. A little dog barked in the house next door, which had a for sale sign on a pole that had snapped in half. And then the door opened and there was the dwarf, only he wasn't a dwarf, just a small roundish man with thinning ginger hair and thick glasses. His eyes jumped out on stalks when he saw us and he visibly recoiled as if I was going to hit him, but I breezed in like Matron, pretending not to notice, asking about the house next door: did it get the sun – sure; how was the neighbourhood – OK; was there a gay bar near by – yeah, maybe for alligators. That was quite funny and I was rather warming to him but David, who was hell-bent on retribution, produced the big round cake we had purchased on the way and threw it at his face. It missed, needless to say, and landed at the dwarf's feet. There was a pause. I think we were all shocked.

'That's for Britney,' David finally screamed and ran off to get the car, leaving the dwarf and me in a face-off during which I was meant to squirt him with the washing-up liquid I was hiding behind my back. It all seemed rather pointless now. This innocuous blob blinked and sighed, bracing himself for whatever was coming next, and it was rather touching. I was lost for words.

'Would you mind awfully not writing stories about me for the *National Enquirer*?' I asked finally.

'OK,' he replied, looking at me with owlish eyes.

'You have no idea just how much these things can fuck one up.'

'Oh yeah.'

'Thanks.'

Another pause. The sun was sinking over the vast green swamp and it suddenly tinged the dwarf's head with radiance as if he were a saint. He was instantly surrounded by a cloud of leggy mosquitoes and the effect was rather mesmerising. The for sale sign, the long blades of grass on the ratty lawn, the windows of the bungalow, were all momentarily lined in gold and the whole thing looked heavenly.

'Oh look . . . ' I said. 'It's going to be a lovely evening.'

The dwarf looked up and agreed as David screeched around the corner in the car.

'Quick. Get in!' he screamed.

I looked at the dwarf and aimed my Mr Dazzle at his face, pulling the trigger a couple of times before jumping in the car. As we shot off I looked back and he was still standing there, no longer bathed in radiance. Just a sad little snitch in the long shadows, living comfortably on the edge of a swamp.

We turned a corner and David said, 'That was West 110th Street, right?'

I craned to look at the street sign.

'No, 109th.'

'Oh dear,' said David and kept on driving.

CHAPTER FIVE

Faint Heart Never Fucked a Pig

The NBC deal took a long time to come off. It all began one night at the end of the last century.

It was a beautiful July evening in 1999, the perfect night for the last great American party, and the day I hit my peak. Harvey Weinstein and Tina Brown were launching a new magazine called *Talk*. It was going to be the most successful magazine the world had ever seen. People still talked – thought – like that in those heady last days of the American Raj.

Harvey was cinema's most enigmatic producer, a New York hoodlum, the essence of that town, as tall and wide as its streets, as dangerous too on occasion. In appearance he was like a vast manatee recently emerged from the sea. Dripping and scarred, addicted to cigarettes, with flapping shirt-tails. In short, he was a brilliant slob, larger than life, Hollywood style. He had a round face with shrewd eyes and a flat boxer's nose. People said he was ugly – he always came up in those Hollywood games that were played during commercial breaks at Oscar parties: who would you rather fuck, Wienstein or Fierstein? – but actually I think he was attractive. He had an enormous energy, a great voice, and the secret of his charm was that somewhere under that blunt exterior you could still glimpse the face of the ten-year-old Harvey, an erased innocence submerged under the bumpy surface of his moon-shaped head. When he wanted you, as he did me *once* and never again, his onslaught was irresistible, unbelievable. He made great films and great turkeys. He interfered with every aspect of a film and his terrible tantrums were legendary. In other words, he was exactly the type of character that made it all worthwhile, a throwback to the Hollywood autocracy.

Tina Brown was his unlikely sidekick in those drunken days, as small and thin as he was tall and wide. She dressed carefully, a Princess of Wales in clumpy shoes, often in white to set off her short blonde hair and her ice-block eyes, and next to her, Harvey looked like a giant old couch that had been left on the street. Tina was perched perfectly on the edge, knees crossed, a journalistic falcon, looking, watching, ready to dive-bomb from a great height at any sign of a scoop.

Together they were a strange combination, a Vaudeville double act. He pushed the barrel organ, while she held the hoops and we all jumped through. They had the makings of the great business marriage *à la mode*. Tina's pedigree was faultless. First she had breathed new life into *Tatler* magazine in England. Then she moved to America and created *Vanity Fair*, and just as that magazine hit its peak she abandoned ship for *The New Yorker*, the jewel in the Condé Nast crown, and made a great success of that. She was vastly intelligent, extremely well read and, along with Anna Wintour, the legendary editor of American *Vogue*, was one of the unlikely British bookends that more or less held the boys' club of Condé Nast together.

Those two fascinating figurines, so physically smashable, you would think, were as tough as nails under their china veneers and didn't seem to care for each other much, giving one another a wide berth. Where one was, the other rarely appeared. Possibly they were the same person. Both women were petite, attractive and frosty with sharp tight voices of extraordinary dialect, peculiar to them and to others like them (Joan and Jackie Collins, Grace Coddington, and all the other various British dominatrices who threw their lots in with Liberty during the seventies and eighties). They are regular treasure troves, vocal collages, replete with all the submerged twangs of north London, the British rag trade, red-brick universities and the Rank charm school, all frosted over with the hilarious compromise an English speaker arrives at with the American dialect.

Now I am standing with Madonna at the end of a jetty at Battery Park, on the eastern tip of Manhattan. Harvey is with us. A thousand paparazzi are crammed on another jetty, a giant porcupine bristling lenses and booms. A thin channel of water divides us from them, the colour of weak tea, slapping against the concrete bollards and jumping up at all those other half-submerged skeletons of ancient wooden piers, which for some reason have never been removed and stick up out of the water like black rotting teeth up and down the Hudson. (These teeth, incidentally, once supported the vast collapsing hangars appropriated by the queen world for crucifixions and cluster fucks. But that faraway Sodom was sucked beneath the waves of Reaganite America. It seems strangely innocent compared with tonight.)

There is a strong breeze, metallic and rancid. It is a beautiful evening at the end of another blistering summer day. Everything, the people, the buildings, the trees even, are visibly relieved that it is over, and there is always a huge collective sigh of relief, a lazy groan that comes with dusk over Manhattan in July. The sky and the sea are milky blue. A giant American sun hangs low over the horizon under a broken ceiling of fluffy clouds that stretch towards the Wild West and the rest of the interior. The sun's rays hurtle down this tunnel between the measurable and the immeasurable, spilling like blood over the marble sea, and turning the clouds into little rashers of pink and grey bacon disappearing into infinity.

Behind us the Manhattan skyline curves into the distance – a gigantic fortress in a blur of exhaust, its billion windows glinting in the setting sun, its Twin Towers flying high above the ramparts. Little red lights blink on pins at their summits, a weird, innocent warning to any low-flying planes in the vicinity. The city is strangely silent. The mad traffic within is only a murmur from the end of this jetty as I stand holding hands with the world's undisputed Most Famous Woman. Before us the Long Island Sound stretches out towards Liberty, Brooklyn and, somewhere out there, Old Europe. Liberty is little more than a red dwarf with cataracts in the setting sun. She has been reduced! The scale of the modern skyline has cut off her balls.

A speedboat carrying Tina, Liam Neeson and Natasha Richardson ploughs across the Sound towards her like a comet with a swirling tail of phosphorescence. (Natasha, the Towers – gone, and that's what's so spooky about this story.) They are on their way to the party, which is taking place at Liberty's sandalled feet. Standing there with Madonna, who is on crutches (she pulled a muscle doing the splits), looking out at all this, I am completely unaware that I have got about as far as I will ever go. And that the whole world is about to collapse.

Harvey is extremely courteous. Madonna leans on my arm. She needs me tonight just to get from A to B. I am her *'ami nécessaire'* and if I'm developing skin cancer from too much basking in her reflected glory, I don't care. (None of those scorched by the nuclear waste that stars exude wears enough protection.) Our film, which in a few short months will tear my career to shreds, is still in that ideal phase, made but not seen, and if our friendship is approaching its sell-by date we don't know it yet. Or at least I don't. (She probably sets a time limit on everything, including orgasm.) For the time being the world is fascinated by us and so are we. Tina is even thinking of putting us on the first cover of *Talk*. (She doesn't in the end.)

Has it all gone to my head? Or do I still feel out of place? Both. It's a befuddled drunken feeling. We climb aboard a cigarette boat, swerve flirtatiously past the phalanx of cameras and roar off towards the island in a wall of spray. The cameras flash like a fabulous firework as we pass by and the screams and shouts of those hysterical freaks blow at us in the breeze, violent and barbaric, so that even when we are arriving at the island their voices are still close. Madahhh-nna! Ruperrrrt! We ignore them, knowing that it will be a great photo op and Madonna has never looked prettier. She too is in the last days of her prime, perched on the edge of a new and delicate reinvention as spiritual leader and offshore earth mother. Harvey and Tina may be launching a magazine. Madonna is launching a new religion. It's the only thing left when you've had it all. Becoming God (or Goop, in Gwyneth Paltrow's case).

We arrive at the party at exactly the right time. Henry Kissinger is already there and I am by Madonna's side as he is introduced. Omygod, I think, this is the man who dragged Cambodia into the Vietnam War, but of course I say nothing even when a waitress comes by to ask us what we want to eat.

'What's on the menu?' asks Kissinger and I can barely restrain myself from shrieking, 'What's on the *menu*, Henry? Would that be *Operation Menu?*'

Instead I obsequiously offer to go and fetch some nibbles. With success comes compromise, and it's amazingly easy to forget two million massacred Cambodians as one is passing around the cheese straws. There is a bit of a hiccough as Tina searches for the right way of introducing Madonna to Henry.

'Miss Ciccone? Mrs Lopez? The queen of pop?' She giggles awkwardly, her face a question mark.

'Madonna,' I say firmly. 'Would you like a cheese straw, Henry?'

'Rupert,' says Tina as we are about to wander onto the next gaggle, 'I want you to come with me to Washington next week. Are you free?'

'No. He charges by the hour. Didn't you know?' answers Madonna, hobbling off.

Chinese lanterns hang in the trees and the beautiful people sit on cushions and chairs on the grass. There are tables, a dance floor with a glitter ball, and a waiter for every star. Queen Latifah gives an address and everyone claps. It's a hollow vulnerable sound in the vastness of Liberty Island. It's a hollow vulnerable party actually, even if it looks like the greatest show on earth, not unlike the dazzling pictures of Studio 54 in its heyday. Many of the same characters are here, in bow ties and silk socks, in fabulous diamonds and couture, but much of it is borrowed or bartered now, and each diamond has its own security guard lurking in the bushes. And anyway there are no waiters in satin hot pants or hungry young garage mechanics from Hoboken to sweeten the pill: just the self-congratulatory drone of all these excessively rich people, frazzled and blinded by power and crazy money. Even the disco queens and pop icons have a sheen of respectability about them and look more like careful heiresses than sex sirens.

Madonna is putting on a brave face but I can tell she is frustrated by her crutches. She needs to be able to swoop into downward dog at any given moment, or at least to be a crab, and feels severely compromised if she can't. She hobbles home after about half an hour, to wrap herself in clingfilm for another sleepless night plotting. She is, as usual, quite sensible and misses the scrum for boats at the end of the party, which isn't when you might imagine, as dawn rises over the city. No.

This party is for a thousand careful Cinderellas and even if their coaches don't turn to taxis at midnight, their serene fascinated faces revert to witches' grimaces if the evening's longevity exceeds by a minute the schedule prescribed by their publicist, which has been mapped out with military precision – from the time they are to be picked up, to the moment of the satellite link up with the E! channel studios in Burbank, to the time they will be getting back home and can get on with their real lives of screaming and throwing things and torturing assistants and complaining about the schedule of their next movie to various vassals in offices still open on the coast. Witchlike, they will kiss their overindulged progeny in bedrooms equipped with hundreds of thousands of dollars' worth of whim and as midnight strikes they will be creamed and chinstrapped, perusing a script, and if they aren't – heads are going to roll.

Yes, this is the bleak reality of tonight in a world that has lost all sense of humour, let alone proportion. Tonight is an important night, because under the orange firmament whose only stars are the tail

lights of aircraft coming and going from the many airports surrounding the city, the life is finally draining out of New York City,
like the colour from a snapshot taken on the best day of your life.
Things will never be like this again and anyway even *this* is not like
this, or *that*, rather. *This* is just Versailles without the style. The only
thing that could be described as – what, touching? – is that none of
us knows what's in store. I certainly have no idea. As far as I'm concerned I should be a national treasure by this time next year.

 And so I prance around, one eye on Madonna and another on the
line for the restroom, because pretty soon I am off my face on booze
and powder, nipping off to the loo with all the usual suspects as soon
as Madge looks the other way, shovelling coke up my nose, con-
torted, five to a portaloo, giggling and chopping and sniffing and
rolling up those damp disease-trap dollar bills and really if I'm looking at me now, I should already be knowing better, because first of all
whatever gland produces saliva has gone on strike inside my mouth
and it feels like a dry paper bag and I am obliged to constantly lube
it by bucketing alcohol down my throat. My eyes are on stalks. I
stumble around.

Soon I am part of a dangerous posse that to anyone in the know is
overlit and exaggeratedly drunk, but to those who aren't, we are just
bright middle-aged things with red cheeks and drippy noses in a
cloud of smoke. We get louder and louder. Then the fireworks start
but we don't watch. One firework is much like another, and all we're
interested in is screaming and drinking and going to the loo for
another line. But the fireworks crack on.

Classical music wafts across the island and then suddenly everyone
in the entire party is struck with the same thought: let's get an early
boat and not get stuck. So a thousand people rush for the jetty. We're
too late and wait for hours, no more drinks or cigarettes, and tempers
fray, but finally I find myself on a boat with one of the nicer couples –
Julianne Moore and her husband Bart Freundlich. They can see
that I am totally wiped out. My mouth is so dry now that I can hardly
talk. My eyes are wide and unseeing. My hair looks as though I have

just stuck my finger in an electric plug. Bart and Julianne are well mannered but I can tell that they are grossed out. The boat trip takes for ever and feels like a scene from *Titanic*. Hundreds of people squashed onto life-rafts in evening dress on the black water. Liberty looks at her watch and says, 'Goodness, is that the time?' and the lights go out. I end up in some restaurant with Kate Moss and Liam Neeson and Baillie Walsh and a few other people.

Liam says, 'Rupert, I'm really happy about your career.'

And someone else says the only true thing of the night: 'Don't worry. It's not going to last!'

At dawn we are back at my house where my dog Mo is sitting by the front door with a disapproving look.

So I put on a pair of dark glasses and take him for a walk, weaving down the street, looking busy as only drunks and junkies can. Bending over to shovel up Mo's shit, I lose my balance and my shades slip from my nose and land splat in the middle of Mo's little present! Mo laughs. I look around to see if anyone is watching and then we hotfoot it round the corner, leaving my Dolce & Gabbana shades stuck jauntily in Mo's shit like a Flake in a Mr Whippy. It looks quite artistic, actually, an apt final 'installation' of the evening, so when we get home I get my camera and race back to take a picture. The shit remains but the glasses have gone. All hail to whosoever had the stomach to take them. Faint heart never fucked a pig.

Now I am on a private plane with Tina and a group of VIBrits on the way to dinner at the British Embassy in Washington. Presumably my behaviour at the party wasn't that bad because here I am. Tina is still talking to me and the world marches on, cloudless like the evening.

To access the broader picture, if I may: in England Tony Blair is still a national hero, flushed and hungry from Kosovo, as it transpires. (We didn't notice. How could we?) England is still in the full throes of Cool Britannia. Clinton is going to leave America with credit in the bank. Tina is at the zenith of her career and the future looks as creamy as the dusk falling on the country as we roar over. It twinkles in the summer haze, a patchwork quilt of fields and woods – the hedgerows dividing them the last whisper of eighteenth-century Maryland.

It's funny how America obliterates the past. You can only see it from the air. Mile upon mile of green woody hills roll into the distance. Thick brown rivers coil through them, with amazing tributaries like the branches of lungs. Strange square towns are superimposed upon this fairy kingdom, their avenues and streets rudely etched into endless tree-lined cubes. Spaghetti junctions and freeways carve across the country, veins and arteries pumping cars and trucks and cheap petrol into the marvellous American mist. It is an enchanted evening.

The interior of the plane is upholstered in beige leather. It's a padded cell for the super rich. Tina sits on a banquette wearing a black dress and pearls, dictating last-minute revisions for the next edition of *Talk* to her secretaries, pretty girls also in black, frozen with attention. The rest of us drink champagne and talk to the guest of honour, Simon Schama, Tina's pet historian. Tina is featuring him in the next edition of the magazine and this trip is one of the last grandiose promotional junkets a magazine will ever take.

Schama doesn't stop talking. He has recently achieved Sufi status in the glare of Tina's sunshine and everyone sits enraptured at his feet. Is he a queen? Actually he isn't. He's one of those peculiar fey straights, a male lesbian, more dangerous even than the lesbian herself. (When riled.) He is impassioned by the surrounding clutch of adoring women and sprays them with words and champagne saliva. He is a great performer, I note sourly, unable to rein myself into the team mindset, and ogle him as if he were Visconti.

(I remember thinking, any minute now she's going to be made a knight. And I was right. Already he is one of the 'artistes' of the Cameron Coalition and has been commissioned by 'Sir' to bring schoolchildren back into the classroom. Good luck. Lollipops and a net are going to be the only way. Bang, Bang, Chitty Chitty Bang, Bang. But I digress. All this is yet to come.)

For the time being he has a gigantic mouth and huge flapping hands and ears, and looks a little like Ian McKellen, and speaks with flat northern drawl. His hands twirl like propellers as he takes off with enthusiasm at some historical yarn. He is very good. Humorous and brimming over with what the Americans call personality, but others would just call blind ambition. He is part of Cool Britannia. Tina looks over at him fondly and I feel a pang of jealousy. I want to be Tina's pet.

More limos are waiting as we touch down. Black whales in impressive rows boiling on the tarmac and our plane comes to a screaming standstill beside the first one. We're at a private airport outside Washington. As the door opens a palpable vibration of power bursts in with the local atmosphere. Dorothy must have felt like this approaching the emerald city. It is claustrophobic and exhilarating.

The airport building itself is quite modest and totally dwarfed by the rows of huge white jets parked around it. They look evil and incongruous against the explosion of summer green that surrounds them. This forest smoulders with heat, livid and threatening, kept at bay by wire fences through which its tendrils creep, clinging to the boiling tarmac, pushing against the fence with all its force. It feels for a chilling moment, as we squawk and clatter to our cars in the setting sun, that nature actually hates us and is seeing us quite clearly for what we are – a line of killer ants in black dresses and patent-leather bags, all set to chomp our way through Washington. The engines of our jet cut out and there is an ear-splitting silence. All life is stunned, but after a second every cicada in the forest rediscovers its voice. Birds begin to chatter and the giant Lyme ticks crackle as they lick their lips and hang from the gently waving branches, scanning the horizon for a passing blood bag to infect. Our shrieks and giggles join this deafening cacophony as we climb into our phalanx of limousines, clunk clunk clunk, and drive into the city.

The NBC deal is born quite suddenly as I walk through the front door of our elegant British Embassy built by Lutyens. It is a sitcom.

The ambassador, good looking, sleek in black tie, greets us at the door with his wife standing by – a pretty, slightly wild-eyed lady with a vaguely German accent. Behind them a vista of dove-grey rooms under glittering chandeliers. Mr Ambassador, or Sir Christopher as this one is called, is full of swishy 'bons mots' and presents us to the ghastly Jack Straw, who grins like a ferret and flings in a few laid-back drolleries himself. They are Blair people, better looking, sharper cut, with their bright engaging smiles of even fluorescent teeth, than their Conservative (smelly retriever) predecessors. Sir Christopher is magnetic, debonair, genuinely interested – or a great diplomat. I look at him and the world falls away. In a blinding flash I see dollars and the future. I must make a sitcom about the British Embassy and play a charming British diplomat installing myself for ever in the minds of America as Mr Ambassador. I can't believe it. I can hardly breathe.

My idea broadens and deepens with every turn around the polished grey rooms where *le tout* Washington congregates. The Queen observes, busty and distant, from above the fireplace. Canapés are served by cheeky young boys in livery with tufty hairdos and forget-me-not eyes. They have fabulous accents from home and I can't help exploding briefly with patriotic fervour, so I drop a Percocet and have a couple of vodka and tonics, and pretty soon, as far as I am concerned, I *am* the British Ambassador. I breeze around the room charming everyone to death.

'Would you like me to get you another drink?'

'Let me light that for you.'

I elbow my way into a Simon Schama huddle of six breathless, strapless, Washington hags. Simon is a gigantic hummingbird flapping above them. Their faces gape, fascinated and slightly terrified, hanging on his every word. How does he do it? I am extremely jealous by now. Well, readers, he has a strange technique. First he confuses them with his hands. These giant paddles bat around his face, which contorts and thrusts, and all this has the same effect as hypnosis. The women sway, numbed by the golden elixir of his repartee. Once they are hypnotised, he does what all stars do and sucks out their energy, and soon he's flapping off to the next cluster of glistening hymens for cross-pollination.

One of the recently sucked-dry hags of our group turns to me. She has a thin rust bouffant, mascara-caked lashes and a turkey's powdered gizzard throttled by aquamarines. She looks drained and clutches my arm.

'Oh my God!' she croaks. 'He knows *everything*!'

'Isn't it ghastly?' I reply, suave, debonair, feeling very cosy by now on the Percocet. 'I wouldn't be at all surprised if his next series is called *History of the Universe*, part one.'

The embassy is a brilliant reflection of our British sense of ownership. It is a Queen Anne mansion on one side and a Southern plantation house on the other. You walk through the British Empire into its American backyard. Now I am standing under the columns of this Southern porch, watching the pageant unfold inside the house. It is about half past nine and the light is going. The gardens are fairy lit behind me. Huge lanterns shine dimly under the colonnade. Crammed behind the windows, the party explodes with colour and noise, the men in black and white crushed against the rainbow of colour worn by the fascinating females of Washington. Smokers observe from the shadows outside, the orange dots of their cigarettes hovering around them like personal fairies as they talk.

Inside, above the crowd, a towering beauty with a long neck and short honey-coloured curls makes her way across the room towards the garden. A path is cleared for her as people recoil and whisper as she moves by. She throbs with an invisible energy, an alien in an empire-line dress. She stops only once – to talk to an ancient man in a chair. He is Alan Greenspan, the keeper of the American purse, and he rises like a failing erection, gloating as she stoops to hug him, his glasses squashed comically against her collarbone. She holds him to her, and then thrusts him away, grasping his shoulders in her manicured hands as if he is a favourite shih tzu scooped up from its basket. Alan's glasses are lopsided as he glares at her beatifically, sustained by the energy of her interest and little else. As soon as the towering beauty moves on, he collapses back into his seat, drained but radiant, and the lady comes out onto the terrace trailed by a small man in spectacles holding a jewel-encrusted handbag.

'Give me my bag,' she orders.

'Her husband,' whispers a horsy voice beside me, as if reading my thoughts.

I turn around. A jolly woman in a sensible black dress has materialised from the gloom.

'You look like you need a top-up. Hi. I'm Amanda Downes. I simply wurship you.' She takes my glass and snaps her fingers at a passing waiter. 'I'm the housekeeper here. Barry darling, look sharp and get Mr Everett another drink.'

'Who is the lady with the tiny man?' I ask.

'You don't know Beth Dozoretz?' she asks incredulously, eyes bulging. 'Fancy that! Is this your first time in town?'

'Yes.'

She leans in close for a theatrical aside. 'She's a rahlie close frund of the President's. Shall I introduce you?' Without waiting for a reply she strides over to the alien Empress, her hand outstretched.

'Why, Amanda,' purrs the beauty. 'What a wonderful night.'

'Thank you, Beth. Ronald, have you met Rupert Everett?' She gestures towards me to join the group. 'He's a part of the delegation.'

Amanda reminds me of my mother. Sensible court shoes, a wide stride and a handsome face. Her dark hair is swept back by a gilded Alice band. She has twinkly eyes and humorous lips made for giving orders rather than head. I immediately love her. More importantly, she will be a marvellous character in *Mr Ambassador*.

We settle on wicker chairs and look out over the garden and Beth quizzes Amanda about the latest drama to unfold at the embassy. The ambassador's wife has apparently lost her children.

'How many?' I ask.

'Two-can-you-beat-it,' replies Amanda.

I try – and fail – to adapt an Oscar Wilde quote. 'Really! To lose one child is unfortunate, et cetera ... '

'It's a terrible story,' drawls Beth, unamused. 'They were kidnapped by her ex-husband. Isn't that right, Amanda?'

'No, Beth. They weren't kidnapped,' Amanda says firmly. 'Right after she divorced they went to see him in Germany and he never let them come back.'

'Maybe they didn't want to,' I venture.

'Oh stop it. They weren't allowed to,' scoffs Amanda, getting up. 'We all want Mummy when we're tots! Well, heels down, toes up! I must trot on. I'll see *you* later, young man!'

Beth and Ronald love me in *My Best Friend's Wedding*. We joke around and the conversation drifts to the political situation and the upcoming election, about which I am blissfully ignorant. Many of the faces we will soon learn to hate are already here tonight, being stuffed and roasted on the diplomat barbecue, should Al Gore not win the White House, and Beth points them all out. She is cool but caged, Washington's Madame du Barry. Her ascendancy will soon be over and touched by scandal. Is she the mystery figure behind the pardoning of America's biggest fugitive, Marc Rich? Either way, she will not make it into the camp of the next administration even if Al Gore wins. She is a Clinton woman and has probably, I muse, looking at her strange alien face, lit a few cigars by rubbing her legs together, and that particular talent will probably not be included in the after-dinner party tricks conjured up by either Mrs Gore or poor Mrs Bush next season. She defends her master casually but her eyes are cut glass as she talks.

I throw in a few political scoops I heard on the plane over. This is a technique I like to think I perfected living in Hollywood, where, never having the energy to go to the cinema, I concocted a game with my best friend Mel. When asked what we thought of a latest film, we simply repeated all the views we heard at lunch and dinner that week. As you know, or maybe you don't, nobody talks about anything else in Hollywood. Just movies. Nothing else exists, to the point that you don't really need to ever go and see one. It has already been accurately and minutely discussed at those lunches and dinners by the wide-ranging circle – from the wannabes to the had-enoughs – of your acquaintance, those intimate friends and professional handlers (and that includes hookers and housekeepers), so that at dinner you can sound so brilliant and perceptive that, on one occasion, my observations about *Dances With Wolves* being so thorough and particular, I was offered a job as a critic on the E! channel. Well, Washington is just the same.

Dinner is announced and we get up.

'You have an extraordinary grasp. You gotta meet the President.' She says it simply as if it is one of the most important things to do next week. (What she probably means, I realise now, is that I am such a spectacular bullshitter that he and I might possibly get along.)

'Yes, I have,' I agree, nonchalant.

'We gotta set that up. Huh, Ron?'

'We really should,' he agrees sagely.

We all move on. Every time I see Ron for the rest of the night he taps his forehead but keeps walking.

(They do organise it. Two weeks later I am *at* the White House, sitting at Chelsea Clinton's table for the last Clinton bash.)

Amanda Downes supervises the serving of the meal with military precision. She may not be an intimate of the President, but she is definitely a Washington star – a diplomatic Cinderella – because everyone lights up when she squeezes behind their chairs, particularly Colin Powell who turns, beckons her down with a finger and whispers in her ear. Her ample bosom brushes against his shoulder, and his little eyes swivel briefly. She prods him with a big bossy finger and he throws back his head roaring with laughter. I wonder if she is CIA? Quite possibly.

I turn my attention to my cash cow – the ambassador. He is deep in discussion with Tina Brown. Assured, casual, vaguely flirtatious, he never flinches under her ice-blue scrutiny. 'Mr Ambassador' on the other hand must be vague and accident prone, dashing and depressive, possibly dyslexic. (A good modern condition is always a crowd pleaser.) He will need a nice, bipolar, semi-alcoholic wife, a leggy blonde (American, obviously) secretary, a diplomatic sidekick and bingo! Imagine: if it works, how rich and successful I will be! I have to clutch the chair to stop myself from passing out. I will be bigger than Dick Van Dyke and Lucille Ball put together. The idea is brilliant.

The speeches begin. Jack Straw is self-congratulatory and much appreciated. He is the warm-up artist. The ambassador speaks next and then introduces the Child Catcher, who responds, flapping and quoting, and bringing the house down. His technique and timing are flawless. He throws his jokes casually into the wind, and watches them with a stagey gloom as they waft over the sea of upturned faces, creating shimmering ripples of glee that he quickly builds into waves that are soon slapping against the sides of the room. The footmen and maids stand by mirrored doors that separate the corridors of power from the back stairs and basements. Unconcerned, they watch the faces of the old regime laughing victoriously in the candlelight. For a moment Beth Dozoretz, taut and unfathomable, is reflected and multiplied in the panes of a closing door, only to be replaced by a laughing jowly Karl Rove at a table of Neo-Conservatives.

It's sheer Visconti. The whole thing – from the dove-grey room itself, sparkling under its priceless chandeliers, to the conga line of tables below, covered with linen, glasses, bottles and candlesticks, curling towards the top table, to the powerful men and women, sprawled on gilt chairs, their polished shoes planted firmly on the polished floor – is like one of those pictures in a gallery, of a sumptuous state feast preceding a period of intense upheaval. The little painted faces have no clue about the bloodbath to come. Tonight we are all overcome with confidence on this shifting sandbar, but strange underwater currents are already preparing to sweep us all away, leaving – possibly – only Amanda Downes, bobbing up and down on the changing tide. Ambassadors, ministers, entire regimes will come and go but a good housekeeper is hard to find.

In the riotous applause that follows Simon's speech, the ambassador surveys his party with pride. Tina claps lovingly, and I go outside
to sit on the terrace and think. Another speech has started. I close my
eyes and soon I am dreaming. Canned laughter, waves of applause
and *me* – a body-building ambassador ruling the airwaves with my
own unique blend of nonchalant glamour and effervescent humour.

CHAPTER SIX

The British Embassy in Burbank

Now I am listening to another speech behind another door. A warm-up artiste – one of the best in the business, I am assured – is regaling a studio audience with the peculiar humour that creates canned laughter. Yes, it actually comes out canned – in short bursts of mechanical glee. Standing next to me is Derek Jacobi. We are both caked in make-up, suited and booted, but no amount of brick-coloured foundation can hide the fact that we are grey and drained and verging on hysteria. I feel like a drowning man. My whole life sweeps over me in waves. Of all the errors I have ever made, one looms higher than the rest, a tsunami of ambition and greed, gathering pace and roaring towards me, ready to smash this makeshift wall of planks and poles against which I cower. Why did I ever set foot in the fucking British Embassy? A young man approaches through the gloom.

'They're nearly ready, gentlemen,' he says.

Derek is manically holding the door handle as if he is clutching at the proverbial straw. His head is cocked like a retriever, listening for a sign from its master. His teeth grind and his forehead gleams with sweat. A brush with a lady on the end emerges whirring from a nook and powders his nose. Somebody starts counting down from ten on the other side of the wall. The audience claps in rhythm. Suddenly Derek grips my arm.

'Darling, I hope you won't think it absolutely vile, but, God, I hope this show is not picked up.'

'Oh me too, darling. Me too,' I gasp, and before I know it Derek has opened that door. His drained face takes on a lunatic gleam, suddenly bathed in tungsten. His eyebrows shoot up and he sashays into the ambassador's office. In Burbank.

My dream has come true. I am NBC's *Mr Ambassador*. For just one night. But no one will ever know. My TV career will start and end here. We will not be picked up.

Three years have passed since that faraway summer's night in Washington with Tina Brown and the Child Catcher. Apart from anything else, the whole world seems to have fallen apart. George Bush is the President. The Twin Towers have fallen, and illegal war has been declared by the free(ish) world. On a personal note, having carefully launched my own jihad on the American networks, tonight I am blowing up with the bombshell of a suicide performance. Luckily no one gets hurt. Apart from me.

TV, or Tired Vaudeville as Tennessee Williams called it, is to be my last Hollywood stand. In one of the unwritten loopholes in the unwritten book of Hollywood rules, TV is still a place to go – a last resort – for many a silver-screen reject. The networks are not as fussy about things like sexuality as the movie studios. Why? God knows. This rule book is constantly being amended.

When I first came to Hollywood in the early eighties, you were either a movie actor or a TV actor. Being in TV was rather like being an Anglo-Indian during the Raj. You were looked down upon by the movie-makers as a hopeless mimic, impossibly common, while a screen star was a gilded maharani, untouchable, both real and unreal, a brilliant actor. Nobody ever called Jane Seymour a craftsman as she ploughed her way through all those cardboard cut-out scripts churned out by Hallmark and NBC, whereas Jane Fonda, similarly screechy, would have been largely considered an artist, protected as she was by the more profound talents of Zinnemann and Kubrick. Until the eighties a movie maharani never considered TV and certainly not advertising. Her image was still guarded like a temple goddess, pristine for the silver screen.

With Reagan in the White House and the emergence of a management culture in Hollywood, the floodgates opened. The stigma of television was drawn out by this new industry of asset strippers, and movement between the two mediums became a well-trodden goat path. So that by the time George Bush steals into the White House in 2000, success for a movie star is no longer simply based on a good performance in a good film. It is measured in perfumes and book deals, clothing contracts and celebrity endorsements, and the perception of success is as important as the actual quality of the product. The wage packet has exploded. Handbags, you will notice, at this point have developed padlocks and metal bars so that these wages can be stuffed safely into their crocodile interiors, and the knuckles of movie stars are gnarled and arthritic from grasping these treasure troves.

I have managed to sell my latest and last idea for world domination to NBC with the help of my new (black) *über* manager Benny Medina. We got a ton of money for the idea, and my head is big, full of plans. I have a new producer. He is a small, neat, good-looking man called Marc Platt. His offices are on the Universal lot. Everything is set up. But first we must find a show runner.

A show runner is the writer who has the initial idea for a series. He writes the first episode and then forms a group of writers to churn out the product for him, should the prevailing winds be in his favour and the show get 'picked up'. He or she will make a whole lot of money if a show makes it to syndication. Syndication – for you civilians – basically means that a show has run for three years and is sold – or syndicated – all over the world. It is at this point that the money begins to pour in. Tens of millions of dollars can be made if the show

he created lasts for even three years. If it goes on for ten then he can
bank hundreds of millions.

I have sold my idea and now have been contracted to produce a
pilot – one episode – which the network will review and decide
whether to pick up or not. Hundreds of pilots are made. Few manage
to jump the various rapids and make it to the breeding pools upriver
and become a series, let alone achieve syndication.

All these minor details are overshadowed by the grandiose
thoughts running through my head as I embark on *Mr Ambassador*.
You could say that I have been thoroughly taken by the flow of
American show business. I think I'm swimming along in its embrace.
Actually I am floundering. I am greedy and ruthless when I can
remember to be – fatal. And the rest of the time I think I'm being
rather marvellous and down to earth, but really what I think is that
the sun shines out of my arsehole. Of course the whole thing is
going to go wrong. I am not built for excessive wealth. (Too tall.)

The first hurdle I encounter is that *as* the person with the idea, but
not the writer – the show runner – I have to find one who is famous
enough for the network, but who still has an interest in my idea.

I commute to Hollywood and stay in the Beverly Hills Hotel. I
love this place. It is ramshackle and jerry-built, the essence of movie
land, and every night I sit plotting with my team in its dark-green
Polo Lounge, merrily observing – sloshed in my booth – as that
marvellous pageant of hookers and frauds peculiar to this corner of
the world parade their wares. I am one of these freaks and it is
almost a religious experience to be there as High Mass is celebrated
each night in all the candlelit booths as another hopeless, flushed
producer with dentures and hair plugs gives communion. The host
is a crumpled, dog-eared idea and he places it carefully on the
caked tongue of the jangly has-been whose soul he is trying to save
from anonymity. We all 'believe' at the Polo Lounge, and to prove it
the odd jewel sometimes shimmers past – a real star – orbiting the
room like a rare comet seen once in a hundred years, and the believ-
ers turn as one, enraptured, but otherwise we buzz and hum – a

thousand infertile bees – as *Cats* tinkles on the piano. I am in heaven, floating in this bubble above the smog. But there is other talk in the Polo Lounge this season.

This is millennium Hollywood. The real world is shifting and so is Tinseltown because now it looks as if we are going back to the Promised Land. George Bush wants to liberate Iraq and the import of this is not lost on our desert community of refugees' grandchildren. The Middle East could soon become a second empire – Son of United States – with Tel Aviv as New York. The idea is mind-boggling and, of course, brilliant. Oil, peace and the Promised Land all rolled into one, and there is a pre-war blitz mentality bubbling up out here in the lubed desert. Quite suddenly Hollywood – so proud in the past of its liberal spurs, won in the last golden age of the seventies – reveals herself in a harsher and more brutal light.

NBC rents a gorgeous car for me in which I crash my way over the hills into the mist of the Valley for meetings with all the famous scribes. Marc, Benny and I are a strange trio, a Vaudeville act from the old days. I am tall and gaunt and terribly British in the middle. They are my Black and White Minstrels, on either side. Together we are the three minorities of the apocalypse: black, Jewish and gay. Anywhere else we would be outcasts but here, for the time being, we are It.

Marc is compact and dressed for a safari. Benny is huge with enormous diamond earrings. (He dramatically loses weight during the course of *Mr Ambassador*, so that if you shot him with a time-release camera he would be like a deflating balloon, ending up on the night of our pilot a size zero wraith and hardly even black any more.) He is a famous manager with the thrilling reputation. He was Puff Daddy's daddy during the famous gun hit-and-run disco scandal. He then became JLo's manager and turned that screechy gonk into a pop star, and now he is going to turn me into an integral part of the American culture. Benny came to fame himself with the original idea for the TV series *Fresh Prince of Bel Air* while managing its star

Will Smith at the same time. This sitcom was based on Benny's real life. He was plucked from the ghetto and adopted by a wealthy family from Beverly Hills. He has a famous temper, and I am absolutely fascinated by him in the same way a chicken is taken by a boa constrictor and pecks and clucks around it, unaware that it is about to be swallowed whole. Benny also uses riveting rappy lingo, which I pretend to understand.

Marc Platt, who is married with kids, comes from the opposite end of the Hollywood spectrum. He has a gunmetal crew-cut and looks a bit like a tentative version of Steve McQueen. His eyes are sky blue. He is impeccably mannered, never swears and is deeply religious. His Christmas present comes in the form of a substantial donation – in your name – to underprivileged Jewish children on a card with 'Happy Holidays' written on it. (God forbid you say Christmas in America.) I must admit to feeling slightly underwhelmed by this generous gift as I survey the jeroboams and hampers sent from the other members of my team and fan club. Next year, I shall play the same trick and make a donation to underprivileged queens in Hollywood and – unlike Marc (he is one of the straightest players I come across in the lubed desert) – I will siphon off all the funds to a numbered Swiss account. It could be a genius accounting scam.

For the time being we set off each day to a different meeting in a different suite of offices at the end of another long corridor, which we march down three abreast, tense like matadors, in a building named after a god from the glorious past that is a part of one of the vast Hollywood studios. Once, not so very long ago, they were surrounded by groves of orange blossom but now are drowned in waves of beige linoleum rooftops.

In the show runner *du jour*'s enclave, we present ourselves to pretty receptionists with wide smiles who chant our names into their headphones and we skim inside past hundreds of drones with vacant faces – they will never need botox – who sit in rows in the outer offices of a show runner's hive. We swish through and are ushered into a priceless room with plantation shutters, white on white on white, where we perform together our 'pitch', the story of our show, with its jokes roughly etched, and with me giving a rough impression of all the spontaneous bubbliness I will be coming up with in the role. My team beam at me encouragingly on either side as I figure-skate to a dramatic halt. Then it is the show runner's turn to whack the bullshit back across the net from the other side of the desk upon which there could be anything from cookie jars filled with jelly-beans to a piece of ancient Greek sculpture (also possibly filled with jellybeans).

No one tells the truth to your face in Hollywood – which face, anyway? This is one of the first rules of engagement – so everyone agrees that yours is the most wonderful idea that has ever been hatched. We – my team and I – jump back into our car, gloating and victorious, even though we have all been through this a thou-sand times and deep inside we know the probable outcome of the encounter. But this is one of the great and extraordinary things about show creatures, and particularly the West Coast breed. We put ourselves through it again and again, like some bizarre mating ritual that unusual animals perform in a wildlife documentary. We throw ourselves over the edge like lemmings, which is rather sweet.

In a few hours we will be informed that our project doesn't quite fit in with what they're up to at the moment and so we have a con-ference call, where I am deflated and my Minstrels pump me back up. There are always innumerable brilliant reasons why this rejection is the best thing that ever happened, and so we move on down our list. Thousands of calls are made but it's not always plain sailing because So-and-So is out of town, somebody else's wife has fallen off a massage table and is in a coma so *he* can't make it. So it goes on until finally the next meeting is negotiated, woven on a web of phone lines slung between giant posts on the boulevards over the hills and far away. Agents call assistants who call managers who call network heads, and soon we're tootling back over the hill into the valley of career death where we regroup in a parking lot, to brief one another about the meeting (act butch; he's really anti-gay – or act as gay as possible because he's just had triplets with his boyfriend and the cleaner). Off we march down another power corridor at another studio, as I readjust all my dials to make myself as perfect as possible for the show queen of the day. And so the merry-go-round whirls on. Past the bar and the doctor and the dealer and the chiropractor and the shrink and the hooker. It takes all that just to get through the afternoon.

Hollywood jumps into the war effort with a terrifying abandon. I am in Marc Platt's office on the morning when French fries are renamed freedom fries on Capitol Hill. In the United Nations the French have vetoed the offensive on Baghdad, and the smearing has begun. Marc is furious. His anger and suspicion go all the way back to Vichy. I try to explain the French side of the current dilemma, but there is no point. Marc says that the French have been in cahoots with Saddam Hussein for years. I reply that Osama Bin Laden was virtually invented by the Americans, and he stares at me as if I have gone mad. We will both look at one another in a different light after this conversation. I realise now that even Marc is brainwashed. *He* realises that I am a communist and (even though he probably doesn't admit this to himself) will be looking out for anti-Semitic traits in our forthcoming dealings. These are dangerous days, and we are all suspicious and slightly hysterical.

Suddenly the Dixie Chicks – an innocuous band – are marginalised for speaking out against the war and the President. Soon the whole of Hollywood is breathless with aquiescence. Only Susan Sarandon and Tim Robbins and Sean Penn have the nerve to speak out. The rest of us cower in the corridors of power, too much in love with our new-found mega wealth, too careful not to upset the shareholders of our new endorsement. On the E! channel we sidestep the issue of war and talk about how much we love working with orphans and our favourite charity. We have turned a corner and we can never go back. Once we had a sort of bohemian credibility. Now we are just a bunch of sluts for rent.

One person who is not for rent, however, is Victor Levin whom we finally land after all the other show runners have rejected us. He ran a ghastly sitcom called *Mad About You* starring my least favourite star, Helen Hunt. Everyone is delirious about the possibility that this *god* of comedy is interested in doing my show, and it has been nearly two years now that we have been looking for a show runner, and the network has intimated that time is running out, so one morning under a flat white sky our dynamic trio arrive in front of a house in Beverly Hills. The first alarm bell rings when I see a pair of tiny scrolls stuck into a crack in the wooden frame of the front door.

'What are those little scrolls?' I ask.

'They are mezuzahs,' says Marc, beaming approval.

'Does that mean he is religious?' I whisper.

'Very,' whispers Benny.

'Do you think religion and comedy are happy bedfellows?' I ask and the door opens.

By the way I am not anti-Semitic. If I saw a giant crucifix in the house of a show runner, or a prayer mat next to the computer, I would run a mile. I just don't think religion is very funny. (When the nut formerly known as Mel Gibson made that hideous film about Jesus, they had Mass every morning before shooting, a really sickening thought.) I should have turned around then and there, but the show business art that I never managed to grasp was the most important one. More important than schmoozing, being talented, looking good, even. Knowing when to say no.

At the initial meeting things go well enough. Perhaps my hatred for Helen Hunt is irrational, and perhaps the show is as marvellous as everyone says. Victor seems nice enough, thin and wiry and slightly theatrical, with silky black hair and thick black eyebrows and a high starched collar to his white shirt. He has one of those anxious, mournful faces that is often built for comedy, a cross between Tony Perkins and Walter Matthau. His house is a nice, Spanish, high-end hissy-enda from the 1920s, which means it looks like something out of *The Flintstones*. Inside it is white with shabby-chic sofas.

We sit down. Coffee is served by his pretty wife. She is *not* wearing a wig and surgical stockings, so I begin to relax and the dance begins. In the first pas de deux he tells me what a fan he is and how excited he is about the possibility of us all working together and I jeté back at him *en pointe*, lying through my teeth, saying how much 'I adored' the Helen Cunt series. It comes out effortlessly by now, all this bullshit. (It's the first of a twelve-step Hollywood programme towards living a life of sheer fantasy.)

Then I launch into my personal version of the 'pitch', sketching portraits of all the characters I am hoping will be in the show. These include my best friend in Hollywood, Meredith, one of the co-stars from my latest failure (unreleased), *Unconditional Love*. She is a little person (aka dwarf). I love this girl and if I'm going to sit around a studio in Burbank for the next ten years (ha ha, wishful thinking), I want to have a few laughs. I don't tell Victor this. I just say that I really believe in her talent (which I do), and I think that she is going to be big even though she's tiny. We all laugh. Victor giggles like a hyena. I explain that I also want to have a Snoop Dogg character in the show, a semi-hoodlum in charge of the boiler room in the bowels of the embassy.

'Do you think that sends out a weird message?' he asks.

'What message?'

'That a black guy can only work in the boiler room.' Political correctness rears its satanic head.

'Where should he work? The Oval Office? Do you know Washington at all?' I ask, perhaps a shade breezily.

'Somewhat,' he replies tightly.

'Well, as far as I can see, it's all black, apart from this tiny masterrace enclave in the middle. I think we should make the most of that weirdness, don't you?'

'Possibly.'

'My other inspiration is a book written by Nancy Mitford called *Don't Tell Alfred* in which the author is the wife of the incoming British ambassador to Paris.'

'I never read that one,' Victor says evenly.

'Well, check it out. The beginning is great.'

Marc Platt looks at his watch, which is a sign that I should wind up, so I do.

At the front door Victor grins and shakes my hand. 'You certainly got a lot of ideas.'

'I know,' I reply guiltily.

'I'd love it if you could write down all these "amazing thoughts" so that I can read them and reflect.'

We all shake hands and quite suddenly the deal is done. I rush home and write all night.

In a nutshell this is my story. Ronnie (mc) and his manic-depressive wife (Miranda Richardson-type) arrive in Washington to take up our posts as UK ambassador to find that the last lady ambassadress (Glenn Close-type), who was insanely popular while her husband was in office, is still in residence, holed up in the housekeeper's flat (Amanda Downes), throwing parties and refusing to leave. (Don't tell Alfred.) It's a very embarrassing situation. (Bill Clinton is discovered sneaking up the back stairs to dinner with Glenn.)

Miranda and I invite Glenn to tea, hoping that we can resolve the crisis. It just so happens that Glenn and Miranda were at school together and hated one another then. (An idea ripped off from *An Ideal Husband* by Wilde, which I have just been in.) Tea goes badly. Glenn has decided that her only chance of staying on is to seduce me and get rid of Miranda. Out of the frying pan into the fire as far as I'm concerned. I escape and decide to explore the embassy to let them hammer it out. In a subterranean corridor I hear hip hop, which I love, and come across the boiler room, which is decked out like a pimp's boudoir. The keeper of the boilers is Snoop Dogg (type). The central relationship is born.

Meanwhile, upstairs, Meredith (little-person-friend from *Unconditional Love*) has arrived as a temp because one of the secretaries is sick. She has come to Washington from Westchester, New Jersey, inspired by *Legally Blonde*, to break into politics. Things get stickier and stickier as Glenn refuses to leave and Miranda sinks into manic depression.

Our first reception is a disaster and everyone leaves early to go upstairs to see Glenn. Snoop Dogg takes Ronnie (me) on a trip to his neighbourhood to cheer him up. In the 'hood Snoop is known as Mr Ambassador. Ronnie adores the real Washington – everyone is much less stuffy than the diplomats at the embassy. Snoop takes Ronnie to meet his mother who is a Cuban witch (Corky, more of her later) and puts a spell on Glenn. All these comings and goings are monitored by the embassy number two, called Vickers, a sticky career diplomat who thought that *he* was going to be the next ambassador and has been having an affair with Glenn. He thinks that Ronnie (me) is remedial.

I send this story to Victor – in a considerably longer and funnier (if I may say so myself) form, go back to New York and forget about the whole thing.

A couple of months later the script arrives. It bears little or, actually, no relation to my original story and, needless to say, I think it is terrible. The rest of my team aren't so gloomy. For them everything is part of a process.

'What does that mean?' I scream down the phone in a conference call to LA.

'It's a journey,' reasons Benny.

'Yes. Into hell.' I am really angry.

'No. Towards making the show you want,' reasons Marc.

Benny and Victor come to New York and we have a very tense meeting in the palatial house of a friend with whom I am staying. I rather hope the magnificence of my natural environment will fill Victor with awe, but it doesn't. If I didn't know he was religious, I would have thought he was on crystal meth. He is coiled and dangerous with glittering eyes, and clearly ready for a punch-up. I have a silver tray all laid for tea, which I begin to pour into priceless Meissen teacups.

'I want this show to be like watching a piece of theatre,' says Victor.

'But I loathe the theatre,' I reply. 'Sugar? And anyway surely this is Television. Not Tired Vaudeville.'

The conversation degenerates over sandwiches. It is very embarrassing to criticise people's work in a friendly, even manner and so, pouring more tea and passing around the cake, we edge the conversation over the precipice. He is as angry with me as I am with him. The discussion becomes more and more heated until at one point I shriek, 'No.' (Too late.) There is a long pause while Victor puts down his cup and saucer.

'Don't say no to me again,' he says simply. His knuckles have turned white and the meeting ends.

Benny and Marc are right. All work in Hollywood is a process and they are brilliant at their jobs because, in the course of three or four rewrites, they manoeuvre the script into something more in line with what I had originally envisaged, but it ain't *Yes Minister*. It's lame and flat and in my opinion not even vaguely funny. But they are brilliant diplomats and creatively astute. Which is lucky because there is no backing out now and we are going to have to roll with the dice, so the 'process' continues. Soon we are sitting in a casting meeting at NBC.

'Do you think Sir Derek Jacobi would play Vickers?' someone from the network gasps.

'Do you think it would be wise to have two poofs in the same parade?' I ask, slightly shocked.

'No one thinks of *Sir* Derek Jacobi as anything but ... a great actor.'

'*I Claudia?*'

'Do you know him?' asks the casting lady.

'Of course.' I laugh. Another lie. I know his agent.

Years ago my English agent Duncan had an assistant who was known as the Flower Fairy.

'Don't worry, darling, the Flower Fairy is on top of it,' Duncan would say.

He was small and good-looking like a Dutch student from a good family. The Flower Fairy learnt fast. Pretty soon he was an agent himself, and not long after that one of the most successful agents in London. About ten years ago he moved to the country and fell in love with fox-hunting. From then on he divided his time between the office and the hunting field where he soon became one of the Masters of a hunt in Sussex. Many a celebrated dame or knight found themselves, slightly mystified, on the phone, talking over a part, only to hear horns and hounds baying in the background, along with various whoops of 'Tally-ho'. Was it 'this wretched new hearing aid', or was it just that the Flower Fairy had such a very good seat, that he could handle a conversation with Sir John Gielgud about a West End transfer and a horse over a five-bar gate at the same time, all the while pretending he was in the office?

'What on earth's going on?' one of his younger clients – Maggie Smith, for example – might whine.

'Someone's birthday in the office,' was the usual reply.

Until the day when Paul – his real name – ('Oh darling, you can't call him the Flower Fairy any more!') was the cover story of a magazine called *Horse and Hound*, the hunting fraternity's bible. He was outed. But no one cared because he was still one of the best agents in the country.

'Paul, it's Rupert. How are you, darling?'

'I have to whisper. We're in a covey. Fox has gone to earth.'

I am in the bath at the Beverly Hills Hotel, and it feels rather thrilling to be in communication with a British hunting field as the palm fronds scratch against the windows of my room and the curtains billow in the warm desert breeze. I feel that sudden rush of brilliance that life sometimes delivers unexpectedly. I used to have to hunt when I was a child and dreamt of being Julie Andrews' daughter to keep myself warm on those freezing winter days. Getting from that to this, from a disgruntled pony on a steep ploughed field to a marble bath like Elvis's tomb, with a spot of room service perched on the edge, is a universal miracle in itself, and suddenly the success of the pilot – or any success, for that matter – takes its proper place in the general scheme of things. It's secondary to this extraordinary moment that has somehow been engineered. Maybe it's successful enough just to be having this conversation.

'Are they bringing in some terriers?' I ask dreamily.

'Not yet. What can I do you for?' whispers Paul.

'Do you think Derek Jacobi would do the pilot for my sitcom?' I explain everything.

'I'm sure he'd love to. When and where?'

'It's here in LA, February. The network are gagging for him.'

'Of course they are.'

Blood-curdling shrieks can be heard in the background as another poor fox is torn apart by a pack of hounds.

'Trot on!' says Paul.

'Are you talking to me?' I ask.

'Yes, actually. We're moving. I'll talk to Derek and get back to you.'

The phone goes dead.

The process chugs on and now I am riding high because poor Derek has finally said yes. After a good deal of vacillating and nudging, like a pinball, he has finally landed in our hole. A pilot is one of those tantalising gambles for an actor of standing, particularly a sir or a madam. The money is very good. The likelihood of the thing going to series is minimal. If it does somehow manage to ride the rapids to that glorious state, then poor Derek will have to move to LA, which he will hate, but on the other hand he will also be rich and, more importantly, able to grab the passing broomstick from Ian McKellen midflight and soar off into the stratosphere – next stop Dumbledore, Middle Earth, or even outer space. If the series is a success Derek will be giving his King Lear in the Hollywood Bowl rather than the Donmar Warehouse.

Anyway, for the time being all that is (or is not) ahead of us. NBC are ecstatic. Give and take is liberally applied in the lubed desert and they have given the go-ahead for Meredith to be in the series. So now we only have to cast Trey (Snoop) and the young female lead that Victor has conjured up to replace Glenn and Miranda who, he says, make the show too old-fashioned.

'But I thought you wanted it to be like theatre,' I whine.

'Yes, but not that kind,' snaps Victor. He is proving to be a real handful, a total megalomaniac.

CHAPTER SEVEN

The Good Witches
of Beverly Glen

On the way to the pool at the Beverly Hills Hotel is a strange little basement coffee shop, a hangover from the old days. It's a thin low bar – a large cupboard really, tucked behind a staircase – with ten high stools against a counter. A TV blares in the corner above the coffee machine. Waitresses in great nylon outfits make and serve the food in one endless movement back and forth behind the counter, crackling with electricity as they squeeze past each other to pour the coffee, flip the eggs and take the orders. They are observed – sometimes lustfully – by a row of locals rather than guests, hags and rats from the seventies, who clamber with difficulty onto their stools and know the girls and each other by name. The whole place is something that Hollywood no longer is, which is cheerful. It's Louis B rather than Mel B.

I am sitting on a bar stool next to a couple of my favourite octogenarian girlfriends in headscarves and trouser suits, having waffles, when suddenly all transmission stops on the TV for an emergency statement from the White House.

Corky clutches Gladys's arm.

'It's war!' she rasps.

'You're hurting me,' squeals Gladys, flapping her off.

There is a sudden hush in the coffee shop as all heads fix the TV with startled eyes. This is the moment we have all been waiting for. Even the waitresses freeze. On the screen, double doors open onto that corridor of ultimate power and Tony Blair and George Bush saunter to their podiums. There might as well be a trumpet voluntary. This is extreme entertainment. Our two leaders proceed to casually write off the United Nations, and declare that soon we shall be at war. Corky, who claims to be psychic and has a spirit guide called the Gypsy, has already declared that Bush is going to save the world.

'We gotta do it,' she says, shaking her head at the screen.

'You're crazy, Corky. You don't know anything. Focus on your area of expertise, my dear. Who'd be better in the sack? George or Tony?' asks Gladys, elbowing me in the ribs and winking, while Corky stares enraptured as Bush squints at his autocue.

'How do I know? I am no longer interesting in these things,' she says.

'You're the clairvoyant, my dear.'

I met Corky – short for Cora – a couple of years ago over breakfast in the coffee shop. She is a Nicaraguan refugee via Cuba with a thick impenetrable accent and a face that has been ravaged by 'the four S's, baby: Sandinistas, surgery, sun and sin'. As a result she looks like the plate that ran away with the spoon. She has tiny humorous eyes like raisins, a flat reorganised nose over a pair of gigantic lips in a face as large and round as a beach ball. She is probably seventy-five years old but no one knows for sure. I have never quite got to the bottom of what she has actually spent her life doing but, like Graham Greene's Aunt Augusta, it seems to have involved a lot of touring.

Her sidekick, the indomitable Gladys, is a strawberry blonde of seventy-eight, married to a producer who 'lost his marbles, honey. I had to put him away!' His name is Maudy and he lives at a home in Encina, while Gladys lives next door to Elsa.

I see Corky a few times, over the course of a couple of years, before we actually speak. She is tall and shapely with an amazing arse and large conical breasts. She is always leaving the bar as I come in. Soon we are saying hello and goodbye but nothing more until one day she turns at the door.

'It seems like we're always saying goodbye,' she says with eyes like slits and a Monroe pout.

'Elizabeth Taylor in *A Place in the Sun!*' I reply without thinking.

'Aiee,' she screams and rushes back in. 'I love that film.'

I quickly discover that much of what she says is lifted from the movies, but there is something enormously warm and true about her, even though she is, as she says herself, 'a fake. But a *yeal* fake.' (*Breakfast at Tiffany's.*) Now, two years later, she is my first visitor when I arrive in LA. She swings into the hotel driveway in an old white Rolls-Royce, which she manoeuvres like a bumper car.

'Aiee!' Crash. 'Sorry,' she shrieks to the boy who parks the car. 'I am a poor yeff-you-hee' (refugee).

'Way to go, Corky.' He laughs.

'I been a long way,' she answers, winking.

Normally we meet in the coffee shop but sometimes she whisks me off to her bungalow in Beverly Glen where she lives with three dogs and 'the Gringo', a large cockatoo who does a brilliant impersonation of his mistress's answering machine: 'Hellooo. Leeve your mesaage, please.' This bungalow is a throwback to a humbler Hollywood long gone. Built in the sixties, custard coloured, it has dog-eared plastic awnings over all the windows. They stick out like old yellow teeth, and the windows beneath them are dark open mouths covered with ripped mosquito nets. The house is shrouded in shadow on the side of a hill under a roof of towering eucalyptus trees. There is an empty liver-shaped pool in the garden. One of Corky's dogs once drowned in it and it has never been refilled, although there are always plans.

She has a coterie of ancient girlfriends – other refugees from all
the various South American coups and counter-coups that exploded
across that continent after the war. These ladies gather at her house
in the evenings for prayer and plantains. They are all deeply religious
and superstitious. Corky is a Madrina (from her days as a croupier in
Havana), which in Cuban voodoo, called Brouharia, is a kind of
witch doctor. Her spirit guide, the Gypsy, speaks through her and
sometimes sends her out of control.

'The Yipsy is drivin' me cazy today. Oy, Roopi!'

On these days Corky nibbles a Xanex and puts her feet up.

'We would like to clean you,' she tells me, climbing off her bar
stool.

'Clean me? Why? Am I dirty?'

'Veery slightly.' She smiles, batting her raisin eyes. 'So that everything yun smoothy for Señor Ambassador! Miguelina – you hear me
mention her – is over wisitin' her cousin. She is vey good! Come to
my place tonight.'

It is one of those wet Februarys, and water gushes down the steep
streets, tumbling into the drains and dragging the odd tiny old lady
into the sewers. There is a cold front and the rain beats down on the
deserted streets as I park outside Corky's house. Lights twinkle inside
and Corky's shadow – conical tits and curvaceous hips – crosses
behind a blinded window. The trees groan in the wind. In the
kitchen a little round Indian lady in a tracksuit sits at the table reading the cards for Gladys, who is crying.

'What's wrong?' I ask.

'Hey, baby. Miguelina says Maudy can't last much longer.'

'It's better that way,' says Corky.

Miguelina looks at me guiltily and breaks into a large toothless
smile. She rattles off in Spanish to Elsa and the two of them laugh
and high-five each other. It's slightly disconcerting. I can tell the
Gypsy is around because Corky is acting weird and wild like Marlene
in A *Touch of Evil*. Gladys looks at me and raises her eyebrows.

Miguelina – who has come all the way from the Dominican Republic – strips me to my underwear, observed by Corky and Gladys, and submerges me in a bath full of flowers and herbs, standing over me, humming and singing. It's quite a tight squeeze in the tiny bathroom, lit by candles. The three women lean over me and I start to get the giggles. The wind rattles on the windows. 'I feel as if I'm in *Rosemary's Baby*.'

'Except that we are good witches, baby,' laughs Gladys.

After the bath Miguelina leads me in to the middle of the sitting room, dripping, half naked, and stares at me while the other ladies light more candles and hang giant oversized rosaries around their necks. We all stand there in silence for a long moment. The only noise is the rain and my racing heart. Gladys and Corky begin to move slowly around the room, murmuring and swatting at the air, as if unseen energies have arrived from another dimension. The hair stands up on the back of my neck. It suddenly feels really scary. The rain beats down on the roof and the eucalyptus trees groan outside and it is suddenly cold. Then Miguelina, who has been looking daggers at me now for at least ten minutes, shrieks and lunges at me. I nearly scream but she puts her hand over my mouth and thrusts her head up close to mine. Her eyes are bulbous and bloodshot.

'Sshh,' she whispers and starts rubbing me all over with her hands, grunting and wailing, throwing back her head and laughing maniacally, going through the A to Z of gesture and expression. I think I might get the giggles again because she puts her hand inside my underwear and grabs my cock and tugs at it. My God, she's going to pull it off. Then she puts her hands right up my bum. After that she places them on my chest, fingers outstretched, nails long and red and gleaming. The other two approach and also put their hands on me. Their moans intensify. They wave and sway. They wield their crucifixes at my face. It is all quite deranged. Miguelina's eyes disappear in their sockets, she emits a blood-curdling scream and is literally thrown across the room, landing on the sofa.

Corky turns on the lights.

'That was a good one,' she says.

'Hellooo,' sings the Gringo. 'Please – leeve – your – mesaage.'

'Now the sky's the limit. That's the message, you silly bird!' shrieks Corky.

The old ladies make Miguelina comfortable on the sofa and she begins to snore.

Every day I plough over the hill with a heavy heart to the auditions, where endless girls and boys parade their wares for us on tape. It is a cattle market and, as you'll know if you've ever done an audition yourself, it makes you want to jump out of the window. One holds one's whole life in one's hands at an audition, offering it up, clothed by the Bard, or Beckett, or by Victor in our case, to the barbarians on the other side of the table. You've learnt the scene. You've rehearsed it obsessively in class with your scene partner or with your steering wheel as you crawl along in the traffic on the freeway, and now – for five minutes – it is looked at, laughed at and rejected, as often as not, in a process that never gets easier, no matter how good or bad you are. It is the hideous hunger state of being a young actor in Hollywood, from which only a lucky few will ever set sail towards the puffy pink sunset of fame, leaving the rest of them – us – staring out to sea, trapped in that infamous circle of the inferno – the Circle of Auditioning – and going down on ... not dick, just tape.

All the girls who come to see us are good. Proficient. Believable, even. But they have no originality. They are all clones of someone else. Their life experience is nil and their emotional language is braille. Some girls do bubbly. Others do neurotic. Some do sultry, but it is Tupperware sex, neatly packed up in clingfilm for a light snack. Many of the girls seem to be fanatically Christian and talk about things like 'my church', which everyone on our side of the table seems to be really thrilled about, while I am literally holding my head so that it doesn't do a three-sixty-degree turn and shriek, 'Your father sucks cocks in hell!'

'She's just not that sexy,' I whine at one point about a particular seminarian.

'What do you want? To be raped in the audition?' snaps Glynn, the casting lady.

'Some chance! That girl is saving herself for the rapture party.'

'Don't you have any beliefs at all?'

'Belief is very Windows 3,' I snigger.

'What does that mean?'

'It means, dear Cindy, that I have more important things to do with my time than conjure up little fantasies about the future when the present is a big gaping hole because we can't find an actress!'

Or an actor.

Casting a black actor who is as edgy as, say, Snoop Dogg proves to be impossible. They just don't exist like that in TV and movies. Despite the fact that there are now some big black stars, America still views black people with some trepidation, and pretty much all the black actors on the scene, from the top to the bottom, strain every nerve to present the wholesome side of being Afro-American. In other words there are no fabulous rough diamonds for hire unless you want to cast the role from the back pages of *Frontiers* magazine (which I would). When one of the guys talking to us says, 'Oh my golly!' I nearly fall off my chair. I've accepted that we can't say 'God' any more but 'golly' is going too far. Besides, they seem to have forgotten that traditionally at the end of 'golly' comes 'wog'. I want to crawl into a hole and die.

However, we do find two great girls and a lovely guy. One of the girls is from Texas and I want her, but the casting ladies think that she is too much like Julia Roberts and so we go for the other who is a sweetheart and good. She is called Megan. The boy we finally land for the role of Trey from the boiler room is really handsome and a very good actor as well, even if he is not genuinely rough.

Rehearsals begin on Monday. The recording of the show is scheduled to take place in nine days' time – next Wednesday. Derek arrives on the dot of ten, looking the very picture of a theatrical

knight in Hollywood, and my heart briefly leaps. Like Marc he is
vaguely dressed for a safari in various shades of biscuit. He is a
sweetheart, very warm to everyone, with a little briefcase like a travelling salesman. What must he be thinking, I wonder, as he is taken
from group to group around the large trestle table? Everyone bobs
and beams. Derek has impeccable manners and chats animatedly to
all and sundry. It's one of the few moments of 'the process' I can
remember actually enjoying. The fact of Derek actually being there.
The joy of watching his English manners – as thorough as a lawn-
mower trundling across a garden making hay (nonny no), leaving
every blade of grass shorn of all prejudice. Derek is an animated
vicar on a prison visit, clutching his script to his chest as he stands
over Trey who is sprawled across a chair. I catch his eye and he
winks. I can tell exactly what he is thinking. 'You got me into this.
Now get me out!'

Victor surges forward in a phalanx of comedy scribes to greet
the English knight. These laughter stooges are an extraordinary
breed in the Hollywood food chain, a strange haunted type of
after-dark animal. They are often failed stand-ups, prone to crip-
pling depression and drug addiction. These scribes wander from
one TV set to another like a weird desert tribe. They leaf through
their books of gags with shaky hands and mumbled complaints,
and they are actually fabulous scruffy outsiders in the sharp overdressed world of Hollywood. They settle down around their
master, trying out jokes on Derek who throws back his head with
glee, even though I bet he probably hasn't got a clue what they're
on about.

Suddenly everything goes quiet because Jeff Zucker arrives. He
is the head of NBC and has given me my deal. We all stand to
attention. He is a small dark stocky man with piercing eyes and a
biting tongue, one of the most important men in Hollywood. He is
very clever and will make the most sensible comments throughout
these last days of 'the process'. More introductions are made.
Meredith, overlooked, or underlooked, watches furiously from

between everyone's legs. Soon we sit down and read the appalling script.

I would bore you with the tragic details – luckily for the most part I have forgotten them – but, just to give you an idea of how TIRED *Mr Ambassador* is, in the first scene I am late for work at the embassy and Derek is complaining about me to Megan, the secretary, because I have apparently spent all night at a party with Jennifer Lopez. *Yawn*.

'How was her bottom?' asks Derek when I finally arrive.

'Absolutely delightful,' I reply, launching into a far-fetched yarn about going back to her hotel and ending up in a jacuzzi with her and some other celebrities.

After the reading Victor disappears with Jeff Zucker, Benny and Marc.

'It isn't that funny, is it?' I ask Derek, whose head sinks slightly into his shirt as he eyes me suspiciously.

'But darling, wasn't it your idea?' he asks carefully.

'Yes, but then it was hijacked by Victor.'

'Oh!' sighs Derek, not wanting to get involved. 'It's all a little bit over my head.'

Victor returns after about half an hour. His face is ashen and drawn. Benny takes me aside.

'Jeff Zucker is furious,' he whispers.

'Oh, good. Why?'

'He says it isn't funny.'

'Well, hello!'

'We're going to rehearse anyway and then they are going to do a rewrite tonight after you all go home. Don't tell the others.'

'Hopefully it won't be a case of out of the frying pan into the fire,' I say, looking at Victor now in a huddle with all the gag hags. They don't look very funny.

'Let's hope,' says Benny.

We start to rehearse. The sets are all marked out in tape on the floor. It is like doing a play. There are yellow lines for doors and some actors like to mime opening them, which I always find hilarious, particularly now when Merrylegs bustles into the room for her first scene. She clomps to the yellow line, stops dead in her tracks and then – on tiptoes – laboriously mimes grasping a big door handle and pushing open a door, peeping through and then clomping on. It's very Marcel Marceau and totally wasted on Victor, who is biting into a giant overflowing jelly doughnut.

'What are you laughing at, asshole?' she snaps.

'Your door-opening technique is flawless.'

She raises a finger. 'Sit and spin.'

Victor is snappy and mad-eyed all day, like the nutty professor, and at about five o'clock we call it a day.

We get back in at ten the next morning. Victor and the scribes have been up all night and look crazed.

Derek, on the other hand, bounds in looking fresher and jauntier than yesterday.

'Darling, sorry to have been a bit *piano* yesterday. I was feeling absolutely exhausted.'

'How's your jet lag?' I ask.

'I passed out at nine but then of course was sitting bolt upright from three on.'

'Oh God, poor thing. What did you do?'

'Actually it was rather useful. I just sat up and learnt the whole script. So now I feel on top of things.'

'Oh, good,' I reply cautiously.

As if on cue, Victor arrives with an assistant holding a huge pile of scripts and gives us both one. I make a quick getaway to the other side of the room because I know what's going to happen next. Derek puts on his glasses and settles down to peruse the new script. It is the last pastoral moment he will know this trip. He leafs through each page, his jaw dropping by degrees, his face turning from pale to pink to purple. He looks as if he is going to faint. He stares out at the room, locates me and rushes over.

'Dear heart. They've changed the whole script. Every word!'

'I know.'

'But I just learnt the whole fucking thing.'

'I know. Me too.'

Lie.

Things go from bad to worse and Victor begins to lose his hair. It falls out in clumps on his signature white shirt. Every day we get a new script. The actors are exhausted, verging on hysteria, and Victor looks grim as Derek nearly slams the latest script down on the table. I say nearly, because actually he doesn't. He is a mild-mannered, gentle creature, but we have pushed him to his limit.

'I don't really understand this joke I mean . . . is it really funny?' He strains every nerve to sound reasonable. He looks around the table for support. The rest of us regard him mournfully.

'No. It's not funny,' says Meredith finally.

The stooges turn on Derek like a row of hungry dogs, ears cocked and earnest eyes. Will they lick him or eat him?

'Oh yeah. I mean, I think so. Potentially *really* funny,' says one.

'Oh definitely. And with your delivery . . . ' says another.

'You are sweet, Brandon. It's just that I really don't know if I can learn any more.'

He is almost crying but Victor ploughs on regardless and in a few minutes we are up and rehearsing the latest version, which involves a meeting with some Russian businessmen where Derek has to mime behind their backs the answers to their questions, which I misinterpret. It's like the word game, and just as ghastly. Derek makes big circles with his arms, tweaks at his ear, and strikes extraordinary poses with bulging eyes. He gives it all he's got, poor darling, but there's no denying that it's a long downhill slalom from *I Claudius* to this. Everyone watches our antics listlessly from chairs around the room. Benny sits in the corner. He is now size zero, like a balloon that has blown away and finally fizzled out on a chair.

Suddenly a fight breaks out. Meredith is in a stand-off with Victor. He towers over her, wagging his finger, and she is grabbing at him with one hand and waving her script at his crotch with the other.

'I can't take any more,' she screams and bursts into floods of tears.

'What did you do to her?' I storm up to Victor.

'I just told her to do it a bit faster.'

'No,' seethes Merrylegs between heaves. 'You have been patronising to me ever since I arrived.'

'I am just trying to get the show up and running before we move to the studio.'

'If you didn't keep rewriting the scenes we might be able to get it together.'

'It's normal. It's a part of the process,' screams Victor. I am about to grab him by his starched white collar. Benny and Marc stand up.

'Put the brakes on, sir,' says Benny evenly.

'I am sick of your fucking process, Victor.' I am screaming now. Benny and Marc stand either side of me, ready to restrain. 'I want to learn my part. I want to rehearse it and be sure about what I'm doing. That's it. I don't want any new fucking jokes that aren't funny. I just want to do the job and get out of here.'

Silence in the room apart from muffled sobs from Merrylegs. Victor says nothing.

'You know, he *is* right!' reasons Derek finally. 'We've *got* to know what we're doing.'

When Corky hears that Victor is losing his hair, she is ecstatic.

'This is great news. Get me six of them and we do a leetle work on him. There is a veery good Brouharia with hairs. Don't give up hope. It's going to be great. The Yipsy told me.'

'I wish the Gypsy was directing,' I joke.

'She could. She first came to me when I was on tour.'

'I bet she did.'

A small spell sounds just the ticket so I brief Merrylegs later that night on the phone. The next day while I am bickering with Victor in the rehearsal room, I see a tiny little hand appear from behind his back where a long black hair lies waving on his shoulder. I hold my breath as two little fingers delicately lift the hair off the shirt and then disappear. A moment later Merrylegs herself materialises behind Victor, holding the hair in her hand, and marches nonchalantly off to the loo. During the next coffee break she sidles up to me.

'It's in a Kleenex in my pocket. I nearly peed myself.'

'We need six,' I whisper.

'*Six?* Don't make me go through it again. I'll have a coronary. You do it. I'm not established like you. If they find out . . . Imagine a dwarf in a black magic scandal. I'll be dead in the water. I'll never work again.' She is ranting now.

'You're never going to work again, period. None of us will.'

I decide on a more direct approach.

'God, Victor! We're making you so miserable, you're losing your hair,' I say breezily, brushing his shoulder with my hand, and hairs fly off like autumn leaves falling. Actually I am feeling quite sorry for Victor by now. He knows we all hate him. He is exhausted. I am exhausting. And I have to hand it to him. He is tenacious. He will be there with Cher and the ants after the nuclear war.

'Yes, you're killing me,' he says wryly. 'OK, let's try it again.'

We all drag ourselves from our chairs while Merrylegs discreetly crawls across the floor on all fours, hair-hunting.

'I got at least ten,' she whispers.

That night I race off to Corky's after work and present the girls with the hairs. Miguelina's leaving and her bags are packed. She is taking the red eye to Miami and then on to Santo Domingo. She holds the black strands up to the light, chuckling.

'You're not going to kill him, are you?'

'Yelax, Roopi. We just give him a leetle smack.'

'That's what the mafia say when they are going to break someone's legs.'

'Oy, Roopi. Is a spiri-uh-ahl smack.'

'What are you going to do?'

'We got two candles blessed by Father Gabriel – very important – and we plait them together and now we burn the hairs. Leave us. You gonna see.'

Nothing happens.

The next day we are on the set in the studio. It looks just like the embassy. There are three sections: the ambassador's office, another office for Merrylegs and Megan the other secretary, and then Trey's boiler room at the end. Facing all this is a bank of empty seats, and above it hangs a firmament of follow-spots and klieg lights. When Derek arrives he clutches his chest.

'Oh, Christ,' he says, looking at his watch. 'In five hours this place will be filled with screaming and disappointed people.'

'It already is! Look over there.'

Victor is having a heated discussion with some NBC executives. They have begun to assemble, like ghouls, watching the proceedings silently, huddling and pointing in small groups, as technicians focus the lights and push around the vast cameras, which look like Daleks, blinking and gliding. Victor is now ensconced in a control room at the back of the studio and has been reduced to a voice. He talks crisply to us over a loudspeaker, like God or Oz.

And so there we are, Sir Derek and me, cowering on the other side of the door. The audience are screaming. Corky and Gladys are there. They are both wearing their giant rosaries. My LA agent Nick has disappeared – an ominous sign. Everyone from NBC is in the house. Jeff Zucker has shaken my hand and told me how happy he is to have me here at NBC. I feel idiotically chuffed. Again, I think – maybe *this* is enough. It doesn't matter what happens next, if he isn't that happy for very long. Backstage we all hug one another – even me and Victor – with the hilarity of condemned men. Finally Derek and I are alone. And the countdown begins. I want to say sorry to Derek. But it just doesn't come out.

'Darling,' he whispers to me instead. 'Would you think it so very awful if I say to you that I hope to fuck we don't get picked up?'

And action.

The first scene goes pretty well. The audience are trained and laugh if you drop a teaspoon, so that by the end of it we are all feeling a bit giddy. The Daleks circle and scrutinise us with their black inhuman eyes. Derek and I possibly overdo it, and play and arch at them as if we were Gloria Swanson at the end of *Sunset Boulevard*, wild-eyed and shrieking. Why not? The audience seem to love it and only when we get to the second half of the show does it all begin to fall apart.

I have hardly had time to learn the new scene with Megan and in the middle of it I stop dead, scouring my mind for the next line, but it is nowhere to be found. The world literally stands still. The audience – so animated until a second ago – watch me silently on the edge of their seats. They have to laugh again and their mouths are open like baby birds craning to be fed. I feel as if I am going to puke at any moment. I try to speak. Nothing comes out. I look at Megan. She stares love and support at me, and mouths the text, but I can't hear. A chasm has formed between us. Tears prick at the back of my eyes. Faces from the shadows stop what they're doing and look. Merry watches from the wings. Everyone in this fucking studio is watching me. Silence. Just the whirring of air and electricity.

'Sorry,' I say finally.

There is an almost palpable exhalation of despair from the viewers as I rip down the fourth wall between us. The tension gone, people converge upon me from all corners. Make-up. Hair. Producers. Writers. All with some instruction or other. Tears begin to leak from my eyes. The first assistant circles me, talking into his headphones to the control room.

'What do I tell him? OK. I'll tell him.'

'Can we go back a bit? I got lost,' I whisper, but nobody is listening.

A brush whirls out and powders all the sweat that is dripping off me into a kind of mudpack on my face. The witch on the end of this mini-broomstick scrutinises me with undisguised horror.

'Wait,' she screams. 'I gotta redo him.' She prods the circling assistant with the brush.

I squint with horror towards the control room. 'No. I'm fine. Honestly.'

'Really?' says the lady, considering. 'No! It's a total redo. He's sweated the whole thing off.'

I am bundled backstage and the warm-up artiste rematerialises. As the witch fixes my foundation I look at the script but it's just words now. I can't take any of them in. Within minutes I am back on the floor. The warm-up artiste is much funnier than I will ever be and the audience is reassured and laughing along again, like a baby who has had its nappy changed. The technicians leave the stage and we start the scene once more. It goes OK for about a minute and then I lose the thread again. I stand there for a moment with my hands on my hips, trying to keep it together, but it feels as though I am about to pass out.

Benny suddenly arrives on the floor. 'Don't let them see you crash, man. Don't let them see you crash.'

'OK,' I say.

He takes me by the arm, turning me away from the audience. 'Breathe,' he orders.

'OK.' I breathe.

'You can do it.' He stares at me solemnly.

I look back. His eyes are the still centre of my collapsing universe, and I think with a rush of gratitude that Benny has been a great manager. It's a moment of empathy, which I will never forget, and that energy – from him to me through his clutching fingers on my arm – sends a surge through my body.

'OK,' I say and we go for it. The script supervisor comes over to me with the script so that I can look at the lines. She has a kind face and regards me with maternal concern. I study the words but they mean nothing. They are in fact jumping out of the page at me, like the reviews of a hit show in a Hollywood film from the thirties.

'OK, I've got it,' I say and off we go. This time it works OK. Hopefully cancer cells have not replicated inside me.

We finish the show. Executives and casting ladies surge backstage and blow the usual hot air up any arsehole that has managed to unclench itself.

'You know,' says one with authority, 'I haven't heard a reaction like this since we shot the pilot for *Friends*.'

PART TWO

CHAPTER EIGHT

Nicky Haslam's Mid-Life Crisis

Needless to say, *Mr Ambassador* is not picked up, and I have never again seen anyone who was involved in it. Nor have I returned to Hollywood. But that's show business. Yesterday's best friend is tomorrow's complete stranger. Like atoms we cluster and dissolve, forming strange exotic bodies that sparkle or writhe across the firmament in a lifespan that can be as short as a moth's or as long as an Andrew Lloyd Webber musical – in either case, death is the endgame – floating back into the ether, only to be born again with other atoms on some other hit or miss, on or off Broadway, TV or radio, Pinewood, Hollywood Bollywood, amen. It is an endless movement of reincarnation or reinvention until the final croak. For the time being I am back to square one: London. The world of Hollywood zips up behind me.

But it is spring and I am lunching under the apple blossom with Nicky Haslam who has just had an amazing facelift and looks like an ageless German general with silver hair and a new Wagnerian jaw. He is unusually lively. On the other hand I feel dead. Spring always does that to me and I moan my way through lunch, an unpardonable crime in Nicky's lightly painted, pouchless eyes.

'You're rather dreary today,' he says as we peruse the menu, under the impatient scrutiny of the waiter.

'I think I might have a—'

Nicky doesn't let me finish my sentence. 'Mid-life crisis?' He enunciates every syllable, like Noël Coward. 'How common. What a terrible waste. I enjoyed every moment of mine.'

'But Nicky, that's the marvellous thing about you. You adore everything. If you had a colostomy bag you would absolutely worship it.'

'Worship is perhaps the wrong word but you know what they say? When you've got one? Bunny Rogers told me. The nurse says, "Welcome to a very exclusive club, sir! You are joining the ranks of the Queen Mother and some of our leading entertainers." You'd never catch any of the royal family having a mid-life crisis.'

'Do women have them?' I wonder.

'Don't you know?' (One of Nicky's catch phrases.) 'They've got more sense. They're too busy washing up. Or being a she-man in the office.'

Possibly they are shell-shocked at having become invisible at thirty-five, unseen entities stacking dishes, while their men oogle (new virtual word incorporating Google and ogle) sixteen-year-old girls or their more successful men friends. Anyway, Nicky is right. *Les girls* normally sail through mid-life into the harbour of old age, playing bridge and gardening, while we men make a terrible business of it, ending up staring glassily into space, collapsed on a deckchair in the garden. Our pectorals have become baboon breasts (moobs) and our cocks leak. As our ladies and their girlfriends can be heard shrieking with laughter through the kitchen window, busy at their tapestries, we begin to wonder who we ever were, and what we are to become, but, as the Buddha points out, it was all an illusion in the first place. Best newcomer, executive of the year, employee of the month, fastest centre forward on the local team: all these absolutes are nothing more than stations, often too insignificant in the main-line scheme of things for our little puffing train even to stop at.

When a man first feels that hurtling sensation, his world has packed up like a travelling stage set and he is quite suddenly falling through thin air, a dot in immeasurable space, with neither ground beneath his feet, nor parachute on his back. He may buy a Harley-Davidson, or grow his hair, or develop a drug habit, or take to the cloth. Anything can happen. If he has led a rather unresolved or sheltered sex life, a giant libido may suddenly bloom like some ghastly flesh-eating flower. Actually, even if he hasn't, he is still quite likely to begin a sexual rampage. Sex, once a pastime, is now a religion. Viagra is the blessed sacrament, and a stack of steroids can be a course in miracles. These diversions will break our fall for a while, create the illusion of ground and control, but it's a game of bumper cars at full speed, and pretty soon a head-on collision necessitates a new chassis, as we limp to the sidelines, exhaust pipe clanking against the superhighway, our big end gone for ever. Without wanting to, we step irretrievably into old age, and may never turn back.

Not if you're Nicky Haslam.

I first met Nicky when I was seventeen and worshipped him immediately. In those days, he was quite conventionally turned out with only a feather-cut silver bouffant and a slightly clipped Noël Coward delivery that set him apart, unless of course you bumped into him off the beaten social track, late one night, as I once did, at the Coleherne pub in Earl's Court. Nicky could fit in anywhere. He always dressed for the occasion, and that night, with deadly aplomb, lurking like a cast member of *Cats* under a lamp, he was decked out in a suit of black bin liners over galoshes.

Today we are reminiscing rather carefully, as only two dowagers in the throes of autobiographical looting missions can, when Nicky, somewhat cagily, I feel, denies this clearly etched memory.

'Don't be silly, dear. I was wearing my fireman's uniform. I would never go out in bin liners. You should take up embroidery. Anyway, what about those leather drainpipes you were wearing with the pixie-hat codpiece!'

'Now *you're* being silly, darling. I would never have worn drain-pipes. I didn't have the calves for them.'

'Until you met that doctor in Brazil.'

'Carlos Fernando has never worked on my legs, Nicky. I would like to make that clear right now.'

'If you say so.' Nicky's face sinks back into itself, always a bad sign.

But the main thing was that even though he was already ancient in our cruel teenage eyes, he was completely unlike the other men we knew. He looked at life with a fascinating mixture of childlike enthusiasm and savage queenery. Nicky was, in fact, the last in line of a certain type of royal. David Herbert and Stephen Tennant, bright young things from between the wars, were his fey trailblazers, and Nicky's psychological roots wrapped around caskets as long buried as Alfred Douglas's. Unfortunately, this type of queer is largely extinct now, but in the seventies there were still quite a few left, and it was in their drawing rooms that one still heard the nuance and timbre of Wilde. Nicky loved a vendetta, and was normally waging wars on several fronts. If he got a bee in his bonnet, it could get stuck in there for years, or days, anyway, as we all found to our cost, at some time or other. But equally, a deeply lodged rancour could dissolve over a lunch or a funny remark, and the milometer would be back at zero.

My first significant public appearance was at Nicky's famous 'Tenue de Chasse' ball at the Hunting Lodge, his newly acquired country seat.

I was determined to make a splash and decided to go as a Masai warrior. After much persuasion, my boyfriend at the time, the eccentric designer Antony Price, knocked up a ruched pouch in rust-coloured ultra suede on the sewing machine that stood in the corner of his bedroom in Earl's Court. I lay in bed while he sat hunched over the machine, deftly sewing under an anglepoise lamp, which was the only light in an empty mauve room that contained a mattress, a pile of clothes and an ironing board. The windows were open and it was raining outside. The curtains flapped about and

Antony looked like an enormous wicked witch, pedalling away under his giant spindle, throwing an enormous shadow across the room. I watched him nervously from the bed – this pouch had taken a lot of persuasion – Antony was a gentle giant but a pathological grumbler as well. Now he was heaving with doomy predictions.

'What are you going to do with that flat arse of yours?'

'Sit on it. Anyway I'll have my cloak.'

I was putting the finishing touches to a cape of butter muslin and threading tons of wooden beads into necklaces. Antony shook his head and chuckled as he inspected the pouch.

'Come on then, Mary. Dress rehearsal.'

As the rain poured down outside we painted my body with Negro Two by Max Factor (those were the days) and my lips with Crimson Lake by Leichner. Then Antony took Polaroids and had his wicked way with me as thunder crackled above and lightning briefly lit our incongruous writhing bodies. The beads broke on my necklace and bounced off all over the floor.

On the night of the party, a beautiful June evening, I set off from my parents' home in Wiltshire with my two best friends in my smashed-up Mini for the party, which was about an hour's drive away.

Liza and Damian were an item. They were also the best-looking people I knew. Already a ruthless snob, I revelled in the reflected glory of being their spokesperson, and they were staying with my family for the party.

Liza had a beautiful body and loved nothing more than to wear a skintight, leopard-skin dress, ravaged by scissors, over stiletto heels and under (but later quite possibly over) a fabulous mane of blonde hair. She teetered on the heels, moved like a caged tigress inside the stretch wrap, and her slightly pouting lips peeped out from beneath the mane of hair. She had incredible allure, with the added bonus of being the daughter of the Thane of Cawdor. She was a descendant of Macbeth. I was her best friend. We both had Minis. Mine was white and falling to pieces. Hers was blue and souped up. Mine had a large gash across the bonnet inflicted during one of those typical hooray accidents – a hit and run with a parked car late one night on Eaton Terrace, on the way home from the Embassy Club. Hers had a House of Lords parking sticker on the windowscreen.

Nobody could persuade Damian to dress up that afternoon before the party. He was extremely shy and his lips too could only be glimpsed, full and sensuous behind his thick long dark hair. All the girls wanted him, and so did some of the boys. Parents said he couldn't look one in the eye, one of their sink-or-swim yardsticks, but we didn't care. We were looking at his lips. He was the richest of my friends. He had a credit card while the rest of us wrote cheques (which invariably bounced). We tore these meaningless contracts with abandon out of large flapping books from such exclusive banking houses as Coutts and Hoare's, or, in my shameful case, Lloyds. Damian's cheques, on the other hand, came from a bank in Nassau. This was indeed glamour. But then Damian's father was a film star, the famous hellraiser, Richard Harris.

Now Damian and Liza were having an affair. She had stalked him through the drawing rooms and discos of SW1 with the intensity of a tigress on a feeding mission. Damian accepted her briefly, but he was a slippery fish when it came to girls and that night of Nicky's party was their spring, summer and autumn merged into one. But everyone was impressed. These were the days when avocado pears were a novelty, and a bottle of plonk washed them down, at dinners and weekends largely populated by chinless creatures with wonky noses and teeth, youthful stoops and potatoes in their mouths. In this milieu Liza and Damian exuded a curious new international glow, and I was right there next to them, bathing in the reflected glory.

And what was I, exactly, that summer night by the river in our garden at home? Certainly no beauty, although straining every nerve to become one. A manic beanpole show-off, with blue-black hair and shaved eyebrows, looking, as Antony Price remarked one night after sex, like a cross between Anne Frank and Snow White.

My poor parents clenched their jaws and barely managed to

restrain themselves from leaping upon me and tearing me limb from limb. Every latest antic, every newest affectation – my refusal to get a job, get up, stand up when grown-ups came into the room, my eccentric appearance – all this had worn their nerves to shreds. A cartoon storm hung over our heads with lightning forks pointing in all directions. Recently a letter had been received from a business associate of my father's – a man currently employing my elder brother – in response to one from my dad, in which he (my dad) had complained that my brother wasn't working hard enough.

'Why worry so much about your elder son,' the letter said, 'when your younger son is a drug addict, a homosexual and a prostitute?'

Very cleverly, my parents never said a word about this letter, although one can imagine the epileptic fit it engendered. My father only mentioned it years later, casually, one evening at dinner, but by then everything had changed.

However, that night of Nicky's party it was all going on. Without knowing it, I was skating on very thin ice, so that what appeared to be an idyllic country evening in the garden held all the potential of a Greek tragedy. The drama was resolutely kept offstage inside buttoned lips and suppressed groans, but any minute now the whole thing could blow up, and I might be dragged to the river and held under water until I saw sense, my whole, short, wasted life passing before me.

'Did you hear? Tony Everett killed his son. Drowned him in their river. There was some awful bust-up on the night of Nicky Haslam's party.'

'No? How ghastly. Sara must be distraught.'

'Yes and no. I think she had come the end of her tether, frankly.'

I had come downstairs in my warrior outfit and sat on the drawing-room sofa, leaving an imprint like the shroud of Turin all over it. My mother had a heart attack. Hardly appeased, but a resolute hostess nonetheless, she bumped a trolley over the lawn towards the summerhouse, rallying her guests from the house, and we all came out and helped ourselves to Pimm's. My father glanced over his paper at

Liza's nipples peeking through cunning little slits in her dress. Liza wasn't fussy where the admiration came from and played up furtively from beneath her bangs, watching my mother from the corner of her eye, just in case that lady noticed, but she needn't have worried. Sex was a myth rather than a reality to my mother, and anyway she never stopped moving, jumping up to dead-head a rose, cantering into the house to answer the telephone, coming out with a fresh jug of Pimm's and inspecting my thong, all in one endless flurry of activity.

Our house, and the valley in which it lay, was several feet below sea level and maybe this was another factor contributing to the pent-up atmosphere in the garden that night. There was a strange magnetic pull, as if gravity there was somehow stronger. When you climbed the hill onto Salisbury Plain above, you suddenly felt weightless. It was true that the people who lived in the clusters of thatched doll's houses on the banks of the meandering river below were strange haunted folk, tinged with inbreeding, from a world poised on the edge of extinction. Soon the tree-tunnelled road that ran along the side of the valley would become a hurtling, murderous short cut for trucks and tourists, and the peace of a thousand years would be shattered for ever. But as dusk fell that summer night on the vast empty plain around us, our little valley, hidden and forgotten behind its hedgerows and woods, shrouded in purple shadows, still held that deep uncanny silence that might have come from the dawn of time. The hill was a black line against the mauve sky, and the quiet was broken only by the odd car changing gear as it went round a corner, its muffled engine a faraway bluebottle banging against a window. Wood pigeons flapped around in the poplar wood. The river gurgled and splashed over the weir. Moorhens squabbled in the water and we squabbled in the garden. Windows and doors were all open in the old house cloaked with wisteria. My father's lurcher loped across the lawn towards us.

'Drat you, darling!' My mother's shriek from inside the house stopped everything in its tracks, including the river. 'You'll have to redo your bottom. Most of it's come off on my sofa. Couldn't you wear some trousers?'

'No!' I shrieked. 'It would ruin everything!'

It never crossed our minds in those days to drink without driving, but the tiny Wiltshire roads were still in a post-war summer haze that night, folded into the plain between the high banks of cow parsley and may that waved us on as we sped towards the ball. Night fell and the heart-stopping smell of the English country evening wafted through the windows on the cool breeze. It was ours, effortlessly, without a thought: all this. We never imagined anything bad could ever happen and so we roared along, screaming, and arrived at the party just after dark.

Nicky presided over the festivities from a throne inside a large striped marquee, dressed as a maharajah. He wore white jodhpurs over high boots, a white safari jacket, a large pink turban and strings of ammunition. He looked like a marvellous villain from a silent film, as if he might pull a gun at any moment on Lady Diana Cooper, sitting beside him. That lady, dressed in a toga with a wreath on her head plucked from the garden, of wisteria, ivy and laurel leaves, still swarming with mosquitoes, glowered lovingly at Nicky like a chihuahua that had been dressed up by its busker master and sat in front of the hat full of coins, smiling or growling – who knew which – at the passing trade. After fifteen years living the American dream – rancher, biker, body-builder: you name it, Nicky did it – his return from exile was perfectly timed. Thatcher, Punk, Safeway's and Nicky. They all came together, and at his ball Nicky threw down the gauntlet to the next chapter of his life. He would grow old disgracefully.

Our arrival didn't cause quite the stir that I had anticipated. A fat lady in a wetsuit with enormous flippers looked daggers at me through her snorkel mask and brandished her harpoon. 'Get away from me, nudist!'

But Nicky was a little more generous. 'You look wonderful, darling. Who are you? Gandhi?'

The party went on all night. There were fireworks, photographers, a band, a discothèque for the young. Liza, Damian and I finally left at about six o'clock in the morning. On the Basingstoke bypass, the engine cut as we ran out of petrol so we glided onto the hard shoulder, had a cigarette and made plans. Cars and lorries roared past, shaking our little vehicle like a leaf. It was a bright summer's morning and we were all desperately hung-over, squinting at one another through the haze of cigarette smoke, tempers slightly frayed. Finally lots were drawn, and Liza, dressed for a Tarzan movie, and Damian for *Miami Vice*, hitched a ride in a lorry to a service station, while I covered myself with my cape and had a quiet nap in the back of the car.

An hour or so later, the two lovers, now in another lorry, with a can of petrol, were thundering back up the other side of the motorway when they saw my poor Mini surrounded by flashing police cars, and me spreadeagled against one of them, cape flying in the wind, naked, being frisked by a policewoman. Arriving at the scene of the crime, they found the whole thing so amusing that we nearly all got arrested. I was trying to explain to the police that the gash in the car's front was an ancient war wound, not recently inflicted, and was being quite convincing, until Tarzan and Jane appeared and were unable to answer the simplest of questions without bursting into tears and clutching their sides as though they were going to explode. The crosser I got, the more they laughed. Finally the police realised we were simply a trio of deranged inbred morons and began to laugh too. We were allowed to go on with our journey, arriving home at about nine o'clock, just in time for breakfast, where we regaled my mother with embroidered stories of the party and our scrape with the law, before going to bed for the rest of the day.

So Nicky was back for the eighties, redecorating Thacherite London with his own brand of throwaway country-house chic. He was pompous – 'My mother was a Ponsonby, you know' – and humble – 'If I wasn't such a wicked old witch, I'd ask you back,' all in the same breath. At dinner he was vastly entertaining, regaling newcomers with all the glittering names from his past, dropped into the conversation,

like commas and semicolons punctuating the long, sometimes complicated phases of his life in America, which sounded like short stories
by Tennessee Williams. Once, for example, Nicky ran over a local
peasant on the road outside Puerta Vallarta in the early sixties. He was
arrested, roughed up and chucked into a paddy wagon by a gang of
thrilling Mexican policemen, to the horror of his two companions,
the society beauties Romana McEwen and Anne von Zigeiser.

'What shall we do?' cried the ladies, as the door of the police van
was slammed shut.

Nicky's face appeared through the bars, purple and bloody. 'Call
Merle Oberon, and tell her to call the President!' he shouted. And
then he was gone.

The girls booked into a hotel, all the while pondering the mystery
of Nicky's final words. Had they heard him right? How on earth
could they get Merle Oberon's number, and what she was going to
do if they did manage to contact her? And maybe he hadn't said
Merle Oberon after all.

'There is an Earl of Oban, I think,' drawled Romana. 'But he's a
frightful bore, and I'm not sure how sympathetic he would be to
Nicky's cause, in any case.'

They were on the point of packing up and going back to Mexico
City, putting the whole thing behind them and into the hands of the
British Embassy there, but they ordered some drinks and got on the
phone anyway. Of course nothing is beyond the network of a well-to-
do beauty, and soon Anne was speaking to the squeaky little midget
herself in Hollywood. Within a matter of hours, Nicky was out of
gaol and aboard a government plane heading for Mexico City.

The great thing about Nicky was that he didn't really care what other
people thought. As far as he was concerned he started life as 'an
ugly little thing' and would soon be an ugly old thing, and that was
enough for him. He didn't look for any further criticism. He was
authentic to himself and that was all that mattered. In Thatcher's
queer nation he remained fairly conservative, but in 1997 – at the

shocking-pink dawn of Cool Britannia, when the whole of Britain rose up in a frenzied euphoria, like the last night of the Proms and the Cup Final all rolled into one, with Tony Blair as conductor and the captain of the English team, heralding a brave new world of all-day drinking in your burka – a curious new character erupted from Nicky. Like a medium drunk on ectoplasm, he was suddenly possessed, and overnight channelled himself from Michael Heseltine into Liam Gallagher. He dyed his hair black, had a brilliant facelift, wore tight torn jeans over cowboy boots with loo chains around his neck, lashings of Egyptian-coloured pancake on his face, and at a hundred yards he was indistinguishable from his new hero. He was the mirage of Oasis and Oasis was the mirage of New Labour. The effect was mesmerising. Until he opened his mouth. Then he was more Noël Coward than Gallagher.

Britain exploded and so did Nicky Haslam. Suddenly he was more famous than he had ever been. 'A proper celebrity!' He wrote a column in *Hello!* and another in the *Evening Standard*. Nobody was safe, and all were grilled at some point or other. He won *The Weakest Link* and his extraordinary wardrobe became legendary as it lurched from Oasis to Biggles to Sid Vicious and back again. He indulged his every whim, and mid-life for Nicky was like the blooming of an exotic orchid, seen once in a lifetime and never forgotten. The crisis was for everybody else.

Nobody knew quite how to handle this new rock legend, except for his Russian clientele, who probably found him the most normal-looking person they had ever met. Suddenly he didn't just know everyone from the pages of *Burke's* or Dun & Bradstreet, he knew *everyone*. Like the White Rabbit, he popped up everywhere in the enchanted forest of New Labour London, one night chatting with Princess Julia, the DJ, in the toilets of a Hoxton pub, the next in a tête-à-tête with the Duchess of Cornwall at Highgrove. Nothing was too high or too low.

One evening I went with him to a club in Shoreditch that was so fast and hip that it later closed down because it was too popular. At the door a cluster of freaks were waiting to be vetted by a vitriolic drag queen in a pink bunny rabbit jumpsuit, waving a clipboard. Nicky elbowed his way to the front. This was madness, I thought. Quite often these girls took a dim view of a barging celebrity, and I always stood firmly in line, terrified lest I should be turned on by some hideous gremlin playing to the crowd.

'Ow yes, dear, Rupert Who? Where's Madonna now, eh? Ask 'er if you can come in! Get to the back of the bloody line an' stop fussin'.'

But Nicky had no such qualms. 'Don't worry. La Bottomy's a friend.'

Sure enough the bunny rabbit shrieked with excitement and bashed Nicky over the head with her clipboard. 'Nickaay, you old tart! What's happenin', babes? How many are you?'

The two hugged and chatted, while I marvelled at Nicky's ease and charm, and we swanned through the velvet rope and into the club. Inside, the place was packed. I immediately spied a brilliant-looking skinhead.

'That's Spence,' said Nicky. 'Hi, Spence, how are you, darling?'

I couldn't believe my eyes. As we made our way around the room it was clear that he knew almost everyone, and by the time we got to the bar we had been given a gram of coke, several drinks tickets, an Ecstasy and an invitation to an orgy.

'I'm exhausted, but Ru might love it,' said Nicky as though he were talking about lunch on Sunday.

One last image. I am walking past the Grill Room at the Savoy Hotel on my way to some dull corporate party. The restaurant is packed and the lights are dimming. A spotlight quivers over a pair of double doors.

'Your Royal Highness, my Lords, Ladies and Gentlemen . . .' commands a voice over the loudspeaker. 'Please welcome Mr Nicholas Haslam and his band.'

I stop dead in my tracks. The double doors are flung dramatically open and there is Nicky wincing slightly in the light, clutching a microphone in one hand and a swathe of notes in the other. He has a deep tan and a crew-cut of bright white hair. He trots into the room and the crowd goes wild, whooping and cheering, while he weaves through the tables, kissing the baubled hand of a deposed royal, whispering in the ear of Andrew Lloyd Webber, blowing another kiss to his ex-boyfriend Paolo, standing at the bar. The piano strikes up and Nicky points dramatically at poor Paolo and launches into 'You Made Me Love You'. The room gasps. Paolo freezes, eyes on stalks. Nicky knows how to work a crowd. He throws his head from side to side between lines at the sheer anguish of the emotion, pouting like Mick Jagger. The effect is mesmerising. The audience watches, aghast.

'I didn't want to do it. I didn't want to do it.'

You could fit a large slice of cake into the open mouth of Lord Lloyd Webber. It is an extraordinary performance. Two American ladies stop at the door beside me.

'Any royals?' one asks.

'Yes. Quite a few queens,' I reply.

Like England, Nicky is slightly more conventional these days. 'Jolly Good Boating Weather' has replaced 'Live For Ever', and Nicky can be heard regularly at the Savoy Hotel, singing Cole Porter, and will probably be minister for the interior (decoration) before very long. Whatever. But for the time being, the crisis of mid-life has been thwarted, and Nicky is sailing into Porto-Vecchio, flying all colours and making an album too.

One night, some time ago, Nicky had dinner with my father and me.

'We are going on a pilgrimage to Lourdes,' said my father.

'How marvellous,' replied Nicky, sweet and attentive, always good with family.

'What?' said my father.

'The pope has issued a plenary indulgence.'

It was like playing to the upper circle, talking to my dad sometimes. One had to enunciate every syllable.

'What's that?' asked Nicky.

'It means that if you take the water, go to confession, have communion and do the candlelight procession, the whole hokey-cokey, this year, the jubilee, a hundred years since the initial apparition, *then* you will go straight to heaven, come what may.'

'Even if you commit a terrible murder on the way?'

'Even if you commit a terrible faux pas!'

'There's a good son for you,' said Nicky to my dad.

'Where?' asked my father.

'That's what I am going to give you, Daddy. Eternal life! You are going straight to heaven.'

'You're screaming, darling,' said Nicky.

'I shall wait for you at the gates,' said my father and we all fell silent.

'Take a good book. You might be waiting an awfully long time,' whispered Nicky.

CHAPTER NINE

The Last Campaign

At some point in 2008 the plan was hatched by my father to make a trip to Lourdes, the village in south-western France where the Virgin Mary appeared to a peasant girl one hundred and fifty years ago. There is a miraculous spring and my father wanted to bathe in it one last time.

'Not for a miracle, you understand,' he said, brave, blind and in bed one morning. 'But to give thanks for a marvellous life.'

Life was marvellous in retrospect and tawdry up close. Daddy was finding it difficult to adapt to old age. Unable to escape to the office, abroad or to the races, and having few interior pursuits to fall back on, he spent most of the day in front of the television, watching the news or sleeping. This pastime was punctuated by visits to the loo, pushing his empty wheelchair in front of him for balance, or to the drinks cupboard before lunch to mix a pink gin. He shuffled along, banging against the furniture like a bumper car. My darling mother, still verging on hyperactivity at seventy, screeched around the house performing her chores, swooping down upon him every fifteen minutes for a spot check.

'Do sit up straight, Tony, for God's sake!'

His own energy paled beside hers although he occasionally rose to her bait and snarled back as of old, at which point she cantered off, satisfied that she was keeping him going. She was, although their world was shrouded in its deep winter freeze, under a blanket of dementia and disease. One by one their vast network of acquaintances began to die, and some of the survivors behaved very oddly at lunch. The men went on ahead. They'd fought a war, after all, and had drunk seriously ever since, so they slid into the fog, mistaking a birthday for D-Day and their wife for the postman, while these poor wives, who had never signed a cheque and had been accustomed to receiving orders, now found themselves in charge. The tables had turned, after a life spent buttoning their husbands' collars and their own lips. Occasionally this new power went to their heads and many a lazy Georgian rectory turned into a Zimbabwean dictatorship, where unspeakable atrocities were committed in the name of progress by a junta comprising of Mummy and Mrs B, the housekeeper, crushing and squeezing some poor crazed brigadier towards the Last Post and the final frontier. Once he was dead, history could quickly be rewritten, and Mummy either sailed off into the sunset memoir with her girlfriends or else she lost her marbles overnight.

But for the time being, funerals were the cocktail parties for the over-eighties. One caught up with a vast network of friends and relations, with people one had watched getting married and divorced and married again. After all the wars and the weekends, now they met in a funeral pew, or waving from a passing wheelchair on the rickety pathways of graveyards, or later over a box, bending low to look at the messages on the floral bouquets. And so, rather brilliantly, living and dying were challenged in the same breath, my parents embarking on these trips and on the big trip itself with their signature blitz sang-froid.

'That was a marvellous funeral.'

'Terrible hymns, though. Not one tune I knew.'

'Boring address. General X looked goofy.'

'He hasn't been right for a long time.'

My father's health had seriously deteriorated over the previous two years, although his will to live still overwhelmed his body's desire to call it a day, and so he ploughed through several shipwrecking storms and miraculously survived. He had a stroke in a swimming pool in Dubai, where on a whim he had gone to the races. According to a racing friend, he was chasing a girl to the shallow end when it happened. That trip lost him the sight in one eye. A few months later his spleen burst one night, and he began to spew a strange black bile like a beer tap. He just opened his mouth and it bubbled from him. He was rushed to the local hospital, ominously named Odstock, where he contracted MRSA and C Difficile, while the condition of his spleen went undetected and untreated. After a week there, when it had poisoned his entire body, he was discharged. The next day he was rushed to the Cromwell Hospital in London.

The Cromwell is a reassuring landmark for the wealthy and ancient returning from Hampshire, Wiltshire, Dorset and Devon after a weekend in the country. Otherwise it is an ugly modern building, unremarkable except for its futuristic windows of blue glass. Inside the large reception area wait an uneasy melting pot of the sick rich and their various dependants. Bony British matriarchs in tweeds and headscarves sit gingerly next to rows of small round Arab ladies swathed in black, whose eyes swivel comically inside their masks. Everyone is waiting for a man. I have rarely seen a woman patient in the Cromwell, although they must have them. The man arrives – sheiken but not stirred, accompanied by the Harley Street specialist *du jour*, pristine in a pinstripe suit, under a handsome head of silver hair. It's the last generation of everyone: of tribal leaders, of empire rulers, and not least of the elegant British private doctor with his Harley Street rooms.

My father lay in a bed surrounded by machines in the limbo of Intensive Care. No night or day – just life held by a thread in an unrecognisable body, wired and masked, in a ghostly pool of light. There was a feeling of theatre in that place, a hushed expectancy, as if a giant curtain might rise up at any moment and we would all find ourselves on stage, confronted by an audience of saints and gods and everyone we had ever fucked or fucked over. I found it deeply exciting. A nurse sat as still as a graveyard angel at the foot of each bed, making notes. The deathless silence was broken only by whispers, clicks and bleeps. Occasionally a sob cut through it, somebody receiving bad news, a loved one seen for the first time, and sometimes one heard the strangled rattle of life evaporating off the planet. Then screens would be rushed towards a bed with a theatrical precision to shield the rest of us from the horrors of death. A silent flurry of doctors and nurses followed, white on white on white, coats, walls, screens and faces. Mummy and I looked at one another, not daring to speak, lest the grim reaper turn his attention towards our bed, although our curiosity always got the better of us, and we did everything but stand on tiptoe to see over the garden fence at the electrical resuscitations going on next door. Unfortunately the nurses were discreet and unresponsive to the energy of our interest.

'How ghastly for them! Did I hear electrocardio massage just then?' sleuthed Mummy, one night, after a particularly dramatic scene change.

'I really couldn't tell you, Mrs Everett,' the nurse replied, smiling.

Mummy tried changing tack. 'Poor Mrs Abu must be beside herself.'

'We're going to wash your husband now, Mrs Everett,' the girl said firmly. 'Would you mind going to the waiting room for a few minutes? We'll call you when we're done.'

In the waiting room lay the answers to all Mummy's questions. It was where we all gathered in the morning, the motley crew of distraught relatives, another place that reminded me of the theatre. It was the quick-change room where you fixed on your smile and covered your drained face before you went on stage.

There was only one other patient in Intensive Care when we arrived. A shrunken grey man from Dubai lay in the bed next to my dad. When you went into the room you were confronted by the two of them, surrounded by their consoles, a pair of undead kings on their thrones, while backstage his wife and my mother waited side by side, both in full burqua (Mother's was from Hermès), and a little girl drew with felt tips in her colouring book. She was wide eyed. Ours were red. Sometimes there were men there. Sometimes another woman, sometimes my brother. Any mutual distrust quickly disappeared in the light of our common hopes and fears, and soon we were a kind of team.

It was touching to find my mother and 'Madame', as we ludicrously called her (when in doubt, use French), chatting together in their own languages, holding hands. They may not have understood the words, but they were fluent in the irregular verb of being a wife. They had both devoted entire lives to these flattened vegetables next door, and had quite possibly received rather less attention in return. The warmth between the two women, and the support she received from the nurses, got my mother through the day. 'Monsieur' was never coming round. They were resigned to that, and sat by his bed talking quietly to one another while he watched through unseeing eyes. Daddy was going to come round. That much was certain. And so my mother sat beside him, held his hand and waited.

Spectacles of intimacy were frowned upon in military circles. One said goodbye to one's husband – whether he was boarding a troopship or being nailed into a coffin – with little more than a wave and a chin stuck out in defiance. Those were the rules of the game and so I had rarely witnessed any gestures of affection between my parents in forty-five years, beyond a distracted peck at the airport. I had a feeling that my father's drugged-out, half-closed eyes registered faint surprise from somewhere in his semi-coma, and I smiled. Intensive care was coming from all directions.

What a far cry, this picture of them now, from their wedding portrait, fifty years ago, that stood by both their beds at home. Between the bleeps and flashes of hospital, and the bells and the thundering organ of St James's, Spanish Place, a lifetime had rushed by. Was it a second ago or fifty years since that spring morning when they stepped from God's house to be photographed for the first time as man and wife? Frozen for ever, surrounded by bridesmaids in crinolines, Edwardian matriarchs in musty hats and veils, friends from the war still carrying swords, in a blur of confetti; the future stretched out in a beautiful haze that day, conjured up and coloured by faith and belief in Britain and Beelzebub. It was a mirage, of course. 'In sickness and in health, for better or for worse' were just words and not a magic receipt to deal with the series of events and experiences that led them towards the valley of death via the swing doors of Intensive Care.

The operation to remove his spleen was a success, and after several days Daddy was brought round.

'I am feeling rather holy at the moment,' he whispered, and began to have hallucinations. 'They are making a marvellous chanting in the mosque next door.'

'What mosque, Daddy?'

'I don't know where it is. They're hiding it from me.'

What recovery he made was painful and slow. A brilliant Scottish sergeant major of a lady, recommended by the wife of a dead friend, stormed into our house, and completely took over. Jean was a slightly unhinged Mary Poppins. She was nearly seventy years old herself and was possibly shell-shocked from the years entrenched in various country houses of the rich and selfish. Her tactics were brilliant but dangerous. She completely identified herself with the patient, usually a man, which inevitably led to rebellion against the lady of the house. She didn't much like women. At coffee time in the kitchen she was deliciously indiscreet about her latest case and we all hung on her every word, as she sat, legs astride, in front of the Aga.

'When she'd come into the room he told her tae bugger off. It's nae wonder. She'd been starving him on plastic ham all the while!' she said about a couple we all knew.

'Oh, Jean. That's simply not true,' said my mother, enthralled. 'She absolutely loved him.'

'Wull, if that's love, I can dae withoot it,' Jean replied, with a snort of derision.

That summer we were infested by field mice, which was a sign, according to country people, that it was going to be a cold winter. It was certainly a hot summer, and at night the old house groaned in the heat. From the ceiling above my bed I could hear the scratches of little feet, as those rodents who had escaped Mummy's executions got ready for the winter. Our valley was quiet under the harvest moon, released from the endless buzz of daytime traffic as if it had been holding its breath all day. The only noise was the screech of the local owl and its mate's distant reply somewhere up on the plain.

But our house was a creaking galleon on the changing tide. Sometimes I woke in the dead of night to hear the ghostly groans of my father's nightmares. I tiptoed to his room across the corridor. There he was bathed in the light of the moon, smoking imaginary cigars in his sleep, puffing and talking distractedly, his hand searching blindly for an elusive ashtray.

'Oh, Crippin! Where is the bloody thing?' he moaned, winding himself up in the tangle of sheets.

Further along the corridor my mother's door was closed. In the old days she hardly slept and no matter how quietly one crept upstairs her voice always sliced through the darkness. 'Is that you, darling? Did you lock up?'

Now she was dead to the world, laid out for a wake, flat on her back with her hands folded across her chest; the light on and the World Service at full blast. Its calm authority conjured up a lost empire, and her post-war youth still whispered around Mummy's face in the bedside light. During the day the harsh reality of old age was a constant challenge to my nerves, but at night I was transported outside time, when both my parents became beautiful and touching as they wrestled with oblivion on the pillow. One didn't need phantoms in that creaky old house. The living were their own ghosts.

Out of the dusty gloom, Jean, insomniac, appeared in a T-shirt and tracksuit, carrying an empty mug.

'I couldnae sleep. Ahm goin' for a quick wee cuppa. Want one?'

And so we all woke up, spent, for another day.

When Jean wasn't coaxing my father back to life, she was up a ladder pruning a tree, or ironing. She never stopped. I adored her. She called Duncan our gardener 'Sexy Legs', then one day she suddenly announced she was leaving and my mother cried.

'I don't think I can manage without you, Jean.'

'It's the right time,' said Jean. 'If I dinnae gae now, he'll never come back.'

And she was right. We had to get on without her. She had pulled Daddy back to life by the sheer force of her will, like an exorcist, exhausting herself and my mother in the process. Now it was up to him, and us. Unfortunately my father's post-operative holiness had vanished. Instead the poor man was spitting with fury at his reduced circumstances and took it out on everyone, particularly his wife. But little by little things got back on track, and one day, when the vicar was visiting, the plan was hatched to go to Lourdes.

And so we flew on the wings of faith towards Plymouth in my father's Lexus. The silver racehorse on the bonnet and the pro-hunting sticker on the back window left no one in any doubt as to the hopes and fears of the travellers within. My father sat in the front, wearing his old straw hat and his new glasses, the lens over his blind eye blacked out. He quickly fell asleep and woke only as we reached Plymouth, after a hair-raising drive down England's worst road, the A303. We were accompanied by his new nurse, a German lady called Marianne. You've probably noticed that sooner or later everything in my world is reduced to a Julie Andrews film and I had already renamed her Fräulein Maria. She was a kind, vulnerable creature, devoted to my dad and, according to him, a good driver. This was one of the ultimate accolades in my family. 'Well parked' was a far greater compliment than 'You look quite sexy.'

Our disabled sticker was like a backstage pass when we arrived at the port. We waved it and drove straight on board. My mother had made the reservations on her computer and, needless to say, had booked us the three cheapest berths. In high spirits we loaded up my father like a packhorse with all our luggage, so that his straw hat was all that could be seen above it, and pushed him through the labyrinth of passages – just wide enough for the wheelchair – towards our tiny windowless cubicles in the bowels of the ship.

Normandy Ferries is a French line, but these floating tanks are in fact the very essence of England, and Dickens, Waugh, Wilde – even Shakespeare – can be found sitting at the bar. There is a charged romance in the air as the engines grind into motion, the thick ropes strain and the boat groans to be released. Passengers crowd the decks for one last look at home, that jewel set in its silver sea, as the lines are cast off by chubby dockhands and the ship finally edges her way from quay and country towards the open sea in a swirling, wailing confetti of seagulls. England is a dripping green jungle under the low sky and Byron must have watched it disappear thus, before dragging his bad foot below for a drink.

As soon as our boat hit the open sea, Fräulein Maria became mortally ill, clutching her jaw.

'I am having the abscess. This is not seasickness! I will burst it with this needle. Don't worry. I have done this many times,' she announced, turning all the colours of the German flag.

I became very frosty. 'Who is going to take my father to the bathroom?'

'Come and get me when he wants to go,' she whispered, clutching her head.

So I parked her in her cubicle and left with my dad for karaoke up on deck. It was raining outside now, pouring down the windows, and there was quite a swell. The ship lurched and listed, perched and swooped on the rolling sea, but nothing detracted from the party within. Snaggle-toothed she-bears with builders' bums swayed through the lounge, juggling six pints of lager and as many packets of crisps, towards groups of purple-faced mechanicals in chains and rings. The smell of beer and aftershave wafted through the saloon.

The revellers sat and laughed at their drinks, all elbows and arms, squeezed as they were into nightclub tables around the periphery of a sort of stage, next to older groups, retired professionals, who were neater, more controlled. They were Old Labour, worlds away from the raucous children of Blair at the next table. These ladies had posture. Their pink, grey and beige hair had been set in rollers and was backcombed and sprayed, ready to withstand the gusty Channel winds. Sensible handbags sat on their laps, surgical tights sparkled on their coffee-coloured legs and they watched entranced later on when oldie hits and magic tricks were performed by some former young hopeful just out of drama school fifteen years ago, applauding politely, as the groups around them bayed louder by the pint.

My father watched from his chair. In his dotage he reminded me of an old dog, surveying the passing world from a corner, occasionally sniffing the wind, in that lazy state between sleep and wakefulness, no energy left to judge, or condone, just pleased to be there.

'I rather miss the smoke,' he said. 'Everything is so terribly clear without cigarettes.'

We had dinner in the restaurant. The rain stopped quite suddenly and the clouds drew back, revealing a creamy dusk, a large orange sun and a cargo ship like a spacecraft on the horizon. As the sun hit the water, dolphins appeared by the side of the ship. They jumped and raced in the waves.

'Aren't they marvellous?' Daddy said, looking in another direction altogether where suddenly a submarine appeared out of the ocean. It sailed beside us for a few minutes and then disappeared.

'That was a very big one.'

'It was a submarine, Daddy.'

'Oh. Are you sure?'

We talked about our trip, and the last time he went to Lourdes, with his mother and sister, in 1954.

'There was a marvellous statue of Our Lady that my mother liked very much. We must find it,' he said.

'Well, I don't expect much has changed.'

'No, but we have,' Daddy replied, staring blindly out to sea.

I had been to Lourdes on a pilgrimage with my school, a Catholic monastery in Yorkshire called Ampleforth College. Accompanied by a few congenial priests, we went by train and boat and train down France to look after the sick, whom we pushed in ancient bath chairs towards the grotto every day to take the water. Our choir sang in the basilica.

One evening I escaped from our dormitory with another student and played around all night in the woods outside Lourdes under the full moon. He was one of the most handsome boys in the school and played in the cricket eleven. We had loved and hated each other for a while in one of those typical school relationships in which childish romance is squashed by guilt and fear. Most of the time we avoided each other – but occasionally our eyes locked across a noisy common room, or in the abbey church. Without a word we would both leave, one following the other at a safe distance down long stone passages, round corners, up a turret staircase, to a classics room high up in the eaves of the school, which had a lock on the door, and in which Greek, if not Greek love, was taught. We'd silently undress and have each other among the desks under a blackboard covered in ancient Greek. Later, reclothed, we'd leave the room without a word, merging back into the traffic of the school.

This was the violence of Catholicism in action. But in the hills outside Lourdes it felt different. Maybe the Virgin was watching from above, thinking: God, I wouldn't mind a bit of that! At any rate something was released in us, and we laughed and talked, and wandered ever further – two escaping puppies – into the woods. By the end of the night, under a sky streaked with thin pink clouds we lay under a tree, exhausted. Looking back, it should have been one of the most beautiful moments of my childish life. But it wasn't. The religious conditioning was too strong, and post-coital remorse flooded through our veins, so without speaking – actually we hardly ever spoke again – we climbed the hill back to the monastery and silently scaled the wall into the same open window, returning to our separate beds.

It felt important to be telling this story to my dad, now, after all this time, sailing back into the jaws of the Catholic Church, and I was looking out to sea, lost in the drama of it all, when I heard an enormous snore. He was fast asleep. Probably just as well.

Ashen-faced, Fräulein Maria stumbled into my father's cabin to undress him while I went back up to the bar and had a drink with four truck drivers who loved me in *St Trinian's*. When I returned she had passed out on the floor, and my father was lying on the bed with his trousers down.

'What's going on?' I asked.

'I don't know what happened to Marianne,' my father replied. 'She was here a minute ago. Could you ask her to come back and finish me off?'

'She's under the bed,' I said.

'Oh really?'

'Sorry, Rupert,' murmured Fräulein Maria. 'Could you take me to my cabin now?'

'Oh yes, madam.'

The clowns were running the circus.

'I shall be invoicing Mummy for this, you know,' I quipped later, as I struggled with Daddy's underwear.

'Isn't she?' replied my dad obliquely. 'Leave my bottle by the bed, would you?'

'Which one? Whisky or . . .?'

'Both,' grunted Daddy, followed by his sing-song 'Thank you.'

I was dismissed.

The next morning Fräulein Maria made a miraculous recovery so we left the boat and began the six-hour drive along the coast of Spain into France. We had lunch at a truck stop outside Bilbao, and arrived in Lourdes at six o'clock.

The grotto of Lourdes is in a deep valley with a wild slate-coloured river running through it. There is a magnificent dam, and the water thunders down it from the mountains. It is the roar of God in a place largely deafened by the industry of faith, but actually, if you can see past the basilica with its Disneyland towers and mawkish statuary – Our Lady should have appeared in Hollywood. Then she would have had statue approval – the kingdom of heaven is all around you in Lourdes. Strangely, it comes as no surprise, even to the hardened cynic, that divinity briefly congealed into human form and appeared here as a woman.

Bernadette Soubirous was a fragile little shepherdess living in one room with her large family during the middle of the nineteenth century. She was weak from having cholera as a child, semi-literate and, some say, backward. One day she was gathering firewood by the cliffs on the banks of the river when she looked up and saw a beautiful young woman standing on a small niche in a kind of half-cave where rubbish was dumped. They began to chat, and Bernadette ran home afterwards and told her mother. She described a small lady in white with a blue mantle, holding a long rosary, with yellow roses on her feet. At first nobody believed her story, but the lady kept appearing, and soon people became intrigued. The local priest told her to ask the lady who she was, but when she did, the lady just smiled and looked down. During one of the visions (sources vary as to which), the lady told Bernadette to dig in the ground, saying that a spring would come up, and that she should drink from it, and eat the surrounding plants.

By now the whole town followed her each day to the grotto, so in front of an audience of hundreds she dug in the mud and tried to suck water from it, covering her face with dirt in the process, but no water came. Then she began to eat the plants as instructed. With her muddy face, and a mouth full of dock leaves, she must have looked unhinged. The townsfolk jeered and drifted off while her mother cleaned the little girl's face. Suddenly the whole family was facing disgrace, but a few days later water began to pour from the spot where Bernadette had been digging. The spring has been active and miraculous ever since. Finally the lady introduced herself: 'I am the Immaculate Conception.'

Interestingly, at that time, the Mother of Jesus had been largely ignored for the previous few hundred years by the Catholic Church. But only a few years before, the pope had issued new dogma concerning the Virgin Mary, claiming that she had been born without sin and was to be known henceforth as 'the immaculate conception'. How could an illiterate peasant girl know these words when few priests at the time were even familiar with them?

The lady instructed Bernadette to tell the local priest to build a chapel over the grotto, and that people should come and drink from the spring and pray for forgiveness. And so a cult was born. Today Lourdes is the most popular pilgrims' destination in Christendom, and countless inexplicable cures have been scientifically witnessed.

Three or four years after the visions ended, Bernadette was unable to cope with the endless scrutiny of the faithful and not so faithful. She took orders and retired to a faraway convent, for a life of contemplation. On her first day the Mother Superior assembled the nuns and ordered her to tell the whole story for the thousandth time. Then she was forbidden to mention it ever again. In the convent, she contracted TB of the knee, and when asked if she would go to Lourdes to bathe in the water, she apparently said, 'It is not for me.' According to Catholic propaganda she lived happily and humbly, loved by her sisters, although I doubt it. The Mother Superior wanted to plead Devil's advocate during the Vatican inquiry thirty years later into Bernadette's sanctity. Nuns were a mean bunch in those days. She was not allowed go to the inauguration of the basilica at Lourdes. In fact, she never went back, nor saw her beloved family again.

The world is cruel to saints while they are on earth. According to a witness, on her deathbed – she was only thirty-three – Bernadette was racked for several hours by a terrible anxiety. Maybe it had all been a dream, the fantasy of an imaginative child. Certainly the yellow flower slippers she described the lady as wearing sound more like the wish-list of a little girl for her Christmas stocking than traditional footwear from BC Judaea. We will never know. Either way, the sisters sat around the bed murmuring the rosary, and slowly she began to calm down. Somehow it is a picture of utter desolation. A sweet little peasant girl, exiled for a vision from her beautiful mountainside home, from rivers and forests that she loved, punished and imprisoned for being simple and trusting and maybe magical, ending her life on a gurney surrounded by the stern, withered faces of a swarm of nuns in starched wimples and snoods buzzing around the honeycomb. '*Je vous salue, Marie, pleine de grâce. Le Seigneur est avec vous.*'

Finally she died, saying the prayer that would make her – and her patron – famous, and Mary, Mother of God, would be the clever new image of late nineteenth-century Catholicism, neatly embracing the exploding women's movement, but also subliminally inferring that only a virgin could know God. Bernadette was disinterred in the 1930s. Her body had not decomposed at all, though some daft nuns washed it with soap and water, and it turned black. This was another sign of her sanctity. (Mind you, Lord Byron's body was exhumed that same year – a hundred after his death – and was found to be in an equally sprightly condition. But then many virgins had appeared to him.)

Whatever the truth, it was a magical May evening as we arrived in Lourdes. The woods and fields were that green one sees on a TV when the colour is turned up too high. The countryside literally blazed. The road wound down a hill towards the basilica, which stood on the remains of the famous cliff in the pastures at the bottom of the valley, and the old village rose above it, cut into the side of the mountain like the backdrop of provincial pantomime. Suddenly we were in the rush-hour traffic, bumper to bumper with the faithful returning from the grotto, through a maze of steep ancient streets crammed with hotels and boarding houses. The Solitude. (Three stars.) The Pope Pius XIV. (Air-conditioned.) The St Francis of Assisi.

(Hot and cold in all rooms.) Nurses in capes and starched head-dresses pushed wheelchairs up the hills. It was like an evacuation scene from a war film. My dad looked out of the window, and I wondered what was going through his mind.

Later that night we pushed the wheelchair down the hill to the basilica, really fast; my dad holding on for dear life with his legs out straight – for some reason he didn't like the footrests on his chair; I think they made it feel too permanent – Marianne running beside us, past the bars overflowing with revelling pilgrims, and the souvenir shops with their rows of statues at all prices, to the amphitheatre in front of the basilica, where pilgrims were preparing for the regular torchlight procession through the hills. It was stunningly beautiful. Blind devotion under the silver moon. A snake of flames winding through the black hills. The hymn to Mary surging on the breeze, ghostly and distant, then suddenly up close. And my dad, incredibly, still alive, me and Marianne beside him, weaving through the crowds. A group from some town in Poland were clustered around the steps of the church, in their nurse's garb, with their sick in chairs in a semicircle in front of them, holding their candles, and in the guttering waxy light they were Rembrandts and Vermeers. Their eyes glittered with belief.

'Ave, ave, ave Maria' sang the torchlight procession from the hills, and the sound was not unlike the roar of a distant football stadium, ecstatic at a goal that was about to be scored.

'I've been here before,' I suddenly remembered.

'Yes, when you were at Ampleforth,' said my dad.

'No, after. Long after. I came here with my dog. My God, I had completely forgotten.'

'One does that,' answered my father knowingly, but I was no longer there.

CHAPTER TEN

Two Boys of Unimaginable Beauty

The house was on a hill above the beach, up a steep bumpy track, hidden by umbrella pines and verging on the vineyard of an aristocratic family whom, by chance I had met once as a child. It was going to be a pretty house one day, pale yellow with blue shutters, but for now, it was the shell of an unfinished dream. Inside, it was mostly a building site where work was often suspended for lack of funds, so that for one whole summer a cement mixer stood defiant in the middle of the sitting room, or a hole in the bathroom floor had to be circumnavigated at one's own risk late at night on the way to the loo. There was no heating. In the winter the wind shook the windows in their frames, and my dog and I huddled in front of an electric fire, wondering what had become of us. The umbrella pines outside scratched against the roof like zombies and we pricked up our ears, ready for the attack. But once the summer came, the slow months by the granite sea were forgotten, and the lonely mists of winter dispersed in the Mediterranean spring. The water sparkled blue and white again. The beach clubs opened, and the season began. The empty house was suddenly alive.

My best friend Tom came from Madrid. He spent every summer in my gypsy caravan wearing a sarong and flip-flops, and that year a group of Hobbity kids from Alsace squatted in various nooks and crannies of the house. Their leader was an hysterical imp called Bruno, a tiny creature with waist-length hair and a laugh like a hyena. He had a little dog, Geppie, that was half fox. Tom was falling in love, I could tell, and together they flirted over the stove as they made dinner every night for the other guests.

And so our summer days were spent surveying the shoals of tourists that washed up on the beach, and our nights trawling them into our nets at the various bars and discos of St Tropez, luring them back to the beach in the dead of night, where the beam of the lighthouse at Cap Camarat grazed my rumpled bed, briefly sketching in silver the tangle of our inert, salty bodies knocked senseless by sun, sea and sex.

We were a famous force, known by the 'gens du coin' as 'La Bande Rupert', neither fish nor fowl, locals nor tourists, and that was the thing I liked best. We took promising newcomers under our wings, and issued fatwahs against our enemies. We were loved by some, loathed by others and mistrusted by all. Everything was on tick, and we were always broke, but somehow we got along. By August our numbers sometimes swelled to fifteen or twenty, as people came and went like the waves on the shore, slapping into the house and being sucked back out a week later, leaving odd bits of driftwood that accumulated over the years, and added to the general feeling of chaos in my unfinished home. Chinese hats, wicker baskets, a solitary espadrille, my dog and I were all that was left by the end of another summer.

In town at night, there were two bars for those of a liberal disposition, on either side of a narrow street behind the port. In a way the whole of France could be understood, grasped, within a week or so of meandering back and forth between the two.

Chez Nano didn't set out to be a gay bar, but its owner, a legendary Tropézien fairy from the glorious sixties, was a man named

Nano. She may have looked fairly butch in those early days, when long hair and afghan coats and winding scarves were a man's attire, but by the time I got to St Tropez she was a lady cow, old, silent and unmilkable, her good looks submerged under a pink quilt of quivering flesh. Long nights on the bottle and days on the beach had done her in, although her hair was still long and thick, cut with a fringe, whiter in winter, blonder in summer, and she dressed, like Antonia Fraser, exclusively in white.

The bar was small; an old cave really, and the jungle-red walls were covered with framed, faded photographs of Nano and the stars. Anyone who was anyone who had ever been beached on that particular strip of the Côte d'Azur was there, laughing intimately with this creature they had never met, sharing some unfunny joke, always glossy, in their prime, while Nano's entire pilgrimage through life was chronicled in uncompromising close-up: winter, spring, summer and fall. The fall came in the eighties when the bar was requisitioned by the cackling old queen world, and it was there, when I got to St Tropez, that they conducted their business, still dressed for *Some Like It Hot* in sailor hats and striped jerseys, while the beauties of Toulon and Nice, Paris, New York and Rome, sprawled next to them on the banquettes wrapping the room, sucking umbrella-ed cocktails through straws.

On the other side of the road was Chez Maggy, owned by two brothers from Toulon who also had a restaurant on the beach. They were tough movers with jet-black Provençal hair and local accents, and they appealed to a younger crowd, the kids who worked the season, and the flocks of visiting drag queens who arrived side-saddle on scooters from the north of Italy. The night-time explosion of sunburnt revellers overflowed from both bars onto the pavement. In high season the whole street was jammed and a car had to honk its way through the jeering crowd, as Nano peeked out, frowning, from across the road, but it was all part of the fun.

One morning two boys of unimaginable beauty appeared on the beach. Binoculars came out of bags as the early bird queens, slithery with suncream, rose as one like Lazarus from their mats and watched the two men as they undressed, wrestling each other, laughing, into the sea. Their two bodies were sheer Michelangelo, although by the looks of things rather more encouragingly sculpted where it mattered. They ploughed into the water, splashing and diving until their thick necks and ears resurfaced far out in the milky void, and a hundred queens flopped back down on their mats. By the time our group came down the hill everyone had agreed that two finer specimens of manhood would not be found that summer and, as if some secret switch had been turned on, the energy level rose and the frenetic, sleepless party mood for which the beach was famous suddenly kicked in. Disco music blared from loudspeakers, and queens danced by the bar. Flags waved, plates clattered, waiters screamed, and the beach was suddenly a magnet, drawing cars, families, bikers, helicopters, yachts – anything metal, in fact – towards it but through the mayhem we all watched out of the corner of our eyes for the boys' return.

The most seasoned seducer on the beach was Antoine, one of the Maggy brothers. Well built, sexy and confident – after all, he owned the beach – he swaggered across the scalding sand to where they were lying and stood over them, arms akimbo, as the rest of us strained every nerve not to drop everything we were doing and run over. The boys sat up on their elbows. Antoine said something and they threw their heads back laughing. We all gasped. What teeth, what jaws, what necks these creatures had.

'Look at the hands.'

'And the ankles.'

'Ankles?'

'Oh yes, dear. Didn't you know?'

They were both from Turin. The taller one, Alfo, worked in a bank. The other, Doriano, was a gym instructor. Alfo was a colossus with Venetian colouring – sandy-coloured hair, brows, lashes and skin, all slightly burnished by salt and sun. Large beckoning lips curled into an earth-shattering smile, replete with Dracula incisors. Doriano was smaller and darker, a gladiator with close-set eyes and a

broken nose. Unfortunately, they didn't seem anxious to participate
in the back and anal rites of endless coffees and cocktails that the rest
of us enjoyed. They had canoes and paddled away every morning to
the accompaniment of our collective groan, and came back only at
sunset, dripping black silhouettes against the orange sea. They sat on
the shore until night fell, and the modest Mediterranean waves gurgled and splashed between their legs while they chatted and laughed
or just looked out to sea. Then they disappeared and no one knew
where they went after that.

Until Melody arrived.

'They are staying at a camping site *vicino a* St Raphael,' she said
with relish.

'Where are they from?' asked a newcomer.

'Turin!' we all shouted angrily.

'*La città rococo*,' explained Melody through half-closed eyes to
the boy who had turned red.

'Pardon?'

Melody leant in, pouting. '*Ro-co-co*, baby!'

Her voice was ethereal, pitched high, and when she giggled it
was like the engine of a car turning over on a frosty morning. She was
quite a genius and we all looked forward to her arrival because it was
officially high season when she stalked on to the beach with her
girlfriends in leopard-skin bikinis and Egyptian tans. They were a
caravan of musk emerging from the desert haze, clinking with
bangles, the last survivors of some ancient tribe. The only things
missing were their spears. Tall and severe, with a handsome, ageless
face framed by Cleopatra hair, Melody wore coloured contact lenses
of apple green with pupils like cat's eyes and she carried a small dog
in a Louis Vuitton shoulder bag.

She raised one eyebrow and thought for a moment, as if she were
weighing something up.

'Trash from Torino,' she said finally and waved.

The boys lumbered to their feet, and everyone held their breath as
they walked across the beach towards the bar.

'Oh my God!' whispered Tom. 'Look. The big one is wearing shorts made out of your mother's bedroom curtains in London.'

It was true. Recently my mother had redecorated her room. The walls, the curtains, the bedspread and the lampshades – everything, even the ceiling – was covered in the same dizzying fabric of tiny blue squiggles against a white background. The effect made you feel faint and lose your balance.

'Do they have Peter Jones in Turin?' I asked, trying not to stare.

'Fasten your seat belts!' replied Tom. 'This is going to be a bumpy flight.'

Melody sat them down at the bar and began a blatant interrogation, punctuating their story with little asides that dripped with innuendo, undermining them brilliantly and placing herself at the same time just where she liked it – centre stage – and she brought down the ever-enlarging house with every gasp. The boys had a big tent.

'Ah, si?' (Huge laugh.) But it was so hot they could hardly sleep. 'Ah, non!' (Hysteria.) But they didn't want to return to Italy for another couple of days. 'Probably they will be stopped at the frontier, by the police.' (The house came down.)

They spoke in Italian and Melody translated into English, Spanish and then Portuguese, as the crowd around the bar soon included the old Brazilian fairy with a wooden leg. She pretended to know them only vaguely, but it was a vague acquaintance that had clearly gone on for years and there was definitely blood under the bridge between these three. They lobbed one-liners back and forth over the head of the little dog, which peeped out growling from the Louis Vuitton bag. But the boys were good-humoured and let her make fun of them. They were on her turf, and anyway it was water off a broad duck's back, and the fact remained that Melody knew a meal ticket when she saw one. They were the real spaghetti, and quite soon everyone was buying them drinks and waving phone numbers on strips of paper napkins.

Melody directed the traffic. If anyone got too bouncy she slapped them playfully or wagged a threatening finger. Hers was a kabuki performance, heightened, ridiculous, like everything on that loopy beach, and we all rose to the occasion. And so corks popped, the rosé flowed and the chatter merged with the music. Alfo had slanted green eyes and at some point we looked at one another and the sound cut out. He smiled and shrugged his shoulders. I could hear my heartbeat and nothing else. Then Melody dug me in the ribs with her elbow and the cacophony rushed back: plates, screams, disco music, and Tom, whispering in my ear in a funny American accent.

'What's hiding under Mummy's bedspread?'

That night in town we all sat together on the pavement outside Maggy's. They were surrounded by a crowd of admirers, and in a moment of desperation I invited them both to move in.

Alfo was simple but knowing, like all the best Italian dishes; a huge hairy bear with elegance and grace. He was funny and sincere, at home in the endless stream of people coming through the house. This first act of our affair was played against the backdrop of a Feydeau farce, on a stage full of surprise entrances and exits, of strangers bursting into rooms, and couples caught in flagrante by the parish priest. Doriano was decoyed by Huge Crack, my trainer from London who was staying that weekend, while I lured Alfo onto the rocks of my bungalow at the bottom of the garden, on the edge of the vines.

There was only one problem. We couldn't understand a word the other was saying, and so our communication swung from the sureness of body language to a hesitant verbal contact that came and went in bursts, sometimes comical, at others a strain. We were crossed wires, worlds apart, but St Tropez was that kind of no man's land, and reality was held at bay by the ropy curtains of the holiday package, like the sunshine, as we lay in bed all morning in my darkened room, sleeping or having sex or smoking. My nerve endings were still young enough to explode at a touch, and when he came near the hair on my arms reached out to meet him. I was in a state of constant breathless anticipation, half ecstasy, half dread, like the expectant bride in the bible.

'Widow, more like!' said Tom grimly.

Luckily Bruno was half Italian. When we arrived at a linguistic impasse, lying in bed in the morning, or out at sea on the raft in the afternoon, we would seek him out. The high-pitched yelp of his laugh usually located him in Tom's caravan. On the morning of his departure, Alfo began to talk earnestly. I didn't understand a word, but said 'Si' and 'Certo' knowingly. It was only when he looked strangely pissed off that I decided to consult the oracle, and so we went in search of Bruno. We knocked on the door of the caravan. Silence. We knocked again. A creak. I opened the door. Inside Tom and Bruno were a frozen guilty tableau, sitting on the unmade bed in the little wooden recess at the end of the caravan. The smoke from an enormous joint was the only thing that moved in the room, curling around in the shafts of light that penetrated the gloom.

'Hi,' said Tom, vacantly.

Their affair was beginning to get on my nerves. There was room for only one grand passion in La Bande Rupert, but we climbed on to the bed with them anyway, folding ourselves protectively into one another, toes interlocking, and Bruno put his hair in a bun as he listened to Alfo explain. Bruno's English, still in its early days, had been learnt from me and his vowel sounds were borrowed from the hooray vernacular, blending spectacularly with his impenetrable Alsatian lilt. Alfo finished and was silent. Bruno fixed a chopstick into his hair, frowning.

'Ee sehs eetz finish aaahftah today,' he said finally.

'What?'

He repeated the phrase, slightly shriller.

Tom and I looked at one another. Bruno tried again.

'Oh. I see,' I said finally, taken aback. 'May I ask why?'

'Perchè?'

There was a long explanation. Tom sat very still, watching like a praying mantis, and I thought I was going to faint. Alfo talked earnestly at Bruno. Bruno yelped with glee.

'Zees eez quoite eembarasseeng, ak-tuy-ah-lee!' he giggled. 'Ee say that euw is leevin' toe faa anyway an' eet weel never be geude.'

'What?' This time it was Tom.

'Ohhhla!' puffed Bruno, swaying his head from side to side, in that gesture of exasperation peculiar to the French. He rummaged around in his little school satchel and produced a small French–Italian dictionary. He threw it at us and stalked out. Tom followed.

We sat on either side of the bed. Alfo held his head in his hands. We were silent for a while in that rickety old wooden tomb. Dust played in the light, and someone giggled near by.

'*Mi dispiace*,' said Alfo finally, offering his hand across the bed, but I didn't take it, because my eyes were filling up with tears and I needed to concentrate.

Was this real, or was I acting? Long ago I had stopped being able to tell the difference. That's what a career in front of the camera does to you. There are only so many times a man can say I love you, and most actors have said it with the most sparkle to a camera rather than a *camarade*. On top of that I had made my whole life into a film, a drama in which I took the leading role, and the line between fantasy and reality was at best a smudge. Who knew what was going on in my head? Certainly not me.

Alfo sighed. He knew. There was no way he could compete with my plotting.

'*Non piange, bello.*' He sighed.

'*Non*,' I whispered, and on cue the tears rolled out of my eyes and onto my face. (Or at least one of them.) Alfo looked at me, half smiling, half groaning, and put his huge arm around my shoulder.

By the time we came out of the caravan, the whole household had congregated at the table outside the kitchen door to say goodbye to the two Italians. In front of them lay our kitchen garden. One tomato plant clung to its pole in a ring of parched lettuces. This vision was my very own circus. I had conjured it up myself. Gypsies, tramps and thieves sprawled across a table in front of a tumbledown house. An overweight Labrador and a scruffy little half-fox fighting in the dust, a strong man leaning out of the door of a gypsy caravan, and, behind him in the shadows, the ventriloquist and the dummy, the Master of Ceremonies, Me. Now I would crack my whip and the pink elephants would lumber off. It was all too good to be true.

La Bande Rupert looked apprehensively at us as we emerged from the caravan. This love affair was everybody's concern. It would make life much easier if it were kept on track. La Rupert could be a tricky number.

'Well?' said Tom.

'Everything's fine. In fact, Alfo's coming back next weekend,' I said as casually as I could.

And so the two boys of unimaginable beauty, one of them now mine, got into their car crammed with camping equipment, top-heavy with canoes, kissing, laughing and hugging, as the doors slammed and they clanked away down the steep dirt track towards Monte Carlo, Menton and the frontier. Huge muscular arms waved from either window, and we all waved back, unaware of the drama that was about to unfold.

CHAPTER ELEVEN

Offshore Company, Sole Beneficiary. The Knights of Malta in Lourdes

And so I was there but not there, wheeling Daddy towards a village church high up in the Pyrenees on the first morning of our pilgrimage. I hadn't slept. I had spent the night excavating the ruins of that ancient affair I'd stumbled upon yesterday. How could I have forgotten that Alfo and me ended at Lourdes in a torchlight procession, snaking through the hills in a conga line of faith and ill health, praying desperately for redemption or a miracle cure. I had simply wiped it from my mind. Was this selective memory at play or the first notes of that Golden Oldie – Dementia? Either way, my poor brain screeched to a halt and must have sent a shock wave to the sludgy backwater where memories of failed romances were stored, because now all the summer hits and street corners of the affair, all its twists and turns, were being dragged from the shadows to the frontal lobe in 3D Technicolor and Sensurround, obliterating the Knights and Dames, my father, his nurse and even Lourdes itself, in waves of crystal-clear recollection.

*

Bartrès is a beautiful hamlet tucked into the hills a few miles outside Lourdes. When her family became too poor to look after her, Bernadette was sent there to live with some slightly wealthier relations. You could walk along the same footpath she took from the valley below and there was a mysterious silence hanging in the air. One half expected to see Bernadette herself – she was certainly there – but instead a pair of patrician English priests sauntered round the corner, arm in arm, engrossed in some urbane celestial debate that led us to the appointed place. Outside the church an eccentric crowd was gathered. Here, finally, were the people we had come to meet.

The Knights and Dames of Malta were busy with their sick: *'malades'* they called them. At first I thought they were talking about ducks. They outnumbered their *'malades'* three to one, and they buzzed around them like a swarm of killer bees. Even if these blue-blooded pilgrims weren't particularly used to helping others, they had at least all mucked out stables at some point in their lives, so wiping bottoms was something they grimly accepted, not so different from curry-combing a favourite pony, but they were sweetly attentive, although possibly getting more out of the experience than the poor *malade* himself. The buzz of chatter reminded one of a cocktail party in Belgravia or a first night at Glyndebourne. The only things missing were nibbles and drinks laid out on the tombs.

The Knights are an extraordinary sect within the Catholic Church. They date back to the sixth century, when they built and ran a hospital in Jerusalem for sick pilgrims. Originally they were nurses, but they soon developed a militant side and became famous fighters, defending themselves to the death in Rhodes and later Malta, where they were besieged by the Spanish in Valletta. They are a very grand organisation, proud and rich. They will tell you how much money they raise each year for various causes, and it is a great deal, but as we know charity is often the net curtain behind which we conduct our real business. Theirs has always been the discreet acquisition of power, and within the Church, along with the Opus Dei, they are the ghoulish *éminences grises* of Christendom. You must have at least four quarterings in your coat of arms to become a Knight, and if you want to be a 'professed Knight', an actual monk, you must submit yourself to poverty, chastity and obedience.

They are a sovereign state, and their ancient centre of operations, in the Eternal City, looks directly down a long vista at the shimmering Vatican. Their leader is traditionally one of the pope's chief advisors, which gives one a little insight into how deeply out of touch the Catholic Church is with the unwashed world it still controls, because apart from being perfectly nice upper-class people – all of them charming, eccentric, humorous, the last generation of an extraordinary species, weaned on that curious mixture of rationing and opulence, of baked-bean suppers under a Van Dyck – they tend to see things through the blinkered perspective of all their tree-lined avenues, where the real world is glimpsed only through dilapidated park gates at one end, shut and padlocked, from an ancient palace window at the other.

The Knights and Dames were mostly older, although some were middle aged. They were dressed for the pilgrimage as if for charades, the men in black dungarees, extras from *Dad's Army*, and the women in cloaks and starched headdresses. Every actor knows the power of dressing up. It is like putting on a mask. One loses oneself and can suddenly do all sorts of strange things. (Like wiping bottoms.) So the Knights and Dames were all feeling sexy and punch drunk at lunch in a marquee after Mass.

I parked my dad at a table with our lovely local vicar from Wiltshire, who, I decided, must have been a bit of a masochist, because being an Anglican vicar in this exclusive group of Catholic monseigneurs was similar to being a leading light of the village amateur dramatics society thrust suddenly into the Comédie Française. At communal services, he and the other Anglicans had to stand one step below the Catholic clergy. He never complained, he was 'a very good man' as my mother loved to say, and, unlike some of the others, had taken seriously the notion of humility.

A Dame my father adored, called Patricia, once a beauty and still strikingly handsome, came over and sat down. A bishop ambled around filling glasses. Various other priests sipped their drinks and leant over the '*malades*', beaming assurance and the wages of gin. All of London's celebrity padres were there. Famous Father Ronald had arrived from Brompton Oratory, the only monastic order where a monk is encouraged to have a private income, and where, until recently, a butler served dinner every night. He had come by private jet 'with darling Rupert Loewenstein' (Mick Jagger's former financial master wizard) and 'was only staying a few days, before going on to a spa'.

Everyone was having a marvellous time. Maybe this was salvation after all, and heaven was nothing more than a giant flapping marquee in the sky. God ambling over, tipsy, slightly overweight, a bottle of red in one hand, white in the other, saying nothing complicated like, 'I am who is,' just 'Aren't we lucky with the weather? Chablis?'

I left them all talking and wandered around the tent, meeting people I had not seen for forty years. I found myself chatting to a man I had known in France, where, according to rumour, he had systematically pilfered the collection box of his local church. Now he drawled that he was taking orders and becoming a professed monk.

'God, how will you manage, Kieran? You were always such a bon viveur.' I was impressed, remembering him from the old days at the Club Sept.

'Well, obedience and chastity are really not a problem. One hasn't bonked for yonks. As for poverty, I've worked that one out too.'

'Oh, how?' I asked, intrigued.

He leant in, speaking softly. God looked around from across the tent. St Bernadette shook her head and sighed.

'Offshore company. Sole beneficiary.'

And we laughed. Extra hard in my case, because I knew it to be a giant double bluff. He was famously penniless, from penniless stock.

That night, my dad and I had a dinner party in a restaurant near our hotel. The cast included Kirsten, a neighbour of ours, and an

Anglican, her friend Jo, Colin our local vicar and one of the more magnetic priests on the Catholic circuit.

Enter Fr Alexander Sherbrook. Tall and swarthy, with the soul-saving eyes of a Jesuit, straining slightly from their sockets at the horror of the world, under the bushiest brows in Christendom, Fr Alexander was the parish priest of St Patrick's, Soho Square. He had been posted there from a rather genteel living in Twickenham. Now he was in the centre of Sodom, and I used to be his neighbour in the days when I lived in Frith Street. He worked tirelessly in that run-down parish of junkies and queens, particularly with the homeless, who all washed up there at some stage or other.

Because underneath the rattle and roar of modern Soho, with its constant change, its amnesia, its facelifted bars and brothels, its tinkling rickshaws and wrangling trannies, it is still the ancient parish of St Giles, the great slum of London from time immemorial, where *Les Mis* was a reality show and not a musical. The lanes and yards still have the same names, but otherwise all that intensity of living has left no trace. St Giles has been bricked up, burnt, bombed and rebuilt and the howls of the poor have been drowned under the rain-splashed asphalt of Shaftesbury Avenue, but at least their gravestones are written in lights. The names of theatrical battleaxes reflected in puddles, splinter and spray into oblivion, driven over by time and a taxi cab on its way to Cambridge Circus. But old St Giles is still there for those who have the eyes to see. The poor, the struggling, the escapees of Bedlam still wander the streets, watching us listlessly or begging for change, and Fr Alexander is their friend. Apart from anything else, he produces sixty free dinners, twice a week, in the basement of the church.

We met thanks to Frith Street's most famous tramp (not me), a Moroccan boy called Omar, with whom we were all friends. Omar made his bed each night in the stage door of the Prince Edward Theatre, surrounded by the books he had nicked from the second-hand shops along the Charing Cross Road. His days were spent laughing on the steps of Ronnie Scott's or having a shower up at the

Regent's Park Mosque. Until he discovered cider. Then he began playing up and was about to go to prison. Father Sherbrook went to court and spoke up for him, and he got off. On that note the priest and I became friends.

I loved to sit in his dilapidated church with its peeling walls, and its damp musty smell of incense and floor polish, for hours sometimes, lulled into a kind of trance by the odd snore of a pilgrim taking his morning nap in the confessional, and the distant roar of Tottenham Court Road that rattled the old windows. A noisy lady arranged sad bunches of flowers on the altar, clattered down the aisle and chatted in an exaggerated whisper, or hoovered just as you were about to have a vision, but St Patrick's was a lovely humble church, and many a troubled soul unrelated to the incomprehensible religion passed its doors and went inside. There we sat in the dusty shafts of light, heads in hands, trying to figure out the latest checkmate in the game of survival thrust upon us in Soho's jungle outside. Soon we drifted off into the void, only to awake to find ourselves surrounded by small Chinese ladies in black trousers and pumps, grimly chirping the Mass in Cantonese. It was multicultural at St Patrick's.

Fr Alexander was a fearless man, a modern Friar Tuck, prepared to go to war for God. On certain feast days I used to watch from my window as he took to the streets, all in white, under a makeshift awning held on poles by Poles, grasping the monstrance containing the blessed sacrament like a riot shield, through the throngs of weekend queens on come down, up Frith Street, through Old Compton Street, and back down Wardour Street, followed by the faithful, singing hymns. Sometimes the procession collided with the Hare Krishnas coming in the opposite direction, and on one occasion they got caught up in Satan's own Gay Pride March.

After that Fr Alexander realised that he needed informers on the inside and made friends with a body-builder called Cinders who worked in a bar called the Admiral Duncan, which was famous for, among other things, being nail-bombed in '92. Together they compared diaries and plotted routes to avoid further confusion, until Cinders and his boyfriend were savagely murdered – kicked to death, actually – on the South Bank a couple of years ago. Fr Alexander was terribly upset.

Like most serious Catholic priests, he is utterly intransigent on all the usual subjects. For the Church, an unrepentant queer is marked for hell and brimstone, and there is no getting away from this fact. He is worse really than a murderer, because at least a murderer kills once or twice and, done with his sin, repents. But as everyone knows, we poofs are remorseless and are at it 24/7, so while Fr Alexander is not exactly judgemental – he is, in fact, quite fond of me, as I am of him – our friendship under God's light is a lampshade fringed with tension. The priest is always waiting for you to change, praying that you will, because God, it seems, is very busy turning a blind eye to every sin but buttfuckery.

All this can be very irritating for the poor poof at the receiving end, particularly when this kind of passive harassment has gone on, in some shape or form, since he was very young and utterly suggestible. The innocence of childhood is systematically abused by the Church, as it fiddles with the brain, if not the genitalia, as soon as it can get its hands on it. Debate and enquiry are forbidden – everything must be accepted without question – and priests are scandalised when confronted, dismissing the enquirer as angry and evil. Actually, poor dears, they are blissfully unaware that anyone could be angry with them, because, as far as they are concerned, even if they have fondled a choirboy in a foxy moment years ago, they are still the anointed mouthpieces of God. Thus they have ridden roughshod over us all for millennia, and apparently we love it.

At dinner that night I was drunk on the local wine and also the local attention. Apparently I had mentioned on a French chat show that I was coming to Lourdes, so I was expected wherever I went. This is the fabulous bonus of stardom, and it felt absolutely marvellous to come into a restaurant in Lourdes and be greeted like an old friend of St Bernadette. And so dinner began congenially. Fr Alexander was in a jovial mood.

'Can you believe it?' he said. 'Someone has one of those flashy silver cars with the number plate RUT 12. Unbelievable!'

It was ours.

'What?' asked my father.

'We're just talking about your number plate, Daddy. Fr Alexander thinks it's rather immoral.'

'Oh, really?' said my dad, concerned, leaning in close to the padre. 'Rou-tee-too. Rather amusing, don't you think?'

'Oh, I see,' said Fr Alexander, unconvinced.

The wine was strong and the conversation inevitably drifted towards the pilgrimage and religion, which was probably a mistake. By the fifth bottle I was losing control, and all the years of pent-up fury surged and spat across the table at poor Fr Alexander, who defended the Church's position, irritatingly unflappable. My father sat between us and sank into himself, sensibly deciding to go extra deaf. Colin Fox, across the table, turned red and remained silent. The rest of us were flushed and raucous, but the axe I was grinding sparked and burnt with a vicious glow and was probably quite unpleasant.

We staggered back to our hotel, ominously named the De la Grotte, for a nightcap and to hammer a few extra nails into the coffin of my friendship with this extraordinary priest. Kirsten and I called various mutual friends and apparently left incoherent messages, screaming with diabolical laughter. In the morning I woke in my tiny room and opened the curtains, only to find the window looked straight onto a cliff face. I was up against the wall with one of the worst hangovers I have ever had, but Fr Alexander had contrived a brilliant revenge.

The pilgrimage had a rendezvous to visit a rehab clinic in the hills, and because it was such a beautiful day, he suggested that we all walk. So, in the baking sun, I pushed my father in his wheelchair three miles up the mountain, as the padre strode ahead, his black cassock flapping in the breeze, the panting faithful dotted in twos and threes behind him. At one stage I thought I would be sick all over my dad's straw hat, as we bumped across a steep field towards a road high above. Suddenly I was Robert De Niro in *The Mission*, clambering up the sheer cliff, dragging my sins behind me. I couldn't help smiling at the genius of Fr Alexander, although Fräulein Maria was indignant. The sins of the son were being visited on the father, whose poor legs were getting tired, continually on point as they were without their footrests. Perhaps Fr Alexander was punishing him too for having such a slutty number plate.

After half a mile on the road, we crossed a railway track. Now Lourdes was a fairy castle below us, and we were in a woody suburb, still climbing, past funny French bungalows with names like 'Ça Me Suffit' (this is enough for me), which stood in pretty walled gardens guarded by lunging Alsatians.

Two hours later we arrived at the centre, which was a kind of farm high up in the woods. It was an amazing place, built by its inmates, young men mostly, all with terrible tales of addiction and depravation, which we listened to in a large chapel. My dad, in the front row with the other '*malades*', quickly dropped off. Fr Alexander sat like *The Thinker*, his chin on his hand, his eyebrows reaching towards the addicts over eyes burning like coals. The addicts themselves sat before us, in a row, relating the intimate details of their tragic lives to the assembled Knights and Dames.

It was a peculiar entertainment for these *Telegraph* and *Mail* readers, whose mantra concerning drugs and users was 'String 'em up'. For this reason, probably, not many of them had come. On the other hand it was hard for them not to be charmed by these young men, all busy cooking, washing, ploughing and building. Their earnest commitment was touching and there was a special atmosphere in the place. They had made it themselves, and they ran it. There was no sign of a ghoulish monk or a grinning nun lurking in the shadows. Just the old hands watching out for the beginners who came from all over the world, not necessarily Christian, although after the initial struggle they all seemed to be fervent Catholics, addicted now to prayer. Some had been there for three years. You could see how hard it might be to tear yourself away from a place like this and return to a small-town bedsit where the past jumped out from every corner. Could they ever leave, or was this another Magic Mountain? They would have to become priests.

I looked over at Fr Alexander, fiercely listening – a sixteenth-century Jesuit in the rainforest. Maybe he had a master plan to replenish the flailing priesthood with these rough diamonds. What a brilliant idea! After all, there is no one more steadfast or compassionate than a thoroughly reformed drug user. Like Jesus, he's been to hell and back, and maybe that's the only qualification a priest needs, rather than the endless rules they learn like parrots in the seminary cage. Even the barbaric act of confession becomes more exciting with some fabulous, suffering, still-raw ex-junkie on the other side of the grille.

With all these thoughts exploding in my head – a new priesthood, an AA pope, condoms for Africa, credibility for queers – I wheeled my dad out into the sunshine.

'What on earth was all that about?' he asked.

'I'm not quite sure.'

'It was very moving,' said Fräulein Maria.

'Yes, it was. It makes you want to stay here.'

'Not me,' said my dad. It was Latin Mass followed by drinks for the major.

'I need to go to the loo, Marianne. Would you do the honours?'

CHAPTER TWELVE

The Shroud of Turin

Towards the end of the summer, Melody suggested a trip to Turin. Bruno and Tom would stay with her and I would stay with Alfo. It was endlessly discussed and planned over lunches on the beach as the season wound down. Alfo did return the next weekend, but otherwise he called me most nights from the central station in Turin – he had no telephone at home – and during our broken conversations I could hear announcements for night trains to Brescia and Milan, Ventimiglia and Naples, adding to our union another thrilling dimension. We were nowhere. At a terminus and a departure point, disembodied voices crackling along the wires, or bouncing back and forth from outer space. Dark thoughts and projections flew alongside our words on the sea of static, and our romantic conversations were tinged with that panic that drives many a boat onto the rocks.

Melody took on the role of matchmaker and chaperone, suddenly prim and matriarchal, and she played it to the gallery, which was full on a good day, so that by the time we left the whole beach could tell one another where we were for each meal on the trip and what we were doing after. So, one Friday morning in late September, we set off in my Renault 25X, leaving the dogs with two girlfriends who were staying from London.

Things would never get better. The funny French pop hits of the summer blared through the ropy speakers of the car. Tom lounged in the back and Bruno drove. The windows were open, and we took the road from Ste Maxime towards the *autoroute* at Le Luc. This is one of the great roads, gliding like a snake through a magical range of hills called Les Maures. They are low and round, a child's drawing, covered with forest, umbrella pines and scrub oaks, full of wild boar and the ruins of long-abandoned villages. I wanted to show the others one I had recently discovered, called Val d'Enfer. The Valley of Hell. It was for sale.

We clanked three miles down an abandoned track until it became overgrown and then we walked. The forest cooked in the heat, smelling of cork and earth. Cicadas croaked an endless deafening vigil. The path curved around the ridge of a barely perceptible valley and ducked into it. Hidden under a roof of pines was a narrow gulley, and five or six dilapidated houses nestled either side of a path that wound through it. It was an astonishing sight, hidden under the trees, like jumping inside an aquarium where a ruined castle bubbled at the bottom. The dappled light swayed with the branches above. It was cool and dark and far away from everything.

Not so long ago these forests were scattered with little hamlets. Cut off from the outside world, inhabited by wild, inbred humans, half animal, with unfathomable guttural accents. They surfaced from time to time in the market places of La Garde-Freinet or Draguignan, but they lived and died in the wild, collecting mysteries and legends around them. Blue murder must have gone on, as they roamed the Valley of Hell, day in, day out, year after year, doing just enough to make ends meet, fucking their daughters and killing their wives.

Bruno appeared at a window, leaning on the sill and acting like a local girl. Actually he fitted right in. He looked like a miniature witch, with his beaky nose and long hair. Soon he and Tom were playing houses while I rolled my eyeballs and explored the rest of the gulley. The last house had a roof. A big oak tree was squeezing it to death with its roots. Soon it would be dragged back into the earth, this village, and there was a strange deadly atmosphere that couldn't be budged by Bruno's shrieks or Tom's caustic replies from the top of the hill. Down at the bottom, huge mosquitoes with the longest legs danced in the shafts of light. I imagined being with Alfo there.

Suddenly I shivered; someone was walking on my grave. I felt one of those weird surges of foreboding, and adrenalin shot through my body. The oak groaned in a gust of wind and I ran from the house, terrified, only to find Bruno laughing hysterically at his windowsill, and Tom marching furiously up the path, towards the road.

'What's the matter?' I asked, running to catch up.

'Nothing,' said Tom, white with rage. Bruno's laughter bounced around the valley.

'Imagine waking up next to that every morning,' I ventured naughtily.

'Precisely,' retorted Tom, giving nothing away.

Back on the road, we hit the *autoroute* with a tangible atmosphere in the car. Tom glowered in the back and Bruno stared crazily at the road ahead, eyes like saucers, hair flying in the wind. Occasionally manic giggles bubbled from his mouth, and Tom snorted in the back. Soon the Alpes-Maritimes appeared through the morning haze and, with them, the promise of Italy. They became clearer and clearer, and what at first seemed to be jagged clouds were in fact their snowy peaks, high above the mountains themselves, suspended and barely distinguishable from the hot white sky. On the plains below, the vast cities of holiday flats, pink and beige, stretched from the sea to the hills, occasionally crowned by an ancient fortified village climbing out of the urban sprawl, a sinking ship in a sea of roofs and windows with a castle on the top.

We sped over a hill and suddenly the bay of Cannes appeared below us, fringed by its long yellow beach. It was tiny and far away. Matchstick figures walked along the Croisette. Most of my life's victories had been grasped there, but now it just flashed past. The *autoroute* curved around the city towards Nice, past Juan-les-Pins, Cap Ferrat and Antibes. I had read about these places in Oscar Wilde, Scott Fitzgerald and David Niven, and they were sacred to me. Now they were nothing more than ugly *favelas*: beach clubs and fish restaurants, villas and flats that had once, not so very long ago, been one of the most enchanted places on earth, where lonely hotels hid in the woods, and Oscar cruised for fisher boys, and Scott conceived Dick Diver. Now, a sprawling city was Californicating before our very eyes, from Marseilles to Menton. It would be the European Union's Los Angeles. Downtown Côte d'Azur. You could feel it coming as you surfed the *autoroute* towards the frontier.

And so we flew along the Corniche, the best road in the world, cut high into the side of the mountains, disappearing into its endless dark tunnels, winding snakes with spines of orange lights. The claustrophobia of the sudden enclosure and the roar of the engine thrilled and terrified one into losing control of the car, screeching around corners, the notion of death as close as the perspiring rock walls with their giant white arrows pointing towards the faraway speck of light. The smell of rubber and diesel; the need for absolute concentration; the notion of travel, of history, of the anticipated love tryst; plus the very fact that we were all there, and that it was all there for us, falling away as we hurled ourselves into the glaring sunshine was as intoxicating a journey as I ever took. Outside there were steep rocks on one side, a precipice on the other. Far below, the terraces of vines, and the remains of the Italian Riviera, squeezed between sky-rise flats and a glittering sea. It reminded one of cheap accordion music and all those American films made in the sixties, *The Yellow Rolls-Royce*, *The Roman Spring of Mrs Stone*. Forget ancient Rome. My references were Shirley MacLaine and Alain Delon in the port at Positano.

As we approached Genoa cargo ships converged out of the haze from all directions as if dragged by a magnet towards the sprawling city, but we bore left and were soon in the forests of Liguria, where

[handwritten margin note: What is cheap accordean music?]

the sleek Corniche degenerated into the road from *Wacky Races*, bridging wide valleys on dangerous-looking stilts. Castles stood on crags and rivers foamed in deep gorges. It was a perilous ballet, driving on the Italian *autostrada*, with its chorus of lorries, belching evil black smoke, overtaking one another on hairpin bends, its prima ballerinas on motorbikes in shiny black helmets jeté-ing at the speed of light through the traffic. Little stupas at the side of the road made of blackened plastic flowers were the mute testaments to these hazardous highways.

We had coffee in an *auto-stop*. Bruno went to the bathroom.

'What's going on with you two?' I asked.

Tom was silent for a moment.

'I told Bruno I loved him, and he just burst out laughing.' Tom smoked furiously.

'Well, I suppose it is quite funny,' I ventured, carefully. 'I mean, he's a pixie really. Not quite human. It would be like having a pet squirrel. You can never tame a squirrel.'

'Yuh,' agreed Tom, blowing smoke and grinding out his cigarette. 'Let alone fuck one.'

He giggled at the idea, and then we both began to laugh.

'Tight, eh?'

'Yuh.'

Turin sits at the foot of the Alps. After the rest of Italy, with its dusty medieval piazzas, its looted church façades of bare bricks, its campaniles and its crumbling palazzos, Rococo Turin seems strained and self-conscious. It is the city of Fiat and the home of the Agnelli dynasty. The local dialect is the first chilling indication of the terrifying mountain twang you will hear as you proceed up the hill into Switzerland.

Alfo met us at the station, dressed up like a teddy bear. I had seen him only in shorts, and suddenly he was a normal person, his breathtaking body reduced to a cube in a sweater and trousers. Nervous in this new environment, conversation lurched and stumbled, and we jerked through the city to Melody's flat where Tom and Bruno were staying. We dropped them off, and drove on to his place.

Alfo's home was on the third floor of a fascist block of flats. You could see the Alps from the long exterior landings that stretched across the building. Front doors, bicycles and pots of flowers were scattered along them with a communal loo at the end. Nothing had changed in Alfo's flat since the war. It was a large bedsit, really, and the last place I would have imagined him living. There was a huge old bed with round posts and a carved headboard, a stained-oak wardrobe, and a chest of drawers with a pretty gilt mirror on top. The walls were a faded green with damp patches by the ceiling and there was a threadbare rug on the tiled floor. A little kitchenette hid behind a screen, with an old sink and a single gas ring. No bathroom or toilet. You had to brave the freeze in winter and nip down the passage to the privy. It was the flat of a little old lady with a body-builder superimposed upon it, and another brilliant vista on a journey packed, so far, with visual thrills.

Alfo lay on the bed talking to his brother on the telephone. The light was vague and honey-coloured through the closed shutters. It was deliciously cool. The pre-war fan over the bed whirred and clanked. I sat on a dowager's chair, unsure in this new territory of my next move. Alfo watched me as he talked, smiling. The loo at the end of the passage flushed, a door slammed and footsteps shuffled past.

Dinner that night was a predictable screaming match between Bruno and the sisters of Turin, a light opera performed at a rather grand restaurant in the centre of town. How *les girls* loved a young boy with a strong effeminate streak. Like vampires, they clustered round him. They wanted him for one of their own. They pinched his cheeks and played with his hair. They lifted his chin and scrutinised his features. Bruno loved the attention. He was always their target and had been chased from Alsace to Austin, Texas, but they always misunderstood. He was an elf trapped in a man's body, not a woman. Actually, shrouded beneath the shrieks and the semi-broken voice, he had a gigantic male ego, as I was to discover to my cost over the years. But he happily played along, as one tigress whipped his hair into a majestic chignon, and another wrapped a shawl around his shoulders.

Melody observed from one end of the table with a detached aristocratic smile ('Moaner Lisa,' whispered Tom) while we watched her from the other. She winked, pointed to Alfo and made a sexy pout. That man was out of sync with the evening, lost in thought, sad and beautiful, just the type of boy I liked; a stranger, it would seem, even at home. Doriano, his friend, the other boy of unimaginable beauty, looked at him strangely, and there was a curious undertow beneath the bursts of applause from the screaming menagerie, as we all got drunker and drunker, and the room began to spin. Our numbers doubled as various freaks from the scene joined the table, nightclub recluses, a steroid dealer and a bent *carabiniere*. A tubby patrician poof with a silk handkerchief in his breast pocket leered over Tom and me with wild watery eyes and a high breathy voice.

'You like Torino? Is first time here? Be veeeery careful. We are crazy peoples.'

Luckily Tom had recovered his sense of humour. He watched Bruno with a bemused smile, and that enormous sense of relief one sometimes encounters when love's light switch is suddenly snapped off.

'Maybe it's a good thing Bruno didn't say yes,' I ventured cautiously. 'You might have found yourself going out with a woman next week.'

'Well, that beats a squirrel.'

'They'd both have your nuts.'

Alfo shut the door behind him and leant against it. He didn't turn on the lights. I stumbled in the dark towards the huge old bed and threw myself down on it, knowing by now that something substantial was about to happen. The springs creaked under my weight. The grainy thick darkness began to subside, a black tide out of which appeared the cupboard, the table, the screen, then Alfo himself, carved in a ghostly light from the street. His eyes were black holes, and the sadness that I had noticed in him at dinner was distilled now that we were back here. A strange feeling of dread surged through my whole body.

'I have something to tell you,' he said, but didn't go on.

After a minute he walked over to the bed and lay down carefully. For a while we just lay there side by side, not moving, not touching, and time stood still. It felt as though the whole room had turned in on us. The furniture watched, the bed cradled us with tenderness, and the universe held its breath until, almost imperceptibly at first, Alfo began to shake. He held his hand over his brow, as if that gesture might somehow quell the storm rising inside, but with a sudden gasp tears began to pour down his face, dripping off his long lashes onto the pillow. Then he cried and cried, with great heaving sobs. Sometimes he tried to speak but he couldn't and anyway he didn't really need to, because I knew what he was going to say. So I cried too. At first for him, then for us, and finally, as the full implication of this wordless confession settled, for myself. For some reason I remembered a line from a play in Glasgow, badly delivered by an overweight cockney ham.

'See, see, where Christ's blood streams in the firmament.'

Later Alfo switched on the bedside lamp. It had a medium's shade with tassels. Estranged by the light, we tried to talk, but there weren't any words to express the sorrow and anxiety, the guilt and fear of one man telling another that he harbours a killer virus. He knew what it would mean to me. I knew what it already meant to him, and I fought the desire to get up, then and there, and run. Alfo caught the mad glint in my eyes and asked if I wanted to go to a hotel. We were stripped of all artifice and there were no more secrets. In the pool of light from the medium's lamp, he was vulnerable, beautiful, simple, living and dying in the same breath, and I couldn't answer. So we just looked at each other and he smiled. Suddenly, without warning, we were in love and everything fell away. A door opened in space. He held out his hand to help me through. I hesitated. I always do.

Aids followed us around like a shadow in those early days, another vampire on the scene that killed with a kiss. So far I had dodged the grim reaper's scythe that had disembowelled so many of my friends, but my nerves were in shreds as a result, and my terror of this disease had become psychotic. I was still infinitely suggestible to all those urban legends propagated by the Christians and Conservatives concerning toilet seats, handshakes, knives and forks, and Alfo and I had done slightly more than share a dessertspoon, although our contact had been largely romantic. On the other hand, during our brief clumsy forays into sex, we had used a pack of condoms from a Christmas cracker produced by Tom on the night of our engagement. How far away that evening seemed now. A dot of light at one end of a long tunnel. At the other – the oncoming train. Tied to the tracks, we held onto each other and cried ourselves to sleep.

I woke fully clothed early the next morning. In that first moment of consciousness there was no trace of the evening's drama. I looked at the cupboard and the bed and the damp green walls, and wondered for a second where I was, but then everything tumbled into place. Our tragedy was scrawled all over the flat. Everything had changed. If this was a film, I remember thinking, it would now turn black and white. Or would it be colour? Alfo's face on the pillow, as he slept, was a picture of health. The morning traffic rumbled outside. Those long lashes vibrated slightly under his thick brows and his large ribcage rose and fell, the swell of an ocean upon which sleep was a ship of fools, rolling towards the rocks of another day. There seemed to be a new dimension to his beauty. Now it was miraculous, and tragic. There but not there. Poignant, fragile and fleeting, because sometime in the near future it would be stretched on the rack, disfigured and broken, made unrecognisable to itself.

Watching him, I was awed that he could sleep so sweetly. I would never be as strong. Already the first twinges of hysteria were bubbling in my stomach. He stirred and turned over, pulling me with him, and I went back to sleep, my face buried in the nape of his neck, hoping never to wake, because I already knew that this moment wouldn't last. My brain was rousing itself, and it would wreak havoc in the name of preservation.

We had decided to leave Tom and Bruno in the capable hands of Melody and the girls while we drove up into the mountains. They were probably busy sawing off Bruno's cock on her kitchen table, held down by Tom, I thought, as we drove higher and higher up the zigzagging roads into the Alps, leaving Turin far below, if not our problems. Our hearts were so heavy that we could hardly walk under the weight of them.

Summer ended that day, abruptly, as it sometimes does, and up in the hills it began to snow. We stopped at a small damp hotel and decided to stay the night. It was the last one we would ever spend together and we both knew it, even though we were busy making plans. Quite suddenly it was deep winter. The universe was our mirror. The ground was white by the time night fell, and soon a storm blew up, shaking the windows and moaning through the cracks under the doors. We sat in the empty dining room, a pair of refugees or deserters. The manageress explained that the heating was broken so she made a fire. Her huge Italian bum and thick stocky legs bending over the hearth were the only funny things on that sombre night. The fire guttered and crackled into life, and was hoovered up the chimney by the icy wind while she covered us in blankets and fussed about. Finally we talked and the truth emerged.

Alfo's was a typical Catholic tragedy. His parents had disowned him when they found out he was gay. There was no information about HIV in eighties Italy – naturally – so he fell into its clutches at the very start of his adult life, condemning him to a secret existence, of which only his brother was aware. He was miserable in Turin, hemmed in by a dreary job, and, like many Italians before him, dreamt of America, the land of the so-called free. There were no answers or solutions. Soon we were silent again, staring listlessly at the fire, and the future. What was going to happen?

The next morning we got up early. It was freezing and we could hardly move. We drove back to Turin in silence. We met Tom and Bruno at the station. They looked exhausted.

'I need to talk to you,' said Tom.

'I need to talk to you,' I said.

'Something terrible has happened.'

'What?'

'Geppie' – Bruno's dog – 'was run over last night. I called the girls. He was knocked down by a motorbike on the beach road.'

'Christ. Have you told him?'

'No. I was waiting for you.'

We watched Bruno camp around with Alfo as they loaded up the car.

'Let's wait and tell him when we get home.'

'That's what I thought,' replied Tom.

I waved goodbye through the back window of the car. Alfo stood alone on the busy street, smiling. He made a 'thumbs-up' sign, turned and walked away. Soon he was a dot in the rush-hour crowd, finally erased by the sweep of a bus. I didn't see him again for twelve years.

I told the boys the whole story. Away from Alfo, hysteria kicked in and Tom and Bruno talked me down. I didn't know what to do next. Tom thought I should give up everything and go back and live in Turin with Alfo. Bruno thought I should get a job. Either way I would have to wait several weeks to know whether I would test positive or not.

'You haven't,' said Tom flatly, and we drove silently back through the forests of Liguria.

We stopped off in the village before going home and went into the church. We all loved that church at Ramatuelle, going every Sunday and often during the week. At Mass a large woman called Madame Ameil sat in the front row. During the offertory she would throw her washerwoman's arms into the air and chant, *'Christ, prends pitié!'* It was very dramatic and utterly ludicrous, because even though she was a saint on Sundays, she was the bitchiest gossip in the village during the rest of the week. As luck would have it, she was sweeping the floor when we came in.

We sat down in a row and I told Bruno that his dog was dead. He gasped and put his hand over his mouth, but otherwise he didn't react. No tears. No words. He just sat there motionless. The only noise was the rhythmic swish of Madame Amiel's broomstick and her flapping ears.

Bruno was ten when he found Geppie in some woods near his village in Alsace. They had lived together for sixteen years. When Bruno left home, Geppie came too, and they roamed France together, not exactly homeless, but never with much of an address, camping out and moving on. They had been a captivating circus act, the little gypsy boy and his pet fox, and Geppie's death was the end of one road for Bruno and the beginning of another. Now he would have to grow up.

After a while we drove home and the girls met us. Sensibly, they had already buried the dog at the bottom of the garden on the edge of the vineyard, and that's where our trip ended. Bruno standing alone over the grave at twilight. The sun threw mauve shadows across the vineyard. The umbrella pines moaned in the breeze, and far away at the end of the woods the sea roared against the beach. The sun set and a mist crept up. The beam from the lighthouse ploughed through it. We closed the shutters and the whole picture reminded us that another summer was over. We sat around the kitchen table, glum and exhausted by all the natural and unnatural shocks. This time events really had overtaken us.

Tom went back to Madrid. The girls left for London. Alone and desperate in the half-built house, Bruno and I resorted to religion. We drove to Mass every morning like a pair of unfucked nuns, and sat around in trances for the rest of the day, lighting candles and building little altars in various nooks around the empty house. Religion works best when things are at their worst and after about a week we were both approaching sainthood, so we decided to make a pilgrimage to Lourdes. We put Mo in the back of the car and set off early one morning, arriving that same evening in the Pyrenees. During this latest dash across Europe we were grim and determined, and Mo watched us suspiciously from the back seat. He wasn't into moping around. Considering that he had witnessed Geppie's death at first hand (paw), he was showing considerable powers of recovery. He had loved Geppie, but dogs are sophisticated. We humans wallow in our memories; they let go of the past and move on.

At Lourdes we found a(nother) rather depressing hotel on the outskirts of the town. It was a half-timbered Norman inn surrounded by dripping shrubs. Inside, it had long creaky corridors straight from a horror film. In our room illness clung to the curtains and the beds, and the smell from the half-hearted central heating merged with the damp-stained carpets in a low fog. The residue of faith and broken dreams made Mo's hackles stand up on end, but we were too tired to move on, so we fed him and then walked down to the basilica.

And so there we were, the neurotic freak, the pixie and the bouncy dog, an unholy trinity, watching the torchlight procession wind around us in a giant halo through the hills above Lourdes, the heavenly music distant and chilling on the breeze, love and death all together, hope and despair, sex, drugs and St Bernadette: everything was included in a moment that was apparently buried alive, only to be stumbled upon twenty-five years later, by the same freak, calcified, with a blind major and his German nurse.

CHAPTER THIRTEEN

Plenary (Self-)Indulgence

An ancient duchess in nurse's garb stood on a podium with a microphone, incanting the 'Hail Mary' in a lethargic drawl, as if she had a cigarette holder clenched between her teeth. The mantra was delivered to the faithful via a clapped-out sound system that echoed and bounced around the sacred spot. It was the day reserved for the Knights of Malta to take the waters, and we were all there, with our '*malades*' at the front of the line, for redemption. Behind us jostled less well-connected pilgrims, other nurses and doctors with different cloaks and costumes, but all wheeling the same the terminally ill creatures, their faces uncannily illuminated by the footlights of faith, extraordinary regards, eyes burning from shrunken faces on bodies twisted and turned by disease.

My father sat upright in his chair, wearing his straw hat and a regimental tie to honour the occasion, and slowly we crept to the head of the line. Finally we were ushered behind a curtain into a marble changing room where three men removed my father from his wheelchair and his body from his clothes with the precision of fishmongers shelling oysters. Hat, shirt, shoes, socks, underpants in his racing colours: they all came off one after another as I gingerly undressed myself beside him. Naked and without his glasses, my father sat on a little stool, wrapped in a loincloth, another animal, really, an old tortoise without its shell, bones draped in thin skin, the pacemaker visible in his chest, and the scar from his heart surgery cutting across it – a botched magician's trick. I couldn't tell if I was touched or horrified. All I knew was that our roles had irreversibly changed. He was the ancient little boy waiting for the holidays, and I was the adult anxious to get back to the office.

The men asked him to stand while they slid a kind of sling underneath him. He stood shakily with his arms stretched out, and they lowered him onto it and fastened him with straps. On a count of three they lifted him and threw aside another curtain, revealing the bath itself, a grey marble tomb of icy water. The duchess's 'Hail Mary' was piped through to these inner recesses of the temple. Suddenly she switched languages and began the prayer in an extraordinary French devoid of any attempt at an accent. 'Joo voo saloo Muree plenda grass . . .'

I always find the French 'Hail Mary' slightly shocking because while we say, 'Blessed is the fruit of thy womb' (Jesus), they say, '*Le fruit de vos entrails*', meaning the fruit of your entrails, which presents a rather grisly image to which the duchess gave a thrilling downward inflection.

'Quite a talented linguist, old Podge,' mentioned my dad as they took him down the steps into the inner sanctum, which was not unlike the RAC Club in London.

These kind sweet men lowered him into the freezing water and I was afraid he would have a heart attack then and there, but he just moaned and shivered. A Knight leant over him; together they said the 'Hail Mary' in low urgent voices and there was something medieval about their two heads close together. Their whole lives were wrapped up in this belief, handed down and adjusted across two millennia. My father's body, like the religion itself, was a mere whisper of its former self, but the faith remained. It was a gilded ship rowing him slowly across the twilight sky towards the faraway star. The old campaigner was heaved out of the water and the kind men put him back together again, while I wrapped my loincloth around my waist and stuck my toes into the freezing font.

CHAPTER FOURTEEN

A Brief Encounter with Mo

There were no lines of aristocrats, no chanting dignitaries, that windswept autumn morning when Bruno, Mo and I arrived at the grotto. Just a cluster of nuns, their robes billowing in the cold wind, chatting by the river. We tied Mo to a bench beside them, having ascertained that he could not take the cure, which was a shame because he loved water almost as much as food, and perhaps would not have got cancer at the end of his life if he had taken a quick dip.

We took off our clothes and wrapped ourselves in loincloths. Everything was full of meaning, and the image of a mother God was never more appealing nor more present. She would forgive Alfo and me, and keep an eye on Geppie, even if that old mood-swinger Yahweh wouldn't, and it felt secure to be there. Mo's furious barks could be heard from the river as we were completely submerged by two local boys in charge, and came out spluttering but glowing into the chilly air. We put our clothes on without drying, which is supposed to be one of the miraculous aspects of the experience, and left, shocked and revitalised. It was all over in five minutes.

Outside, the nuns were making a fuss of Mo and he was tugging

at their robes. They were screaming with delight, and the whites of
Mo's eyes informed anyone in the know that he was getting turned
on. As we sat down he saw his moment and leapt on one of the poor
novitiates, the glistening pink lipstick of his member peeking
through its furry foreskin, and humped her with urgency. An older
nun intervened, as the young sister turned red and screamed louder.
This was probably as near as she would ever get to having sex, which
was a gruesome thought, because Mo was not a gentle lover. He was
in the full vigour of his youth. Consensual sex was anathema to him,
and he liked his partner to put up a spirited resistance. I finally managed to disengage him, without having to throw the proverbial
bucket of water over them both, apologising profusely while giving a
sharp tap on the nose to my dog, who lay down with a grunt and
sulked for as long as his memory served him, which was about fifteen
minutes.

The sisters were French, from Toulouse, with pink scrubbed faces
under their wimples, and bright virginal eyes, unclouded by desire.

'What brings you to Lourdes?' the older nun asked, clearly in
charge.

'I want a miracle for my friend Alfo,' I replied.

'And my dog died,' said Bruno, and we both burst into tears.

With the grotto in front of us, our story spilt out. The ladies listened with compassion and dignity, the elder nun invigilating the
proceedings with concern. They were a small flock of tame black-
birds, their little beaks framed in starched linen, perched on the
bench, gripping it against the wind, leaning towards us to hear better,
while we were a pair of lost parrots from a faraway jungle, shivering
in tie-dyed T-shirts and ripped jeans. (It was the first summer of love,
that year.) Bruno's hair flew in the wind. Mo looked up from his sulk,
from one group to the other, and thought we had all gone mad, but
actually this was religion, an affectionate contact from opposite ends
of the earth, and there was no trace of judgement in these girls' eyes.

'This Aids,' asked one of them. 'Is it very easy to catch?'

'Yes,' I replied. 'I think so.'

'Then you must be very careful.'

I began to sob again.

She took my hand and looked into my eyes. 'I'm sure you'll be all right. As for your friend, why don't you come with us to the basilica and say a rosary for him. You could even make a novena!'

'A *novena*?' For the uninitiated that's nine rosaries a day for nine days.

'Yes. I think that would be very beautiful.'

I did say a novena for Alfo. But praying can be sidestepping and is not always really religious. It gave me a sense that I was doing something, but Alfo needed support, an actual shoulder to lean on, not the distant buzz of a thousand 'Ave Marias' said in a village church three hundred miles away. In reality, I had stolen his tragedy for myself.

My test came back negative. Of course it would. My paranoia had run amok and I had more or less destroyed poor Alfo under the weight of it. He had been careful and responsible, while I had behaved like a 'rich tourist witch', Tom said, out of my depth, not tough enough to play the game.

During our late-night calls from the station in Turin I began to disengage. I couldn't, wouldn't, deal with the very real problems Alfo had. Finally he cracked one night as a train to Viareggio was delayed, and shouted at me down the line. He accused me of playing with him, of being utterly selfish, and finally of being a typical Catholic, all noise and no compassion.

He was right.

CHAPTER FIFTEEN

New Year's Eve in Amsterdam

Twelve years later, I was walking down a rainy street in Amsterdam with my friend Rifat from Turkey. It was a freezing New Year's Eve at the beginning of the new century, and Christmas trees swayed in the wind outside the big hotels. Their lights and tinsel were wavy blurs in the rain. The potheads looked out dreamily from the warmth of the coffee shops, and freezing tourists hurried through the streets, wrapped in scarves and hats.

'Mum, look at that number in the window,' said Rifat.

I looked around and there was Alfo. Older, tougher, no boyishness left; a marine, in fact, with short-cropped hair, wearing army fatigues He sat with a thin blond Dutchman at a table behind a large window.

I banged on the pane and he looked round. His brain's machinery flew through a series of images before matching up the ghoul in the window with that uppity lover from the last century. Then his eyes bulged and a huge smile cracked his unshaven face in half. He bounded from the bar, and there we were again, the same but completely different, weathered and harder, but amazed and thrilled at the universe throwing us together. We exchanged numbers and party plans. Later that night, as midnight struck in some dungeon dance hall, and klaxons blasted, and streamers and glitter fell through the air, someone tapped me on the shoulder. It was him. We hugged as the chimes banged out. My Turkish friend arrived with some other friends. I turned around to introduce them, but Alfo was gone.

A couple of evenings later, as the festivities wound down, I was lying, toxic, in my room when there was a knock on my door. It was him. On closer inspection he had a haunted look about him. He produced a huge bag of cocaine and chopped out lines as he told me all that had happened since that faraway morning in Turin.

He no longer worked in a bank. Obviously. He had fled Italy, first to America, where he met a man, and things were OK for a while. But then the disease kicked in and he nearly died. Only for the fact that he had been a body-builder, and was massive, had he survived the onslaught of Kaposi's sarcoma, which had grown over his entire body and eaten him away. In a sense he had been lucky, because his immune system had held on just long enough for the miraculous anti-retroviral drugs to become available. He was saved, but as soon as he was in a fit state was forced to leave America. He was too proud to go back to Italy. So now he was on the high seas, waiting for something to happen. In the meantime he had become a dealer. Soon, he said, he would try escorting.

He was matter-of-fact, light-hearted, still a graceful colossus, but Aids had hollowed him out. He had survived it but it had marginalised him, exiling him to a life of muddling through and moving on. He wanted to go back to the States, but that was pretty much impossible, considering his condition, so for the time being he was stuck, roaming Europe.

'Just think,' he said, 'what a normal life I had. And now this!'

We stayed up until dawn, talking. I could speak Italian now, and many things were clarified that had been lost in translation. As he was leaving we promised to meet again.

'I'm sorry for everything,' I blurted out as we hugged goodbye.

He laughed, and his eyes glittered. 'Everything ended well. That's the main thing. Do you want some valium?'

It was still raining outside, and I watched him through the window, hunched against the cold, hands dug deep into his pockets, as he walked across a bridge over the canal and disappeared in the deep blue darkness. I never saw him again.

Charitable Feelings

'I am feeling very holy,' said my father as we left the grotto. 'I think I shall make a substantial donation to charity.'

Charity? Now it was my turn to feign deafness.

PART THREE

The End of Charity

It is five o'clock in the morning deep in the Cambodian jungle. A twelfth-century temple called Bayon with fifty-four towers looms black against the purple sky. A full watery moon glides through space above us, outlining the vast temple in silver and throwing long shadows from the forest onto the clearing upon which it stands. It is like a day-for-night scene in a movie from the fifties. The woods behind us are silent, shredded with moonbeams and fragrant with weird Cambodian night flowers. The air is still and warm, and the beauty is so intense that for a moment our anxious lives – with their situation comedies and dramas – briefly stand back and dissolve into the night.

We are not alone. A few other tourists grope their way, beetles in the half-light, up the steep, ruined stairways. Banyan trees weave through the walls, across the balustrades, sucking this forgotten civilisation back into the earth. Huge porticos balance precariously on teetering columns and vaulted ceilings are caught in the branches' embrace, as they fall in ghostly freeze-frames like broken card houses. It's probably quite dangerous, and it won't be long before someone is buried alive, and there are signs and barriers and officious tour guides with megaphones, but for the moment we are watched by a few young Buddhist monks – just kids, really – who are the keepers of these temples of Angkor.

I'm soon separated from the rest of the group in a maze of black stone corridors deep in the temple. A little girl beckons me to follow her. We enter a small room where sits an enormous Buddha and a tiny old nun. There are offerings at the feet of the statue including a packet of Lays crisps, and the nun is arranging things as I come in. She has no teeth, a shaved head and unwavering blue eyes. She sits on her haunches, proffers some sticks of incense, which I light from a candle on the floor. She motions for me to kneel beside her and pray. I gaze up at the huge face of the Buddha; his smile is inscrutable through the wisps of smoke that billow and curl my prayers to the heavens. I'm transfixed. He seems to be looking straight at me. The nun nudges me in the ribs, and motions for me to bow. I do.

'One,' she says in English.

'Two.' She's bowing with me this time, showing me the way.

'Three,' we say in unison. And then:

'*Peace!*' she explains, as if it were that simple.

Charity may begin at home, but it ends in Cambodia. I am here in my new capacity as ambassador for the Global Fund, a G8 invention to combat Aids, malaria and TB in the third world. They have pledged $59 million to this country and I am here to see how it is being spent. I have in my entourage this moonlit night: a TV crew from the BBC, a photographer from *Vanity Fair* – a German prince, no less – and an extraordinary woman from Geneva (that mountain spring from whence all rivers of charity coil) called Mariangela Bavicchi. My Sancho Panza on this escapade is David from Miami, without whom I cannot take one charity step. He is standing right next to me this morning, looking like Frankenstein's monster in the moonlight.

We have become an unusual double act on the scene. Our previous field trips include Haiti, India and Africa. We have lobbied in

Washington and Moscow, and even headlined the disastrous Aids Walk in Miami where no one showed up, but I got the keys of the city anyway. (Where are those keys, by the way?) David helps me write my speeches and is a world expert on Aids, when he is not larking around.

This morning we are going to take a moody dawn shot of me for the *Vanity Fair* article I shall write about the situation. We have been driven to the forest by a rabble of gorgeous Cambodian boys on scooters and I have even done some jaunty shots riding side-saddle, whizzing past a monk taking a shit. Dawn arrives and I am standing on a parapet surveying the jungle. The German prince is shooting me from below – not my favourite angle. He has nicknamed me Frosty.

'Frosty, stop worrying. You are looking marvellous. Just like a lesbian explorer.'

'Good,' I reply. 'I don't want to set a frivolous tone.'

The view from up here is better than *The Jungle Book*. The abandoned towers of a thousand other temples reach out from the swaying forest. They are drowning in it. Their sharp black silhouettes flail against the green ocean, which is now screeching and squawking with life. Mist swirls from the ground and curls into the morning air. The smell of woodsmoke chases off the subtle fragrance of night as we jump back onto our scooters and drive all the way to the Tonlc Sap River where a boat is waiting to take us back to the capital, fifteen hours away.

'If today's newspaper is anything to go by,' I lazily observe over breakfast the next morning, 'it seems as if there's a coup brewing.'

The government here in Phnom Penh is at a standstill, and the king, Norodom Sihanouk, has fled (as usual) to his chum Kim Il-Sung's state-of-the-art hospital in North Korea. There goes my introduction from Nicky Haslam!

But the really big story in the local morning paper is that Angelina Jolie has been offered Cambodian citizenship. She's in Phnom Penh with her adopted Cambodian baby to lobby against the building of a

dam, and they are staying in our hotel. On page three of this remarkable, bumper edition, we learn that Gary Glitter is appealing his
extradition. All in all, it's a very show-business week. No sooner do I
arrive in my room than a smart manila envelope slides under the
door, inviting me to a cocktail party, given by the actress Ashley
Judd, in the American Embassy. I look out of my window and there's
Kirsten Dunst, poolside with a couple of Kampucheans. I swear.

We are staying in the Raffles Hotel, abandoned for many years,
but recently restored to its no-nonsense, colonial, custard-coloured
comfort. Long cloisters with the most polished black and white floors
I have ever seen stretch along the back of the entire building on six
storeys, flanked by rows of identical doors. Dim lanterns like street
lights thread along their ceilings into the distance and wooden
balustrades look over the gardens at the back of the hotel. They are
the corridors we run down in troubled dreams, never reaching the
end.

At night the heat and the scent from the garden are claustrophobic. There is no movement in the air, just the faintest rustling in the
atmosphere – a vibrational trace perhaps, or maybe my newly diag-
nosed tinnitus is playing me up – but I am hearing silent screams
everywhere and hardly have to close my eyes to see the bloodstained
bodies being dragged down these halls, not so long ago, by the monstrous hit men of the Khmer Rouge who used the deserted hotel
during the terror for private torture parties. Inside my room the swel-
tering heat is sharply reduced by the efforts of the grinding
air-conditioning machine, which freezes the place to the tempera-
ture of Regan's bedroom in *The Exorcist* or Michael Jackson's oxygen
coffin. I wake up the next morning with the beginnings of third-
world, third-degree flu.

Looking at our breakfast table in the opulent old dining room,
we could be a group of big game hunters off to shoot some tigers as
we lounge around, sipping from beautiful pink and white china
cups and listening to Mariangela Bavicchi, our man in Geneva, as
she tells us about the day's work ahead. She is the person who must

nurture and control our vision of what is going on here in Cambodia. We must see it through her eyes, the eyes of the fund, and we must wear our special rose-coloured 3-D specs, provided by the G8, when communicating the nightmare to the outside world. It is her responsibility that we never go off piste, or see things we are not meant to see.

Mariangela is one of charity's top handlers. Watching her now, sipping an espresso, I wonder if she is CIA. She is certainly as inscrutable as a James Bond girl. Tall, blonde, attractive but not pretty, laid back and yet irrepressible, shaken not stirred. Her voice vibrates from somewhere behind her nose, making her sound at times like a duck, at others like a German, although she is in fact Italian – and the only one I ever met who rolls her Rs. But that's the UN for you. They are unfathomable folk with untraceable accents, and they all seem to possess three passports. MA has humorous, slightly droopy eyes and the thing that makes her more than just pretty is that when she talks she always seems to be on the verge of laughing. She dresses simply but well in jeans and shirts and expensive shoes, like a Roman lesbian. In fact she is married to a Swiss banker, but we never meet him in the course of our three-year friendship.

If I have conjured up a picture of Marie Antoinette in drainpipes, then I am getting it wrong. MA is committed to her job and extremely good at it, but she is a different animal to the charity girls from Oxfam with whom I have previously rattled the begging bowl. Their faces were blotchy with compassion and panic. MA is poised with a creamy complexion and she never hurries, except perhaps when she nips off to the spa, should we be charioteering at a good hotel and there is a break in the schedule. Between the UN in Geneva and Oxfam on the Banbury Road, there is obviously a wide gap. It's five stars all the way for the bearer of the baby-blue passport, even if the rest of us have to pay our way. Luckily *Vanity Fair* is underwriting our entire trip.

After breakfast our 'mission' moves with military precision, from project to project, morning after morning, in the blazing heat, as I get sicker and sicker. Not a moment is wasted: the cars arrive at eight o'clock with our people on the ground. One is an extremely bossy girl from Poland, named Inga, and the other is a matchstick-thin, wild-eyed pharmacist from France, Emanuel. We clamber aboard, making sure we are sitting next to our new best friend on the trip – mine is the German prince; David's is Emanuel – and off we go, beep-beep through the traffic, past scooters carrying whole families side-saddle, taxi bikes with stately matriarchs looking daggers from the back, SUVs with diplomatic number plates and black windows sealed against the heat and the rest of humanity, and brightly painted trucks crammed with half-naked men, all honking and belching towards one another in a cloud of dust and diesel. A traffic conductor stands ignored at the very epicentre of the crush in what at first glance seems to be white tie and tails but in fact is just white gloves. He is in a trance, pointing this way and that, his forearms rotating from his elbows, blowing his whistle as another lorry screeches to a halt before his outstretched arm. He is Marcel Marceau searching for the opening to an invisible door. He finds it and motions us through and suddenly the crazy city has disappeared like a magic trick and we are driving over a low flat horizon into the huge pale Cambodian sky.

It's a strange third-world phenomenon, that dusty caravan of care that grinds and bumps its way towards some faraway clinic in Cambodia. The vans are packed with total strangers. Collisions from different worlds. Chat starts cautiously about conditions in the field, but I drift off with the view – after all, I've never seen a paddy field before. Solitary palm trees are scattered across the horizon. Little naked kids play in the muddy waters by the road. The red-tiled roofs of distant temples (*wats*) flash past and a man waves from a small canoe on an emerald-coloured field. In the bus MA tells us about the Global Fund.

'Rrrruperrrrt! Arre you listening?'

'Yes, Mariangela. I've got my notebook out.'

Formed in the wake of the G8 convention in Genoa of 2001, the Fund is mostly underwritten by government and to a certain extent the private sector. It is an unusual charity in that it does not seek to control its recipients.

'Just its celebrities,' I whisper to the prince.

'Frosty!' he warns.

MA continues.

The Fund simply responds to the needs and requests of each individual organisation in each country. However, every time a new major player enters the field of international health care, whole new systems and protocols are created. The money must be protected, as it navigates its way from the banks of Geneva, through greedy drug companies, corrupt governments (first and third world) and sometimes dodgy recipients, to the patient on the ground.

'Yes. Which means that now, if I want a new photocopier,' says Emanuel, 'I must send a memo to my superior. But if he is in the field, then I must send this memo to myself! Then I must have quotations of four different machines, which I must send to Geneva. *Putain merde!*' (Whore shit.)

Today we are visiting the Wat Opot clinic, two hours outside of Phnom Penh. It's a Christian mission in the grounds of a Buddhist *wat* at the end of a long straight track surrounded by paddy fields. The centre comprises a couple of shacks and an outdoor kitchen under a flapping green tarpaulin. In its green shade sits a large bear of a man with a grizzly beard and half-dead eyes in the middle of a group of kids. A teenage girl stands over an ironing board. The kids scream and play and the man stares into the distance. He is the spitting image of Bruce Weber and for a moment I think it is the great photographer himself. Perhaps he is shooting the new Abercrombie & Fitch campaign and I can strip off and take part.

The bus has hardly stopped but Inga leaps from it with Iron Curtain mania and frogmarches us through introductions – she is already really getting on my nerves – while Bruce shuffles around finding chairs and our cameras flash and focus. Our sound man holds his boom in that ludicrous way and a little child points and they all laugh and imitate him, making us all feel suddenly bashful and stupid. I fix my charity beam in place and soon I am sitting with Bruce in this makeshift pagoda, ready for the first interview of the trip. The kids are tiny shimmering things in the underwater light. They have no inhibitions and they climb on us and jump off or hang their arms around our shoulders, inspecting us closely, fixing us with their large innocent eyes. Bruce is in fact called Wayne and he sits there, a leftover from *Apocalypse Now*, dishevelled and distant, a huge octopus on the seabed, wrangling a child here with one long tentacle, while stopping a table from falling over with another. The girl irons on regardless.

'Welcome to Wat Opot.'

He even sounds like Bruce Weber. We face each other and the cameras zoom in for the interview. I explain that I am from the BBC and want to find out what is going on here in Cambodia.

'What's going on?' he repeats in a dead voice.

He looks deep into my eyes. His are ringed watery moons. They are saying this is a waste of time. But Inga has persuaded him to let us come. Us and all the other do-gooders who make it up the bumpy track to Wat Opot and never return. And so he sighs and launches into his story for the thousandth time. He is a Vietnam vet, invalided out in 1977.

'What made you come back?'

He doesn't answer for a moment. 'I needed a change,' he says finally. 'The States wasn't working out.' He's been back in Cambodia for seven years and he takes children on their last journey. 'Nobody dies alone here.' The result is that he hardly sleeps. The kids adore him. One, a six-year-old, is almost attached to his shoulder. 'He's only got two T-cells.'

'Do you get back to the States much?' I ask.

'Only for funerals.'

Paul Schrader could have written this.

Wayne used to burn the bodies of the kids outside on a bonfire.

'But sometimes the rains would come and put the whole thing out, and then we'd have to wait for everything to dry.' Now he has built a crematorium, which he shows us. It's a square building, like a little tomb, with a corrugated-iron roof, divided into three rooms. In the first there are two plastic chairs, 'where I sit sometimes when there's a lot of people around'.

On the walls are pinned photographs he's taken of all the kids while they were alive. Underneath, on a shelf, are little gold plastic urns that hold their ashes. Through a window you can see some woods and the red tower of the nearby *wat*. The trees are waving in the wind. We sit down among the ashes and Wayne tells many stories in a slow deliberate voice.

The one that moves me the most is of a man called Arun who died here last year. He was in his early thirties. His father was an American soldier who was evacuated from Cambodia in 1975. They never met. Throughout his childhood, during the terror, Arun became angrier and angrier with his mother. He blamed her for driving his father away. Of course, in reality it had probably been the other way around. But the boy got worse and worse, violent and dangerous, did terrible things to his mother and then got Aids. It was some years before he came limping up the track to Wat Opot.

'Arun was a tough cookie,' says Wayne, 'but three weeks before he died he softened up.'

He asked Wayne for some money to go and make peace with his mother, but the trip was a disaster and the mother sent a message to Wayne never to let the boy come near her again.

'Funnily enough,' says Wayne, 'he's the only one here who died alone. We came in the morning and he was lying there with his arm behind his back, looking up at the ceiling. Just how he always was. But dead. That was Arun all over. He did everything alone.'

A large American lady appears in the doorway of the little hut.

'Hey, Jeanie,' says Wayne.

Jeanie is Wayne's best friend from home. She is a large Southern woman of sixty built like a prison warden. She shrinks the tiny room with her size and energy.

'I came to visit and – when was it, Way?'

''Bout five years ago.'

'That long? Well, I couldn't just leave him here, all alone, could I?'

'So you moved from Oregon to Cambodia just like that?'

'Just like that!'

She laughs and looks at Wayne. Childhood sweethearts. He stares back at her, sombre, broken somehow.

'Are you getting money from the Global Fund?' I ask him.

'Ha!' laughs Jeanie, leaving.

'So much paperwork,' he replies.

Wayne and Jeanie take us across the field to visit the *wat*. It is deserted. A large garish statue of the Buddha, looking like a tricky tranny with Gary Glitter eyes, dominates the interior, which is open to the four winds. A monk looks sleepily from a window in one of the outhouses that surround the temple but otherwise there is nobody around. We walk to a nearby village where the ladies are making silk scarves on huge wooden looms and the men are seated around an enormous piece of paper on a low stage. They are writing a communal will. Strangely enough, the atmosphere is quite festive but there is a lot of debate. Everyone has an opinion. The kids play on the ground, unaware that their dying parents are assigning them new lives as orphans. There are no grandparents. Nixon, Kissinger and Pol Pot took them; now Aids is taking their children. The women listen but keep on weaving and it makes one wonder about all those scarves and rugs and things one acquires and loses, the little Christmas presents and birthday gifts. We have no idea of the living drama sewn into them as the needle slides endlessly on. If only they were labelled: 'Handmade by a dying woman in Cambodia. A living will.'

It becomes clear as the trip continues that there is a lot of tension between the NGOs and the Global Fund. The money that the fund pledged is not getting through and there is a lot of frustration.

'It's early days,' is all Mariangela will say, but the fact of the matter seems to be that Cambodia is so corrupt, nobody has managed yet to find a way of getting money onto the ground without it being stolen en route. One nurse, talking secretly to David, begins to scream, while near by – on camera – I am hearing the official version from Mariangela. The other truth confronts us each day in the perplexed faces of the doctors and nurses on the ground. Debate lasts late into the night but Mariangela gives nothing away. She is a genius actually, because we all get pretty heated and drunk, which is a bad combination, while she sips at a sparkling water and denies nothing.

'It's not easy,' is all she will admit, laughing as usual. 'By the way, you're not going to write all this in *Vanity Fair*, are you?' she asks, suddenly serious.

In the evenings we take to the streets of the capital. Boys on mopeds jostle for our trade, and soon we're off in opposite directions. It's as exciting as the bumper cars when you were a kid. The stifling heat is finally bearable as we speed across intersections and dart through the oncoming traffic. We peel off the main boulevards with their French colonial mansions and fairy-lit *wats* onto the lampless side streets, where guys sleep in the backs of their rickshaws. Every night, back from the field, we jump on our moped taxis – our favourite scooter boys are always waiting for us. They have heard the prince call me Frosty.

'Come inside, Fosty,' they scream and off we go.

We speed along the river front to where the Tonle Sap meets the Mekong River. At last there's a cool breeze on the promenade that overlooks this famous junction and it blows away all the smells and noises of the city behind us – the cabbage and the cheap gas, the honking scooters and the tinkling bikes. It also blows away all remaining sense one has of one's own world. Before us the two rivers are a vast shimmering blanket under the stars. The other bank is miles away – just a black line and a string of tiny lights that divide the river from the sky. Strange oversized thrushes sit in the flowery trees near by, their large blind eyes staring at the moon. Far out, men in straw hats are perched on the prows of their canoes and throw their nets into the water in breathtaking silhouettes. Their voices carry on the breeze. So this is the Tonle Sap. Its very name sounds magical and in fact it is the only river in the world that flows in two different directions. Once a year she turns around and flows backwards. Perhaps this is the elusive piece of the Cambodian jigsaw.

Emanuel takes us to a bar called Heart of Darkness where girls in sawn-off miniskirts play pool with travelling hippies, and there on the TV as we walk in is Madonna yapping away in Chinese. Suddenly there is a big close-up of me, also dubbed by some Hong Kong tranny. I freeze. Normally the reaction to this film has been rather violent so I slink into the shadows with a beer without mentioning anything to the other members of the group but the prince has eyes in the back of his head.

'Oh my God, Frosty, you're on the TV,' he screams but luckily no one hears.

David and Mariangela are deep in conversation with Emanuel but the rest of the clientele are completely wrapped up in the film. It's the scene where Madonna tells me she is having my baby. All action has come to a halt around the pool table as the boys and girls watch, horrified or entranced – one can never tell in the Orient. Their eyes are narrow and their faces are bathed in the weird light from the TV. They lean on their billiard cues, strange warrior folk from another planet. They hardly move during the whole film, and a big tear rolls down the alabaster cheek of a girl sitting on a bar stool at the end. I am thrilled. I'm a star in Cambodia, if not California, and I feel vindicated. Lying in bed later at the Raffles Hotel, writing my diary, I realise that as usual I am getting a whole lot more out of this trip than the people I am supposed to be helping.

There is a roaring sex trade here in Phnom Penh and our friends from Pharmaciens sans Frontières take us to the 'karaoke houses' where young teenage girls work to support their families. The girls sit on red-velvet stairs behind plate-glass walls, dressed in virginal white slips. They are sometimes beautiful, at other times homely. It is just like being in a zoo. They chat together in twos and threes behind the glass wall and men peruse them from the other side. They too are zoo animals, impounded apes running back and forth along the glass, eyeing the girls, who wave hopelessly back or just return their gaze with tired, frightened eyes.

The Pharmaciens have done a brilliant – and almost impossible – job, infiltrating and educating this secret world, and, according to Emanuel, the girls have more or less got the message. Now they say no to unsafe sex, and infection rates are on the decrease. We are not allowed to film even though we have been promised we can, but I don't want to. There is a terrible feeling in this place. These kids are sometimes as young as thirteen or fourteen. But this is the crème de la crème of the sex trade. In the poorer parts of town the safe-sex message seems less clear and for a dollar more anything goes. But the Pharmaciens are welcomed as friends here too, by the girls who live and work together (six to a tiny hovel) and also by their fem.pimp boyfriends who lounge together in the shade outside, giving one another facials, if you can believe it!

There is something really touching about the Khmers. They seem so gentle. Fragile. Trusting. But a visit to the Tuol Sleng genocide museum brings home another facet to these sweet childlike people. Like the river, they can turn. Mercilessly.

The Khmer Rouge, led by Pol Pot, with his agenda of continuous revolution, finally took Phnom Penh on 17 April 1975. Within days the city's entire population was marched into the countryside at gunpoint. 'Year Zero' was declared with a ruthless programme to purge Cambodian society of capitalism, Western culture and religion. Phnom Penh was left empty for three and a half years. Except for the Tuol Sleng Prison – code name S21. The murderers of Tuol Sleng kept an intimate photographic record of each and every one of their victims. Today the walls of this former school are covered with the most moving portraits I have ever seen. Literally, they take your breath away. Terrified little children trying to smile for the camera, their arms shackled tightly behind their backs. Emaciated young men and women smashed to bits but still alive on bloody stretchers. All smiling.

We walk silently through the museum, past the rooms with their torture beds still in place, the iron shackles still cemented into the floor, the tools of destruction standing by. Hammers, screwdrivers, electric wires, and the rules! The rules are written on the walls:

6. While getting lashes or electrification you must not cry out at all.
7. Do nothing. Sit still, and wait for my orders.

What has to happen in a country to turn a high school into a concentration camp? The answers are all in a brilliant book I got at the airport by a man called Shawcross. It's about American policy in Cambodia during the time of the Vietnam War. I cannot put this book down. Reading it feels like walking on one's own grave.

On 18 March 1969, President Nixon launched a secret, illegal bombing campaign against Cambodia that was to last for three and a half years at a cost of $7 billion. It was called Operation Menu, and its various targets were named breakfast, lunch, tea and dinner. An estimated 600,000 people were killed during this period. Cambodia was tricked by Nixon and Kissinger out of its neutrality and dragged into the Vietnam War. For what? In the end the country was simply abandoned. Not just abandoned, but destroyed. This state of shock and awe gave the Khmer Rouge all the leverage it needed to take over and continue where America had left off. Over the next three years 1.7 million people were starved or killed. Maybe that's what happens when you bomb the wrong country for the wrong reasons. America's ill-conceived military action, based on faulty intelligence and wishful thinking, unleashed a reign of terror and turned a whole people against themselves.

It sounds familiar.

A video plays every afternoon in Tuol Sleng Prison. It's of a guy who used to be a guard. He tells how, every evening before nightfall, he would herd twenty or thirty prisoners into a truck. They knew better than to ask where they were going, although they were often told that they were being taken to have extra study. They'd drive to a field outside the ghost city and be made to kneel blindfolded in front of huge pits the soldiers had dug. Then they were bludgeoned, garroted, dumped and buried. 'Still alive sometimes,' the guard says genially in the video. He's talking to one of the seven survivors from the prison. Strangely enough, he's smiling too.

Taking the same route to these killing fields in our SUVs, all these years later, as a beautiful creamy Cambodian dusk settles, it's hard to imagine those terrified people bumping their way in the dark through the empty suburbs towards their final terror. It's hard to imagine how life picks up and goes on, but it does. The killing field of Choeung Ek is a place where life meets death head-on.

In a grassy park there is a huge tower filled to the brim with skulls. The glass doors are open so you can reach inside and touch them. There is no guard, no security system. No one minds what you do here, and I can't stop myself. I pick one up. I'm holding a little skull in my hand. A huge crater has been knocked in the side of it. Further off, near the few excavated graves, the clothes and the bones of the dead can be seen sticking out of the hard earth. But chickens with the longest legs cluck and peck through the crime scene and a gang of boisterous kids run around and scream. This is their playground. One girl has a tiny plastic bow and arrow, which she fires at me, and ludicrously I feign death. They are happy kids. Full of life. The sun sets behind the tower and casts a huge shadow over the park but the kids play on. Ironically, Choeung Ek is a very peaceful place.

It's our last night in Phnom Penh and we're all really sad. We're going to the park with Emanuel and our new friends from Pharmaciens sans Frontières. It's Big Wednesday Night for Phnom Penh's emerging gay culture. There's a small white bandstand at one end of the park and hundreds of kids listen and watch. There is no cheering here in Cambodia. The audience are as still as statues, drinking in the music. A girl with a mop of short black hair, in black trousers and an untucked white shirt, takes the stage. She begins a warbling, haunting lament to some romantic oriental classic. Her voice echoes through the clapped-out, third-world sound system and drifts across the sea of upturned faces. Boys are perched elegantly on the handlebars of their rickshaws and mopeds. They are beautiful, and they've been through so much just to get here tonight. War. Genocide. Famine. And now this. They don't need weapons of mass destruction here in Cambodia. They have Aids and TB, and poverty is their billowing mushroom cloud. The HIV virus is spreading its message through this crowd tonight, at this very moment, and they don't even know it.

A boy in a baseball hat with a beautiful neck looks at me and gestures to the stage. 'Good?' he asks.

'Very good,' I reply.

He leans his elbow on my shoulder and his eyes sparkle with joy and I nearly burst into tears.

Suddenly we're at the airport. Greetings and goodbyes are intense in Asia and I have a lump in my throat through all the bows, the hands joined in prayer and the eyes locked for the last time. We huddle on their side of the international divide, unwilling to tear ourselves away. We've been looked after so considerately by the people here. Nothing has been too much trouble for them.

But eventually we move through the glass partition to the customs booth, bleary-eyed and sleepless. Our Cambodian friends stand together – Emanuel, incongruous, towers over them in the middle: a marvellous, modern-day Knight – and they are waving and laughing as an electric door swings shut and they disappear.

The paddy fields recede through the clouds into a patchwork quilt stretching into the haze. The fragile huts on their spindly stilts are just little grey smudges now and the gilded tower of a *wat* sparkles in the morning sun, winking a last goodbye. We're off to the International Aids Conference in Bangkok to rub shoulders with diplomats, politicians, drug company executives and activists. I'm scheduled to talk about my experiences in Cambodia and about the work of the Global Fund. I get out my notebook to jot down a few thoughts. All I have written down, during the entire trip, in a mad spidery scrawl is, 'Funny old nun says one two three peace.'

I can't deal with it, so I take refuge in the *Herald Tribune*. In America elections are brewing. There's a picture of John Kerry in front of a line of Vietnam vets. He is having his war record questioned. It says he defended America on the Mekong River. I look out of the window, slightly exasperated, and there *is* the Mekong River, shimmering goodbye as it limps (dammed three times in China) towards the sea, from occupied Tibet.

I think of Arun's father who is probably still at large in the USA. A retired soldier with a grown-up family, a grating, overweight wife, and no clue of the tragedy he helped to create. I suppose he too defended America on the Mekong River. I wonder what he'd defend if he was told the story of his son's life. After all, what would it be like to learn that your child was starved, displaced, forced into labour and driven mad with longing for you all his life, and that he died painfully and alone, staring at the ceiling? You would probably sit down and never get up.

CHAPTER EIGHTEEN

From Russia Without Love

There is a low inky sky over St Petersburg today as I arrive with David and Mariangela for this – the end of my charity career. Mariangela has moved from the Global Fund to UNAids and taken me with her, but pretty soon I won't be worth my keep, since it is now clear, even to her, that my star is dimming and I will not be able to engender the necessary international interest. Actually it is one aspect of my latest fall about which I am slightly relieved. One needs nerves of steel to dip in and out of other people's sorrow, and anyway I have rarely, if ever, even in my singing and dancing heyday, managed to do anything of any use on the charity circuit. One is a decoy – largely to oneself.

But for the time being we are driving into Petersburg, talking to our UN man on the ground, a small Swedish gentleman with longish ex-blond hair, a kind face and blue eyes. He outlines the situation on the ground with the cosy bedside manner of a gynaecologist. His sidekick is a wiry American lady in her late thirties with a great figure and luxuriant hair. She is the type of woman you would normally expect to see on the board of a charity in New York.

She is expensively and well dressed, and looks as tough as old boots. They remind me of Robert Wagner and Stephanie Powers in *Hart to Hart*.

'Definitely CIA,' I whisper to David.

'You always say that.'

We are staying in the Grand Hotel on Nevsky Prospect. It is a far cry from the hotel I stayed in when I first arrived in Russia twenty years ago. Then you could make a phone call only using your credit card in the foyer under the beady lighthouse sweep of the hallway *dievotchka*. That foyer was dingy and neon-lit, with orange furniture and brown carpet upon which waves of packaged tourists flooded. In and out they came, on a revolving door from grimy buses outside, dragging with them into the dry, hot interior clouds of exhaust and the freezing air. I would sit in that foyer with my dog beside me – on the first days of the long year I spent in Russia – feeling completely isolated, waiting for hours for a call from home. In the quiet of the low tide, between one coachload and another, only a few scruffy salesmen remained, dealers of contraband baby foods and Wonderbras smuggled from the West. They were probably all future oligarchs. We were united briefly in that bubble between worlds by our common aim.

'Telephon,' the *dievotchka*'s command would ring out, the beam of her scrutiny spotlighting its recipient, and up one of us would jump to squeeze into the tiny booth – with a dog in my case – and listen to the news, accompanied by crossed lines and strange beeps and clicks, from the other side of the Iron Curtain.

Now the foyer of the Grand has been garishly restored to its former glory. The gold leaf is blinding and so is the staggering display of wealth that is being paraded before this Disneyland backdrop. Stick-insect women swathed in furs with gigantic superimposed features – almost Neanderthal, from the needle of Dr Sebag in London or Dr Sandrine in Paris – stalk through the foyer, knocking people over with their cheekbones, followed by porters loaded down with every shape and size of bag in the Louis Vuitton catalogue. They are greeted or eyed by the suited eunuchs of oligarchs posing as their masters in dark suits and gold watches, fixing and folding up deals with a new breed of visiting tradesmen, oil and gas people, over tea and muffins. Russia has been stolen by these gangsters and their molls – or actually it has been inherited by the sons and daughters of the old gangsters.

Outside, the early dusk is falling and I go for a walk. The same palaces are still tumbling down by the sides of the same roads, the yellows and greens of autumn leaves, funny Soviet entrances carved into their classical flanks. They still rise with miraculous elegance above the grime of the treacherous streets, jammed no longer with thousands of belching Ladas, but instead with fleets of Bentleys and Ferraris. The old ladies who used to sit proudly on the corners, selling pickled gherkins, have now been driven wild. New Russia overlooked them and they have lost their Soviet dignity. Progress has reduced them to howling beggars; their careworn faces are riverbeds of tears long dried up. One follows me now over a bridge, screaming, her arms outstretched like a soprano in an opera. I give her some money. She sobs hysterically but no sound comes out.

The city is on the verge of winter. The water in the canals is black and ready to freeze, perfect conditions for suicide. Splosh and the clock's ticking. Two minutes till hypothermia. The bridges over the canals are crumbling and, like Venice, Petersburg has a sinking feeling. Sandwiched between the low slate sky and the ground, you feel as if your bones and your spirit could be crushed at any minute. I stand on the bridge and look out over the city. A row of Hummers with flashing lights and sirens ploughs through the traffic in a flotilla of motorbikes. This is how the powerful move in Russia. People run to get out of the way, and cars screech to a halt as the caravan speeds by. When I lived here I fell in love with Russia. Something tells me that on this trip I will learn to loathe it.

The next morning we drive for an hour outside the city, leaving the smart new highways for the roads I remember from the old days: dangerous torrents full of potholes around which the traffic swerves at breakneck speed, with banks of crusted rubbish and the submerged skeleton of the odd car. The countryside is flat and misty and you can suddenly feel the vastness of Russia. We drive beside a wide river for a few miles and then turn off into a tree-lined avenue towards a cluster of modest buildings on the edge of some woods. Perhaps we are in the stable block of some long-forgotten villa. Through an archway a red-brick asylum, built in the Soviet style, is pale in the mist. The noise of children playing and the shrieks of rooks in the bare trees above remind me of my schooldays and my blood runs cold.

A man appears through the fog, wearing a white laboratory coat. He introduces himself as Dr Veronin. He is a gentle giant, built in the tradition of Soviet Reality, with a pronounced jaw, extended limbs and large hands. He takes us to his office where we have coffee and he tells us about the children in his care. They are all abandoned, most of them with HIV and some with full-blown Aids. He is joined by a pretty nurse, and we all set off to look around.

The children have put on a show for us. A sweet lady plays a piano and the kids sing. They sit on little chairs in a circle but one of them is in a bad mood and refuses to take part. He sits with his head in his hands while the others dance and scream around him. We are all enraptured. There is something indescribable in the eyes of these children. They leap trustingly into our arms while we walk around the hospital, chattering, pointing and showing us their beds, while Dr Veronin explains how each one comes to be here. They all adore him and every child has his or her favourite nurse or, in one case, the cleaning lady. These ladies care for them so selflessly that you want to burst into tears. Some of the older children go out in the morning to the local school, but they are often bullied for being HIV positive and have to leave.

The four-year-old boy sits away from the others in the large playroom, silent and motionless in the blur of activity around him. The other kids scream about, being planes and monsters, but this boy just sits on his stool as though time has stopped. He has a thin worried face with black eyes, tense lips and thinning hair. He could be four or forty. He arrived at the hospital with his younger brother two years ago. Theirs is a familiar story. The elder one inherited the HIV virus from his mother, who injected drugs. The younger one, however, did not. Even though he was hardly a couple of years older, the big boy looked after and protected his younger brother and was always by his side. They lived in squalor in a suburb of Petersburg. Their mother rarely fed or washed them – when they were found, they were nearly feral – she spent most of her time gagged out on heroin. The father of the boys died of an overdose, in the flat. She met another man and immediately got pregnant. As soon as she had the new baby, she abandoned the other two. On the street. According to Dr Veronin, when they arrived at the orphanage they communicated in a special language and were happy as long as they were together. But then one day, the mother's mother, *babushka*, arrived and took the healthy boy away to live with her, leaving the older brother on his own. That was a year ago. The boy hasn't spoken since.

That afternoon we visit the Botkin hospital in the heart of St Petersburg, another rambling Soviet edifice, and a labyrinth of passages and staircases. It is a twenty-minute walk from the entrance, about which a few clapped-out ambulances are cluttered, to the bright airy showroom on the third floor where three smart doctors in crisp white coats stand in the corner with their stethoscopes around their necks, looking busy. The room is white. The floor is white. The large windows are spotlessly clean. One of the doctors is a stocky woman with cruel eyes and grey, wiry hair, swept back like Einstein. She would have been nominated *luchshiye rabotnik* in the old days – best worker – and she is probably still a KGB grass.

'There you go again,' says David.

Well. Her feet are planted far apart on the floor and she wears white clogs. She talks to Stephanie Powers and ignores the rest of us. Stephanie is careful and acquiescent, which is strange because most of what this woman is saying is a pack of lies. Her pearls of Russian wisdom are strung into English by a weird activist queen who runs an outpatients group and also works for the Elton John Foundation. He has a red face with a handlebar moustache and wears camouflage pants. Translating the woman's lies, he looks at us intensely, daring us to confront her. She insists that it is mostly drug users who are being infected with HIV in Russia, and that the epidemic began only in 1997. She says that medication is available to all. She says that there are hardly any homosexuals with HIV.

'But that can't be true,' I say.

'It isn't!' says the translator, under his breath.

'*Da!*' she clucks defensively.

'But surely one in ten people all over the world are gay?'

'Not in Russia.'

'Is that because they are forced to live in secret?'

'Certainly not. '

The meeting quickly freezes over. *Hart to Hart* are hell-bent on diplomacy and begin to wind things up. The translator winks and gestures for us to follow him out of the room. David and I slip out after him.

'I show you the Aids Department,' he whispers, and leads us down a warren of back staircases and narrow corridors.

With every step the hospital gets shabbier and hotter. Gone is the pristine spaceship of the third-floor consulting room. Soon we are rushing down a subterranean passage towards a large pair of double doors. Any minute now red lights are going to start flashing and a klaxon will go off and we shall be dragged back up to the Einstein dyke on the third floor. You need a card to get through the double doors. The translator produces one with a flourish.

'Da-dah!' He swipes triumphantly and the doors click open. Now the cameraman materialises at the end of the passage along with the photographer and journalist from Russian *Vogue* who are covering the trip.

The translator swears under his breath. 'Quick. They are following us.'

We rush through the door which closes mechanically although the others manage to squeeze through as it clicks shut.

Here finally is the situation with Russian Aids.

Rows of empty metal beds stand in wards of peeling green walls off a wide gloomy corridor. Naked light bulbs hang from the ceiling. There is a rancid dusty smell of floors washed with dirty water. Mosfilm was cleaner than this. The place is deserted.

Finally we discover a solitary man in a dressing gown and three sweaters. He is sitting on a bed in an empty dormitory at the end of the corridor, startled and upset by the sudden invasion of TV crew and photographer, celebrity and journalist. He comes to the door and tries to shut us out but our (Russian) cameraman stands in the way, engaging him all the while through the lens. He has no sympathy. The patient's eyes bulge with impotent fury as he tries to tuck his head into his dressing gown and escape across the corridor but the cameraman follows. A weird, slow-motion, split-second scuffle ensues. The cameraman holds onto the patient with his free hand, trying to turn him round, but the patient keeps on going, charging down the corridor towards the sanctuary of the toilets, while the translator, horrified, grabs the cameraman's arm, trying to pull him away. The cameraman, still filming, loses his balance. The camera falls from his shoulder and smashes onto the stone floor.

During the moment of stunned silence that follows, the photographer from *Vogue* takes my picture. Flash! With a howl the patient makes a final dash and locks himself into the loo.

It is a tragic scene with comic undertones, another masterclass in Chekhov, and not unlike a wildlife documentary in which some poor wildebeest escapes a crocodile while trying to cross a river. We have completely violated this poor man's space, and we have observed his humiliation in our UN high heels, and the translator is – quite rightly – livid. Emotionally and physically. He is now a purple gargoyle. He shrieks at the cameraman, who bellows right back, while the couple from *Vogue* have a half-hearted nervous breakdown that 'all this could be happening in their country'. The translator and the cameraman shout and point and tap their heads, more animal than human as they lumber round each other, while the two fashionistas swoon in shawls and patent-leather shoes in this curious drama in the diabolical corridor of the Aids wing.

Mariangela appears from a door far away, giggling as usual.

'There you are. What's going on?'

Hart to Hart are frosty when we regroup outside the hospital and in the car give us a talking-to about going off piste, and that things are very delicate here in Russia at the moment, and that they have worked so hard to get this far, and that we all have to be very careful. The translator, who is with us in the car, rolls his eyes.

'But it's good for them to see what's really going on,' he says. 'The truth is that gay people are afraid to go to the doctor.'

'Why?'

'Because the doctors normally report them to the police. Most gay people with Aids pretend they are drug addicts.'

'There you go,' sneers David. 'Its better to be a junkie than a queer. This place is disgusting.'

It seems impossible that the world goes on as usual after a day like today, but here we are, listless or anxious, laughing or smoking, bumper to bumper, oblivious to everything outside the four walls of our own world. Dr Veronin's orphanage, the speechless boy on his stool, the man in the three sweaters, are just the undertow of the great suffering wave upon which the rest of us mindlessly surf, desperate to keep afloat, beeping and swearing, inching along on a belch of exhaust. The rain pours down now, and the palaces and pepper pots by the side of the road melt in the deluge like wedding cakes. Similarly the lost boys and the solitary patient, bathed perhaps in tears tonight, will pass by and disappear, stretched by time into thin shadows. This is the terrible truth and I plunge into the usual field-trip depression – it always happens: that raw feeling of utter futility that makes one want to curl up and die. There's a lull in the conversation, as if the same void has struck us all.

'It still amazes me,' muses David, thinking aloud, 'that one disease can inspire so much hate.'

'Or apathy.'

Or love.

Now it is evening. We are in one of St Petersburg's few gay bars. It's rather like Joe Allen's. Brick walls, low lights and checked table-cloths. We are here to meet Andrei, a doctor from Siberia, and his cohort of twenty young activists. They have come from all over Russia and are determined to educate Russia's homosexual commu-nity about the threat of HIV. As Andrei says, whether we like it or not, about ten per cent of all Russians are gay.

'See!' says David.

In a completely hostile environment most of them are forced to live secretly, adding greatly to the danger posed by HIV.

'Remember,' Andrei says, 'this is a country where every other person is still an informer.'

The fact is that most gay people have little or no idea about the disease. How could they have? The government more or less refuses to accept that homosexuals exist, so naturally there is no state fund-ing to inform them about safe sex.

I am standing with Andrei on a podium, looking down at the innocent, upturned faces of his army in the half-light of the bar: the blunt noses, the deep-set eyes, the high cheekbones, the Nureyev lips over broad jaws and, in one case, a delicious pair of cauliflower ears (my favourite), but mostly what is striking about them is their sober attention. The liberated queen of the West has none of this inner grace as she flings herself from the dance floor to the dark room, high on lavatory cleaner. These boys are giving their time to help others, putting themselves on the line just by being here tonight. And yet on the evolutionary ladder of this cruel cloud cuckoo land they are only a rung above murderers and not as good as junkies.

I ask them how many of them have 'come out' to their parents. Only two put up their hands. It's not a surprise. After all, even men working at *Vogue* prefer to stay in the closet.

'If you can't be gay in *Vogue*, then where can you?' asks David, and I agree, but no one sees the funny side.

After the meeting we rush to Moskovsky Station, another crumbling, blue-and-white wedding cake. We are taking the night train to Moscow. It is a trip I used to make with my dog at weekends to get away from Moscow in the old days, and I loved it. Through the nineteenth-century halls of the terminal building, the station itself is a Stalinist shoebox, similar in scale and style to the fascist stations of Italy. The place is crowded and it could be 1950. Men still wear astrakhan hats and moustaches. They jostle with small wide women in shawls and scarves. Occasionally a New Russian strides through the crowd like a superimposed cartoon figure – a gazelle in furs with a bodyguard, but mostly the station is still in the hands of the poor. Their world hasn't much changed since those pre-neon days of red flags and military caps, and tonight there are still women sitting on their haunches selling pickled *gorchik*. Thank God, two of the activist boys are with us and take us to the platform, or we would never find the train. The fierce-looking couchette girl studies our tickets for clues to a murder, then grudgingly lets us on board. The whistle blows and the boys wave us off.

We settle down in our bunks and make preliminary grunts and gestures at our new room-mates. One is a bald gentleman already in his pyjamas and the other is a sozzled young man with a round face who smells of booze. I feel like a student again, but David says he may be having one of his panic attacks and lies down facing the wall, doing breathing exercises.

'Oh no! It's not one of your acute paroxysmal positional vertigo attacks, is it?' I ask wearily.

'I think so.'

Serious panic attacks are not funny. Rooms expand and contract. Colours flare and blind you. You think you are having a heart attack, but actually you're just panicking. I once went with David to an air show in Fort Lauderdale just as one was starting. As the latest jets screeched over our heads at the speed of a neutrino, David went from white to grey to green. His face visibly shrank and he clasped his chair with his hands, as the whole world turned upside down. But that's another story.

For the time being our two new friends chat in Russian on the upper bunks, their legs swinging over the edge. The sozzled one's feet are in smelly socks, with all the trimmings – bunions and giant hammer-head toes, which wiggle and stretch as he lays out a picnic above and offers us both an egg. He leans his head over the side of the bunk, his long hair trailing from his head, cheeks and lips flapping. David nearly pukes.

'Do you want some of my lithium?' I ask, trying to cheer him up.

'Have you got any?' He laughs half-heartedly, turning back to the wall, and I look out of the window. He may be having an attack but I am in heaven.

As the weight of the world is measured and debated in beautiful Russian on the top bunks, the train groans laboriously from the station through tunnels and sidings, on stilts at one moment, clattering above a shiny boulevard and diving underground at another, leaving the city behind. Buildings tower over the tracks, a collage of walls and windows under a jagged fringe of rooftops and chimneystacks. Life flashes by. An old woman washes plates. A man observes the train. A silhouette behind a curtain turns off a light. It is enchanting.

David rallies slightly and we decide to hit the restaurant car but when we open the pass door from our coach into the next, our way is blocked by the hippo attendant. It's a Bond moment, and I half expect her to expose rows of metal teeth and sink them into David's neck. We try to get past but she begins to shout in Russian. She shoves David quite hard in the chest.

'Don't you push me!' he shrieks rather pathetically and she screams back, shoving him, bulldozing back into our carriage.

Our bald travelling companion's head leans out from our berth, shouting over the noise of the train. 'Lady say you must not go.'

'Why?'

'I don't know. Is like that. You must go in half an hour.' He disappears again.

The woman locks the pass door with a key hanging from a chain around her waist before squeezing past us and barrelling down the narrow corridor to her lair at the end of the compartment. (I pass her little office later in the night and she is standing in a bra with the door open.)

I am now seriously worried that a full-blown panic attack is going to erupt from David at any moment, but actually the confrontation has cheered him up.

'That was very *Prisoner Cell Block H*,' is all he gasps, the colour returning to his cheeks.

'I can't believe she's locked us in.' I try the door. 'Imagine if our carriage catches fire!' Oops. David's face twitches.

We weave our way back to the couchette and sit on our bunks. The two Russians have spread their picnics about them, and the smell of egg and coriander and feet makes quite a good eau de toilette. But now we're both giggling, holding our hands over our noses, trying not to be seen or heard.

This is only the hors d'oeuvres. After lights out, the bald man grinds his teeth all night. He sounds like a whale calling his mate, while the sozzled one does death-rattle farts. As a result we both spend half the night in the corridor smoking and are still up when the flat white Russian dawn creeps over the plains. This is when we spy the attendant in her over-shoulder boulder-holder, also watching through her little window as the sun peeps over the horizon at another gruesome Russian day.

'*Krasyeeva*,' she says with a vulnerable smile, winking at the streaky sky.

Soon she is back proffering two elegant glasses of tea, with silver handles, on a tray. There is no trace on her big round cheese of a face of last night's battle. That's Russia for you. The fury comes and then it goes. (Another Chekhov masterclass.)

'It's probably poisoned,' says David, sipping cheerfully.

'Let's hope so,' I reply and we clink glasses between the beds. The train gives a wail of approval and we thunder on.

A kind of gallows humour engulfs us. Russia is simply too grim to take seriously. The policemen, the hotel staff, the stupid priests in their fancy hats all looking murderous, stagger around as though they have all been dealt a blow on the head by a giant hammer. They are thick and cruel and cunning. Six generations of alcohol poisoning have taken their toll, and the place looks horrible too. The countryside is a devastated mess and during the last two days I have become almost hysterical, like Uncle Albert in *Mary Poppins*. I just can't stop laughing.

From the station we drive to a small town two hours from Moscow to visit a needle drop-off centre in action. It is in fact an old caravan at the edge of a park in the middle of a dreary town unchanged since Soviet days. The trees are leafless and it is beginning to snow. Lenin still presides over the flat central square – a black fairy on a Christmas cake. It is a town that would drive anyone to drugs.

In all this gloom – the place, the sky, the people on the street – the faces of today's activists literally shine with radiance. They are two young men running a needle drop-off caravan. They look exhausted in their dirty white coats, but their eyes blaze. They drive to a different location every day, awaited in the usual place at the usual time – normally a discreet corner in the local park – by the faithful, their congregation, the poor junkies of Russia, who brave the elements in worn-out clothes under the naked trees, with their bags of used needles and their nerves in shreds.

Today a long line of strangely respectable folk wait obediently to climb on board. Some of them are skinheads and Goths and geeks, the characters one might imagine being there, but others are simple housewives and middle-aged men, conventional and polite. They stand in the falling snow and come to the caravan one at a time, into a kind of waiting room where some forms are filled out, then go through to the other section where they give up their old needles and are given new ones. It is a heartbreaking grind to watch, and as usual it feels sick to be there.

One lady comes on board with black hair and a bird face, wearing an old coat with a fake fur collar. She is sitting quite happily with the doctor when suddenly she begins to scream and jump up and down.

Everyone is shocked. The doctor tries to calm her down but she just screams more and now she is struggling out of her clothes. People leap in to help. It is a tiny space and it quickly turns into a scrum of arms and legs, and, in the middle of it all, this woman's head, all veins and teeth and eyes as she screams. She has enormous strength for such a tiny thing and she elbows her way through the crowd, then pulls down her trousers and throws her coat on the floor. There is a moment of silence, then everyone starts to laugh. Including the lady herself. They become hysterical. Tears are now running down the woman's cheeks. Is she laughing or crying? Who knows? The world is upside down. Someone shouts out of the bus to the line who are all looking up anxiously and they start to laugh as well.

'What on earth is going on?' I ask. 'I nearly had a heart attack.'

The doctors are purple with laughing. One of them explains to Stephanie Powers in Russian, but she doesn't find it the least bit amusing.

'There was a cockroach in her clothes and it was crawling into her underwear,' she says.

'Oh I see. Yes. That *is* funny. It's like the beginning of *Victor Victoria.*'

The little lady hugs the two doctors. The drama and the laughter have broken down an invisible wall and for a moment we are all normal people, unreserved, uncomplicated, and everyone hugs her and she hugs everyone. She gets her needles and leaves the caravan a star. Everyone in the line claps her on the back. She re-enacts some of the high points of the escapade to a couple of people and then totters off into the park, presumably to have a fix.

By the next afternoon it's really snowing hard and we are all worried about our imminent escape. We still have a UN cocktail party to get through and more meetings with activists and NGOs. One of them is a stunning beauty of a girl who has started an information magazine for people living with HIV. She has HIV herself, although she appears to be the picture of effervescent health. She is tall and curvy with thick dark hair falling over her neck and shoulders. We go out into the nearby park to take some pictures for her magazine. She is incredibly vivid and there is enormous warmth in her regard. She is clearly a ball-breaker and would be a seducer if she could be bothered, but, like many Russian ladies, one gets the impression that she has little sympathy for the male sex.

Women who have been sucked unknowingly into the world of Aids by their men look at us all in a new light. Our animal force is smoke and mirrors to them now, a terrible pantomime that crumbles as the virus takes its grip. This lady is made of sterner stuff than any man, although she is completely feminine. She talks about the difficulties of getting treatment. There is not much help from the health system. You have to bribe your way into hospital and sometimes even bribe your way out. More Kafka. She tells scandalous stories of corruption, particularly concerning the Ministry of Health. Everyone falls in love with her and she laughs it off.

As she is leaving, she asks me the question I have been asking myself. 'What are you doing here?'

'I don't know.'

'What can you do?'

'Not much. Talk about it. Write something.'

She laughs. Her eyes sparkle, slightly mocking, and she leaves to continue the fight while I fly home to New York.

We are all going in opposite directions. It's a strange airport, Moscow, and it hasn't changed since the night my dog and I arrived back in 1990. The same brown marble is bathed in the same green light. There are still the same long lines getting in and getting out. It's difficult to do either. Being a part of a UN delegation, we are swept through on a magic carpet, no check-in, no customs, straight through to the diplomatic lounge, where an African king is already enthroned, surrounded by wives and courtiers, all swathed in shawls and turbans. Together we accept canapés and champagne from government lackeys, while officials look at our tickets and bring us our boarding cards.

Mariangela is going back to Geneva. David is going to Berlin. We will never see Mariangela again, and our goodbye already feels like a memory. We both know this is my last trip.

'You were great,' she says.

'I was a handful,' I reply.

'You're always a handful. Call me when you come to Geneva,' Mariangela says and walks off, waving.

My flight is late at night and I sit in the airport wondering about the trip. I never want to come back to Russia, but I do write something, a long explanation of what I have seen and what I understand about Aids, for a magazine in Moscow. I send it – translated – but it is never published.

PART FOUR

CHAPTER NINETEEN

Head Girl

I had locked myself in the loo at Charles Finch's pre-Bafta party at Annabelle's the other night, for a bit of a rest, when I overheard the following conversation.

'Five books, two films and a documentary are being made about the life and times of Isabella Blow,' said a voice.

'They're going to be slim volumes,' sneered another.

'But she discovered Alexander McQueen!'

'Alexander McQueen discovered himself.'

'I thought the housekeeper did.' Shrieks. 'Well, she had an eye. You can't deny that.'

'Yes. Like a smashed plate.'

A door swung open with the noise of the party, and the voices trailed off.

I sat there for a few minutes, wondering what Isabella would have made of the conversation. Would she laugh or be hurt, or would she conclude, like Oscar Wilde, that it was better to be talked about than not to be mentioned at all?

It has been nearly three years since Isabella died, and no matter how slim the volumes, how short the films, people are still talking about her and trying to unlock her riddle.

One thing is certain. Despite the energy, the humour and the eye like a smashed plate, she probably didn't achieve much during her short sentence in earthly shackles. In fact, she managed to fuck up every opportunity she ever had, burn every bridge, test every friendship to its hilt, and perhaps it was for this that she was remarkable. Despite these considerable drawbacks she still managed to inspire unfaltering devotion from all the friends she occasionally needled (rather than stabbed) in the back, and she lit up every room she entered, whether it was the emergency room or the ballroom. Her tragedy was, quite simply, to be born in the right place at the wrong time. During her twenty years as a soldier of fashion, the landscape of that world completely changed. Isabella charged on regardless, dressed as a damsel in distress, Milady de Winter, largely written off by the pretentious rag-trade freaks that so lavishly praised her, post mortem. Fashion was no longer, as Wilde brilliantly put it, what one wore oneself. It was what other people wore. Isabella never grasped this, and for the last few years of her life she was haunted by a terrible feeling of failure.

'I even managed to fail at suicide,' she said wryly one day in hospital.

Depression and madness are incomprehensible to the uninflicted. 'Just snap out of it,' the rest of us said. We were never forgiven. Suicide was our ultimate punishment.

I came out of the loo and decided to walk home. By now I was allergic to the endless awards ceremonies with their deathless pre-parties and after-parties. There was no glamour left, no fabulous monsters, no Isabellas, actually, in the glare of success. Outside I buried myself in my coat and might have been a ghost as I left the club, unnoticed by the paparazzi, all huddled against the spitting February rain, and walked across Mayfair, past the empty temples of fashion, their faceless mannequins in ridiculous shoes staring blindly out at the glittering streets.

An arctic wind bounced down Regent Street, fanning the rain into pretty rainbows around the street lights and whirlpools around the drains. The whole evening, from the candlelit stars at the awards dinner, through the overheard conversation in the bog, to the dark shuttered cathedral of Abercrombie & Fitch, conjured up winterish thoughts. Many phantoms moaned beside me as I crossed the road into Soho, all forgotten and painted over, refaced and bricked up, from Caroline Lamb to Isabella Blow.

According to Isabella – on the first day I met her, at a tea party in a stately home one wet Sunday before Easter in 1977 – she was summoned to her headmistress's study on the last day of school for a final chat before setting off into the world. In contrast to the black tulip 'McQueen' she wore to the potting shed where she drank the fatal pint of weedkiller thirty short years later, she was in her school uniform that day, a grey tweed skirt, pleated and below the knee, lace-up shoes, an Aertex shirt and an Alice band in her sensibly cut, ash-blonde hair.

'Isabella,' said the head, 'there's something you must know!'

Isabella's heart sank. She felt guilty at the drop of a hat. 'If anyone came into this room right now and said there'd been a murder, I'd just *know* I'd done it.'

Our hostess looked slightly uncomfortable. Isabella's storytelling was mesmerising and had one on the edge of one's seat.

'Don't worry, Lavinia. I haven't knocked anyone off this weekend,' she chortled before collecting herself and her audience. She lit a cigarette, inhaled for inspiration, and on a stream of smoke flew the first of countless improbable stories I was to hear over the next twenty-five years.

'We are extremely proud of you, here at Heathfield,' said the headmistress. 'You have been a really super head girl, and a great support to me personally. You may not have excelled at Maths but, by God, you made up for it in the fencing team.'

Another big drag.

'You have always been there to help in a crisis. The girls look up to you. You are, in short, one of the best pupils it has been my privilege to have here in the school.' The list went on.

'How lovely for you,' cut in our hostess.

'But now look at me!' drawled Issie, through a cloud of smoke. 'Two years later. A charwoman. Can you believe it?'

She was certainly dressed as one, albeit a music-hall version, more Carmen Miranda than Elsie Tanner. She wore a spotted scarf around her head tied in a comical knot and a cleaner's flowered housecoat. All that was missing was a dustpan and brush.

We were sitting in the drawing room of Cholmondeley Castle, the Gothic seat of the Marquess of Cholmondeley (pronounced Chummly), and, more importantly, his very dishy son, David Rocksavage. It had rained all weekend, and it streamed down the vast cathedral windows that afternoon while we sat snugly around a roaring fire. I had been invited for the weekend with my best friend Vivienne. It had not been the greatest success, as David's mother, Lady Cholmondeley, or Lavinia to her friends, had taken against me from the moment I set foot in the house. She was a small, neat woman, formal and suspicious.

'Not very Chummy,' I remarked to Vivienne the first night in bed. We were sharing a room.

'There are the chummy Cholmondelyes and the unchummy ones,' she said.

'Well, Lady Chummy is definitely one of the uns.' We had discovered Nancy Mitford that year.

Perhaps it was the knee-length cape I was wearing. She could sense that I was one of 'those' and thought that I would undoubtedly have designs on her fabulously wealthy son and heir.

How right she was. Apart from anything else the word Cholmondeley struck an ancient chord for me, not because of David's willowy beauty or any particular person in that illustrious family, but because of another house they owned, one I had known for as long as I could remember. It was called Houghton Hall, and on the endless (two-hour) drive from my family's home in Essex to my grandparents' house in Norfolk, as I lay in the back of our Hillman, green with car-sickness, at a certain point my mother would say, 'Look, darling, we've got to the Houghton wall.' I would sit up and wait to see the great gates, hoping against hope to spot some of the famous white deer that grazed on the park inside. We hardly ever saw them. You had to be very quick, because the wall stopped only for a moment, and my father would never slow down.

'Slow down, Daddy!' we all whined, but the major paid no attention.

Between two gingerbread gatehouses with tall twirling chim-neystacks, through the black and gold bars of a gigantic wrought-iron gate, flashed a tree-lined park and in the distance a vast grey house. Occasionally hundreds of deer stood motionless as we shot past, like little clouds hovering over the grass, but then it was over, and the wall came back. But my carsickness was always gone by then, because in five minutes we would be at my favourite place in the world, my grandmother's house.

Punch-drunk and competitive with Isabella's success as a racon-teur, I launched into this story to a rather underwhelming response. She alone egged me on, eyes wide like saucers, while one by one the rest of the party began to talk among themselves. Her reactions were as large as her own yarns, and quite brilliant, because, as I learnt years later, she was probably thinking about something else alto-gether. But who cared? Her gasps of 'God, no!' and 'I love it!' kept me going through Lady Chummy's clear revulsion.

'How very Proustian,' was all that lady said as the story finished.

'Exactly!' I replied, wondering who the fuck was Proustian.

There had been a drama that morning because footprints had been found climbing the shiny black stone staircase in the great hall. Some of us were lodged downstairs, and somebody had crept up with bare feet and not come down. As it happened the footprints were not mine, but Lady Chummy was looking daggers, and they were all directed at me. So by teatime conversation had become strained and minimal, punctuated now by the clinking of china, the pouring of tea, and all the various house-party inanities about delicious cake, terrible weather, Mrs Thatcher, or Vivienne's neck, which had recently broken.

Then Isabella arrived.

She was one of those people whose energy was so intense that it burst into a room before her. There was a weird movement in the air and a clattering outside followed by screams and a crash. We all sat up. Somebody outside started laughing. It was one of those infectious laughs that cracked a smile even on Lady Chummy's vice-regal features.

'That must be Isabella,' she said with pleasure. 'She's a neighbour.'

The door burst open and Issie appeared, dressed, as I have already mentioned, as a music-hall maid.

'God, everyone! Sorry. I just tripped over that rug in the hall. I fell flat on my face. Thank God Caro was there. Darling, are you all right?'

The laughter gurgled up again as she clutched David's sister and tumbled into the room.

Lady Chummy made introductions.

'And this is Rupert Everitt,' she said finally through gritted teeth.

'Everett, actually, Lady Cholmondeley,' I ventured obsequiously.

'Oh my God. I love that cape. Look at the buckles,' screamed Isabella.

'Thanks,' I said. 'It was my grandfather's when he was in the navy.'

'Should you be wearing it?' demanded Lady C.

'Probably not, but I couldn't resist. It's so gorgeous.'

'Really?' scoffed Chummy.

I caught Isabella's eye and she began to laugh again.

'God. You're naughty!'

'Isabella,' asked the Marchioness, when everyone had settled back down, 'how is your life in London?'

'Fabulous. I'm a charlady.'

'Is that satisfactory?'

Issie lit a cigarette, blew out a cloud of smoke and looked at her hostess through hooded blue eyes for a long dramatic moment.

Then she began the story of her last day of school. She spoke effortlessly but with enormous energy, sprawled on a chair, to the manor born. She was built for humour and when she laughed a set of teeth jumped out that might have come from a Christmas cracker or a joke shop. They protruded almost at right angles to her mouth, perhaps the result of some witch's spell because the rest of her was quite like a fairy princess. She was petite with beautiful skin, large blue eyes like saucers (as yet unsmashed), an hourglass waist and, as she was the first to point out, she had 'fabulous tits'. Strangely her teeth were not unattractive, and on the rare occasions her mouth was closed they made her look as though she were about to blow a kiss, but they had directed the whole course of her life. She would have been someone completely different without them. They possessed her. They forced her to perform, to live up to them and to live them down. They had the effect of making her face one of the most memorable and expressive I have ever seen. It could make you laugh and later on it could make you cry.

'Do you mean that, after all that, you are a cleaning lady?' asked David, who had listened, silent and beautiful, in the corner.

'God, yuh! I thought you knew. That's my job. I'm a charwoman.' She leapt up and gave a demonstration of hoovering and dusting and knocking things over, all in the course of two minutes, before slumping back in her chair, on the verge of fainting.

'Vapours!' she gasped. 'I shouldn't really be overdoing it right now.'

'Why?' I asked.

'It's my Crohn's disease.'

'What's that?'

'Oh, it just eats you inside until there's nothing left.'

'Sounds ghastly.'

'Yuh. It's terminal. Could I have another cup of tea, please, Lavinia?'

Her stories were too good to be true. Two crumpets later we had already learnt that her little brother had drowned in front of her, and that her mother had simply gone down to the edge of the estate at home, where the railway tracks passed a lodge, and waved down the London train, got on and was never seen again. Her delivery was dramatic and witty, punctuated by greedy mouthfuls that overflowed from that curious beak. Her outfit was sheer Vaudeville, and it was hard to imagine this creature had recently been a model pupil in a strict girls' boarding school. She was enormously vivid and the intensity that would later turn to madness literally sparkled at this point with youth. She was hypnotic, and I immediately adored her, even if I was a little bit jealous because somehow she had managed to take this neurotic tea party and turn it into a platform for her own display of fireworks.

She had a sixth sense when it came to making trouble. After a brief lull in the laughter, she looked around to see if we were ready for the next bit.

'Caro told me somebody has been creeping about all night,' she said with great innocence, in a stage whisper. The room stiffened. Lady C pretended not to hear and adjusted her skirt. Isabella scanned our faces with her mascara'd satellite dishes. They got the picture in ten seconds.

'I bet I can guess who it was,' she continued, giggling.

Please, not me, I thought.

'Was it you, Rupert? Were you after that Cock Sausage?' It was her name for Rock Savage.

'No, it wasn't me,' I said turning red.

'God, you're naughty,' she said again. 'Come on, let's see your foot. Get your shoes off. I'm really good at detective work. You have to be as a charwoman.'

There was nothing she loved more than to work a victim's nerves. (That Easter it was still at the playful stage.) She loved watching me squirm.

'Oh my God, you've got a verruca! I don't think it is him, Lavinia!'

she said, waving one of my bare feet in her hand, giving me another big lascivious wink at the same time. Before very long she had moved the whole party into the hall to examine the staircase to see if my foot fitted the print. Even Lady Chummy came. Isabella had swept everyone into a state of utter hysteria.

'God, it's like *Cinderella*. Were you at the balls last night?' she screamed.

Now it was my turn to feel guilty for something I hadn't done. I just knew that the shoe would fit. And then what?

Mercifully, the footprint was a whole three sizes smaller than mine, so we all went back to the drawing room and sat down.

'God, is that the time?' said Isabella, like a character from a drawing room comedy. 'I've got to dash.'

In a flash she was gone. The scream and the crash and the laughter and the clattering heels rewound and receded as she left the house, and the void in the room was as remarkable as her presence had been. We all slumped visibly, dreaming of an early night with a good book.

Isabella was quite exhausting.

CHAPTER TWENTY

Our Dinner with André

Eight years later everything had changed. Isabella was a professional (sort of) divorcee living in New York. She and fashion had found their way to each other and the time bomb was set, because now, little by little, life began to overcome her, imperceptibly at first, but her intense high spirits had a new note of strain woven into the frenetic soundtrack of champagne corks flying, taxi brakes screeching, doors slamming and high heels galloping off into the distance. She found a job working for Anna Wintour, the fashion editor at American *Vogue*.

Life at Condé Nast was still like something out of a Jacqueline Susann novel, and Nuclear Wintour had not yet emerged from Chrysalis Anna. It would soon become *American Psycho*, and everything was about to change, but for the time being New York was poised on the edge of the abyss, enjoying the Indian summer of a memorable season that had stretched long and lazy since the sixties. There were still neighbourhoods. Forty-Second Street was a maze of glory-holes and strip shows where dealers and hookers and bent cops happily rubbed shoulder pads on their various beats through the delightful swamp. The East Village was to be penetrated at your own risk. Italian Americans spoke their own dialect, and in the summer months everyone sat on the neighbourhood stoops and actually knew each other. The rules of engagement in society were still those of the *belle époque*, a constitution laid down at the Factory and on the dance floor of Studio 54.

But the cracks were showing. Steve Rubell had lost his hair and turned yellow. Thousands of other queens, skin and bone, slunk into the shadows to die. They were terrified to go out because they looked Martian, and people would gather their children to them and shoo the queen away like a rabid dog. The disease was everywhere, contributing to the sinking-ship hysteria of the city. The grim reaper stood above it all, waiting for the moment Andy Warhol's night nurse went out for a cigarette. Until that precise moment New York was still careering on like a train without brakes, and Isabella was a part of that last hot summer crash.

One hot dusty afternoon in 1985 I arrived from LA where I was living, jumped into my Condé Nast limo (courtesy of Issie) and drove into the city. I had my own key to the house of Fred Hughes, the business partner of Andy Warhol. I let myself in. The place was empty and cool and smelt of floor polish. I went up to my room and called Isabella

'Shall I come over?'

'If you have to.'

'All right, I'll be there in half an hour.'

'God!' she groaned and hung up.

There was no point taking Isabella seriously when she said she was too tired. The conversation would always end in the same place.

'I have just had half my insides out, you know!' And then we went out.

A taxi journey on a hot New York night was like riding the rapids of a dangerous river. Fred lived uptown on Lexington Avenue. There, the natives were from orderly, non-violent tribes. Families waited politely at the traffic lights. Preppies in Gloria Vanderbilt jeans and rich old leather queens with blind poodles (Dangerous Top Sir, a famous sadist, lived on 77th and Lexington) ambled along to the shops. The taxi lurched over potholes, a tugboat on a choppy stretch, narrowly avoiding endless collisions in an intricate screeching ballet. The windows were open, and the metallic breeze had a pinch of sea air and a tiny note of garbage in its famous perfume. It was invigorating and sexy, and made one want to let it all go. No city on earth gave one a craving for drugs more than New York.

The wide expanse suddenly contracted, and out of nowhere we were in a bottleneck of honking traffic pouring into Times Square. The air billowed with exhaust fumes and jets of white smoke exploded from the ground. Hell was definitely underneath New York, waiting for its moment when the streets would collapse. The swarms on the sidewalk looked undead, ready at a signal to lurch into 'Thriller', smash one's taxi and tear one limb from limb. Heaven was above in the spray of a million lights that between them described the package, as large as an office block, of some household god in Calvin Klein underwear. Leaning back and looking through the rear window was a high of its own. The flashing skyscrapers towered into the pink night, falling away – the turning pages of a pop-out book – as the traffic evaporated as quickly as it had congealed. The driver stepped on the gas, screeching to a standstill only as weirder downtown folk, little old ladies, fat backward freaks, queens and punks, crossed Seventh Avenue as the light turned red and we were finally downtown.

Isabella lived in a first-floor flat on the leafy corner of Charles Street and West 4th, in the Village. It was next to a miniature synagogue like a doll's house, and across the road from a down-at-heel Spanish restaurant she adored that served poussin flambé, a flaming chicken on a wooden board that came with a knife like a dagger. It was a step down from the street in a half-basement. If you looked out of the windows you could see up the skirts of the passers-by. Isabella, already obsessed by underwear, loved it.

'God, darling, I could almost see the skid marks on that one.'

The restaurant was dark and traditional, with sagging red-leather banquettes, wooden walls, pink tablecloths and low lights. It catered for an older crowd, gentrified beatniks, fubsy now in cardigans and spectacles, and from another planet to the two freaks squeezed into a narrow booth that night. Isabella (tiny) sat with a gigantic black man dressed in what appeared to be a mattress.

'Hi, darling. This is André.'

The giant extended a huge hand. To be kissed rather than shaken.

'Isabella's told me so much about you, and we *love* the shoot you did with Helmut,' he squealed.

He was straight out of *Gone with the Wind*. He had the physical gravitas of Hattie McDaniel (Mammy) and the vocal energy of Butterfly McQueen (Prissy). ('I don't know *nothin'* 'bout birthin' babies!') You may have to be a queen of a certain age and outlook to grasp the full impact of these particular allusions, but suffice to say his Southern tones stretched across four octaves, although he usually favoured the upper registers (Butterfly) since he seemed to be constantly exasperated (Hattie). He spoke extremely fast. This must be what it was like, I remember thinking, taking dictation, because if you lost a word, you lost the thread.

'Say it again,' I said for the third time and the big hands came crashing down on the table.

'Oh my God, Isabella? Do we have to use sign language with this child? I know movie stars are meant to be stupid, but this is ridiculous!'

I probably looked taken aback, because he patted my hand and laughed.

'I'm joking, darling! Tell him I'm joking, Isabella! Oh my God, you English. So sensitive. So correct.'

He was speaking faster and faster, as if the words just couldn't stop coming out. His eyes looked down at his lips, wondering, like the rest of us, if they were ever going to stop. They did, and then they laughed again, cracking open like a yawning hippopotamus exposing rows of teeth like sugar lumps. He was utterly fascinating, like a billboard, so much larger than life you didn't quite know where to look.

'You were saying?' he concluded like a duchess at a tea party.

'I was saying,' continued Issie, 'that André has such a big cock that he has never dared to have sex. Isn't that true, André?'

'Isabella!' he screeched, his eyeballs nearly popping out. 'Don't talk like that. What will your friend think?'

'He'll probably want to get under the table and suck you off,' guffawed Issie. More squealing from André.

'Mrs Vreeland would never tolerate this kind of talk. You would never get away with this.' He wagged his finger in her face.

'Lucky she's dead, then! André was found by Diana Vreeland,' explained Issie.

'I was not found by Mrs Vreeland. I was found by Mr Warhol.'

'Do you think that Issie could be the next Mrs Vreeland, André?' I asked innocently.

André nearly choked. 'No. No. Absolutely *not*, Isabella! Not at all. You don't have the style. How could you *say* such a thing? Shame on you! The poor woman is still warm in her grave. You don't know what you're saying. You have no respect, you English. You think you can come here . . .'

He flagged momentarily, slumped in his seat, visibly exhausted, disappearing inside the mattress, but then he rallied and concentrated his mind on this sacrilegious comparison.

'You do have style, Isabella. We will admit that. But Mrs Vreeland? Never!'

The poussin flambé arrived.

'Waiter! Please have a fire extinguisher standing by. This is "Comme" couture.' André grabbed a bottle of water and poured it over his plate. 'I love you, Isabella, but this is rayon and it's highly inflammable.'

The chicken fizzled in a bubbling pool of Perrier, but André tucked into it with abandon. Now it was his turn to torture.

'How's Colin?' He looked at me, winked, then pursed his lips and looked busy.

'Fine. He's here with his girlfriend,' sighed Isabella.

'Isabella! This is not right. This is not *comme il faut*. He's staying at your place *with* his girlfriend.'

'Yuh!'

'Rupert! What do you think? You look sane. Should Isabella be receiving this child with his courtesan?'

'Well, he is her best friend's little brother,' I reasoned.

'Liza is *your* best friend. Not mine. Anyway I rather like being a cradle-snatcher. God, he's good looking, though, you must admit?'

'Once a cradle-snatcher ...' giggled André, wagging the finger.

Colin was Liza's eighteen-year-old brother, a shy blond student with thick eyebrows, just out of Eton, and Issie was secretly in love with him. Partly because he was about to inherit one of the most romantic titles in *Burke's Peerage*.

'How could I *not* be in love with him. He'll be the Thane of Cawdor!' crowed Issie. She was very medieval.

'Thane of Cawdor? What do you mean, Isabella?' asked André, eyes wide.

'Macbeth. He is the descendant of Macbeth. Out, damned spot. You know? That one.'

'I know who Macbeth is!'

This Macbeth (actually his name was Campbell) used Isabella's flat as his crash pad. He and I both benefited, unbeknown to André and Anna Wintour, from endless Condé Nast limousines, which Isabella ordered whenever we asked.

'Anyway, we're meeting him later, aren't we, Rupey?'

'I've no idea. You said you were tired.'

'I am. Exhausted!'

Actually she had never looked better. She was dressed fashionably at this point in her life, not in costume, and she was in her physical prime. Furthermore she had discovered sex in the interval between that faraway frosty tea in Cheshire and this hot New York night. She still had her own style, a personal twist on the boytoy street look of eighties New York. She was an upper-class version of *Desperately Seeking Susan*. That night she wore an old navy-blue dinner jacket over a corset (Rigby and Peller), fishnet tights and heels, and a scarf around her head tied in a large bow, which drooped over her face like a wilting plant. A rather stately diamond brooch was pinned to her lapel, and her lips were jungle red.

It was no accident that Isabella ended up in fashion. She had a body that was made for clothes. She had wonderful feet that were to her obsess her later on and, unlike many girls, she knew how to walk in heels. Only her eyes had changed. They had lost the fresh, startled regard of the teenager. They hung ever so slightly now, like a St Bernard's. They still weren't smashed plates, just a little tired and disorientated. Real life, with its phone bills, receipts and overdrafts, was already one step ahead of Isabella. Her typical and disastrous reaction was to ignore and spend.

'It's the only thing I can do to stop myself from screaming,' she said.

But she was a great success. André obviously loved her, and she was good at her job. The confines of Condé Nast were possibly similar to the confines of boarding school. A bell rang and you went somewhere.

Outside the restaurant, two limos on that empire's account were purring at the kerb.

'Isabella, is that car Condé Nast?' quizzed André, peering through the window like a detective.

'God, no! It's Rupert's. I would never ...'

Luckily André's attention was soon diverted as he squeezed his mattress into the back of his car.

'Well, it better not be,' he groaned, 'because Anna' – which he pronounced Ahnna – 'will not be happy. Now don't be too late. You have work tomorrow.'

'Oh, no, I'm only going out for one drink.'

And we got into our car.

*

Andy Warhol sat on a banquette at a club called Area with his latest protégé, a young black artist named Jean-Michel Basquiat. That season the two men were inseparable. They were well matched. Andy was an arts-seasoned vampire and went out to feed on new blood at night. Jean-Michel, also a hungry opportunist but green, blunt and addicted, was learning the ropes. It was here in the coloured shards of light thrown from the glitter ball, where the rich and famous got messy, that they conducted their business. It was here, and possibly only here, in this corner of that rat-infested isle, that you could sell a printed silk-screen signed by an assistant for a $100,000. They sat motionless, these two household gods, neither talking nor moving, just waiting, a pair of flesh-eating vegetables, for some mosquito with a bladder full of plasma to buzz by.

Isabella stalked into the club, looking from right to left. Flanked by the beautiful Colin on one side and me on the other, both of us moving instinctively into a sort of flotilla, with Colin's girlfriend taking (it) up the rear, Isabella ploughed ahead, our wooden figurehead, breasts exposed, a demonic smile fixed on her face, and laughter already gurgling up from inside her like water from faulty drains.

Andy Warhol acknowledged our arrival with a helpless wave. It was all we needed. Our formation wheeled, banked and dive-bombed onto the banquette next to him. In the game of Snakes and Ladders we had thrown double sixes and were flying up the big ladder right to the jackpot.

'We're so naughty!' screamed Isabella over the music, winking at Colin and me as we sat down. There was no room for Colin's girlfriend and Isabella rolled her eyeballs. She had a short fuse when it came to girlfriends.

'Andy, would you mind moving up a bit,' she said, and then burst into honks of laughter. 'I can't believe I'm telling Andy Warhol to budge up,' she told the photographer who had appeared out of nowhere. *Flash*. When we had all settled down she introduced Colin to Andy and Jean-Michel, careful to leave no detail of Colin's ancestry uncharted.

'Aaaww gee, Jean-Michel. Who knew? We're sitting with Macbeth,' said Andy, stony-faced.

'Who's Macbeth?' asked Basquiat, also stony-faced.

Isabella was about to relaunch into Colin's complicated genealogy but the boy himself interrupted. 'Issie, please,' he begged, and she stopped dead in her tracks.

'Oh. God. Sorry.' She giggled. 'Am I being a bit over the top?'

'A bit.'

Momentarily chastised, she listened to the music for a minute, bouncing up and down slightly to the rhythm, lips looking as if they were about to blow a kiss, Marilyn in a wonky mirror. She wiggled her bum on the leather banquette and looked out of the corners of her eyes at Jean-Michel, who was nodding off beside her. She had an animal passion for him that summer, and there was not much room for Colin, once Isabella was under the spell of Basquiat. The world disappeared, and the rest of us were no more than foils to get his attention. She was quite like a queen in this respect. When the cruise was on, don't try having acute appendicitis.

'God, would you look at Basquiat?' she said in a deafening aside. 'I'd really like to get that big black cock in my mouth. Wouldn't you, Andy?'

'Aaww gee, Isssie,' said Andy, the tip of his nose turning pink, and his mouth, in response to such an indelicate question, unpeeling into a record smile revealing rows of grey shark's fangs.

'I don't think you should say things like that,' said Jean-Michel solemnly through half-closed eyes, leaning in close to Isabella. He was beautiful, cruel and insolent, and off his face on smack.

'Things like what?'

'Things about my cock. It's inappropriate.'

'This is making me really wet,' squirmed Issie, ecstatically.

'Oh yeah?' said Basquiat.

'Oh yeah,' she replied, imitating his lethargic black accent. 'It's not just the big black cock,' she said, addressing the rest of the table

'Oh, isn't it?'

'There has to be talent,' she went on, winking at Andy. 'I *love* your work. It really gives me a hard-on.'

'A hard-on, huh?'

'Yeah.' (The terrible impersonation again.) 'A big hard-on.'

'Awww, Issie.'

Through eyes like cracks, Jean-Michel surveyed Isabella from the feet up, lingering first on the thighs, then the cleavage, before coming to rest on the infamous mouth. That mouth snapped shut like an oyster, aware that it was being scrutinised, either with a 'tongue sandwich' (hopefully) in view, or more likely, for reproduction at a later date on canvas. (I'm sure if you sift through the Basquiats of this period, you will find various little monsters with Isabella teeth.) Their two faces were very close. It was a moment of drama, and we all leant in. Was he going to snog her, right here, in front of everyone? Just for a second, she was speechless.

'Hi,' was all she could muster, as those lips she had eulogised for months came within suction radius. Her own lips quivered, straining towards the unattainable goal. Andy got his camera out and *flash*, another moment was engraved for posterity.

Clubs are worlds of their own. Shabby black rooms by day, lit by neon, in which a throbbing crowd of third-world cleaners dance to the drone of the vacuum cleaner, clambering over the revellers' debris, decked out in overalls and rubber gloves, unblocking toilets filled with last night's various excretions. Little by little the ambience begins to change. Deliveries are made. Bars are stocked. Glasses are polished. Some mafia moll accountant bimbo who knows where the skeletons are buried waddles in with cash and change for the tills. The owner arrives in the afternoon to examine the books. The lights and music are checked, briefly throwing this shanty dwelling into its star-spangled cloak of night.

Finally, as the evening draws in, the busboys, the bouncers and the barmaids arrive, the glitter ball is turned on, and the magic roundabout is off again, empty and ghostly for the time being, but still magically transformed from the morning's ugly warehouse, with its damp, peeling walls and threadbare carpets, into a kind of time capsule, a sovereign state, a world of its own with alternative leaders, stars, police, markets and schools; a kingdom where reality is held at bay by the muscular arms of the bouncer and a velvet rope.

If you became a proper clubber, particularly in those final days of the New York Empire, when people went out every night from dinner or a disco nap, that particular peeling warehouse became a part of your identity. It was where you lost yourself, or at least your virginity. Billionaires danced with bent cops. Trannies swapped beauty tips with game hags from Dun & Bradstreet. Stars from the real world left their crowns outside. They were more down to earth in those days. They didn't arrive in a phalanx of security guards, as they do today, shoved through the crowds like a battering ram, trampling underfoot the fans they pretend to love. (I remember going out one night with Cher, just after she had won the Oscar. Feeling jet-lagged, I wanted to leave. 'Fine, babe,' she said, pecking me on the cheek. 'I'll call you tomorrow.' And without a word she swayed off to the dance floor and disappeared into the crowd.)

Movie and rock royalty were still stars inside the disco planet, but no more so than the club stars themselves, that strange array of 'ordinary' people whose extreme looks or habits or dance moves set them apart, and without whom a night could not be complete, could never be 'one of those nights'. These characters were, still are, like the old stars of Vaudeville or the circus, music-hall acts once loved, fêted, on kissing terms with kings, or at least Jackie O, but instantly forgotten. A club scene dwindles, another epoch ends and the clubber, with a reluctant sigh, moves back to the ordinary world, only to be remembered years later in cosy conversations of reminiscence, or because of some terrible misfortune. 'Do you remember that awful guy John X? Well, you'll never guess! She was stabbed sixty-eight times by that Moroccan number she forced to go and live with her in the country.'

Area was my club. The invitation to its opening was a pill like an Alka-Seltzer, which when put in water bubbled up into an invitation.

Isabella and I fell out. In her flat one night, I borrowed her diamond brooch. I was a terrible magpie in those days. She gave it to me reluctantly. Poor Isabella, she could never say no. That was a part of her tragedy.

'I can't believe I'm giving this to you.' She laughed, honking and smoking to cover up her anxiety as she handed over the jewel. Of course I lost it. It flew off my lapel onto the dance floor at Area later that night, never to be found. Isabella was furious, but since she was unable to confront – behind the back was the only position from which she dared to fuck you – I never took her very seriously when she asked me to reimburse her, particularly since I was flat broke at the time.

'Oh God, don't worry about it, then,' she said with droopy eyes and a sigh, meaning 'Give me back my fucking brooch.' But I wasn't much of a linguist in those days.

Months later I paid her back, but she never forgot.

She moved back to England. I moved to France. At first she went to work for Michael Roberts at *Tatler*. It was a successful union, but then she landed a job in one of the crustiest institutions in the country. She became fashion editor of the *Sunday Times* and everything took off, exploded in fact. As usual Isabella was in the right place at the wrong time

The *Sunday Times* was no longer a club of brilliant eccentrics harbouring such stately galleons as Violet Wyndham, James Fox, Mark Boxer and Bruce Chatwin. Now it was a snitty, petty, rather common institution, and try as she might, or might not – the energy of her interest waxed and waned with the moon – Isabella was never going to fit in. The *Sunday Times* of the late eighties was a worthy institution of faceless bores, and she was constantly undermined, 'gaslit by them, actually', she always said. They all pretended to like her, but actually they couldn't stand her.

Pretty soon she was a fully developed fashion freak, complicated, bitchy, treacherous and incredibly funny. She had developed some bad habits in America. The extravagance of Condé Nast was anathema to the penny-pinching world of the *Sunday Times*. What did Isabella care? Wads of fifty-pound notes were crammed into extraordinary bird's nest clutch bags. Whether they were hers or just petty cash was not of the least interest to Isabella, as she gaily paid for lunch for sixteen, snorting with laughter as she unscrunched the cash from various pockets and purses.

'There goes the whole budget for this month. God, I'm naughty.'

She developed a talent for talent. She found marvellous photographers, beautiful girls, fey Etonians, Philip Treacy and finally Alexander McQueen, at which point she became extremely grand, which was perhaps a mistake, because even though she was credited with all these discoveries, she was not Christopher Columbus. In fact, she was living in a world that didn't particularly appreciate her medieval value system or aesthetic. The age of chivalry was over, and so Isabella lived on a knife edge, always homeless, or about to be evicted, always broke but addicted to spending. In the nineteenth century she would have ended her days in a debtors' prison. In the twenty-first the final act was played out in an asylum.

CHAPTER TWENTY-ONE

Going Mad on the National Health

One beautiful spring afternoon in 2007 I was on my way to visit Issie in a run-down National Health mental institution somewhere in Victoria, the name of which eludes me. (In fact, I went to look for it the other day, and got lost and confused in that maze of identical mansion blocks behind the cathedral, streets of madness, one leading back into another, until I finally gave up the search. Maybe it disappeared with Isabella, a fortress in a myth where the spell had been broken.) It was one of those large ugly hangovers of nineteenth-century health, built in smog-caked yellow brick that reminded one of iron lungs, padded cells, polio and sleepy sickness. If you shut your eyes, you could still hear the screams of the insane as they were pinned down and subjected to those gigantic charges of electricity that Isabella had become partial to. (Now, they give them to you when you are unconscious. Then, it took four people to hold a patient down.)

The hospital overlooked a small park, which was sandwiched between the backs of three streets. It was throbbing with spring that day. Beds of daffodils and red tulips swayed in the breeze on the freshly mown lawn. Builders sprawled on the grass drinking beer, half naked and paint-splattered. Secretaries ate sandwiches in little neat groups. Mothers sat on benches dozing with an eye half open as their kids played in the sun.

It was the first hot day, and we all looked like ghosts, emerging from another dark wet winter. There is nothing like that first warm afternoon in spring in London. There was a palpable release of tension in the air, as if the earth was yawning and stretching, its grassy breath dusty and metallic perhaps, but elixir to us Londoners, weaned on exhaust fumes and rain. I sat down on a bench and closed my eyes. I had been out all night and was toxic and exhausted. The muted roar of the traffic, the screams of delighted children, and the sun bringing my dead skin back to life, lulled me into a trance from which I suddenly woke to find the park empty.

Hours must have gone by because the shadows had grown long. A girl in high heels stalked across the grass, singing. She held a bouquet of flowers in her arms and disappeared inside the hospital. Perhaps it was Posh Spice visiting La Blow. You never knew with Isabella. I looked up at the dirty Gothic windows of the asylum and couldn't help smiling at the thought. Somewhere in there, dressed for a beggars' ball, lipstick smeared across her mouth and teeth, sat Isabella, wondering already if all this was real or an illusion, when suddenly Posh Spice spins into the room.

I girded myself but remained rooted to my bench. Isabella was recovering from another half-hearted suicide attempt. A few weeks ago she had thrown herself from a bridge onto the motorway, breaking both ankles in the process, but still, unfortunately, very much alive.

'Actually it was a footbridge,' corrected Nicky Haslam, who always knew about these things. We were having lunch when the news broke. 'According to Detmar, she held onto the railings as she jumped, so she only slid actually, if you want the real truth. She wouldn't have broken her feet if she hadn't been wearing silly heels.'

Nicky never had much time for her. Either way it was not the first time that Isabella had tried to kill herself.

One evening, a year earlier, she had taken a Condé Nast car and ploughed in it through a stormy night with a bemused driver, whom she entertained on the drive with her whole life's story, including, rather imprudently, its planned grand finale, to Cheshire, in order to drown herself in the lake of her childhood home. (Isabella's sense of drama was always impeccable. It was in this very lake that her only brother had drowned forty years previously.) Exhausted by the journey, she booked into a hotel, giving the driver enough time to alert the police. So that attempt was thwarted, as she was dragged to a police car and hauled off to another rehab. But the cards were on the table. Isabella wanted to be taken seriously, even if she wasn't quite serious herself. Everyone was held to ransom.

Then she tried again, but this time she crashed her car into the back of an ambulance and was rushed straight to hospital. It may have been an unlucky throw in Snakes and Ladders, but she got the maximum mileage from it (if not from the car, which was totalled). She had us all eating out of the palm of her hand. She was mesmerising in her madness, sweeter and funnier than she had ever been before, brutally honest or dishonest, depending on the occasion, or on how mad she was feeling.

That madness looked like acting to me. Perhaps I have a warped view, but once you become an actor, a strange thing happens. Everything begins to look like acting. Isabella's had gone out of control. She had nurtured the mad streak inside herself and now it had swamped her. Life became a self-fulfilling prophecy. I don't mean that Isabella didn't have serious issues to combat. She did. She was abandoned by her evil father from beyond the grave, which was a terrible trick, but the drama she made of the calamity, the Chekhovian heroine she delightedly created out of it, corseted, deranged, was sheer theatre. This performance electrified us all, at dinner tables, at fashion week, in taxis, or in a sleepless night ill-advisedly sharing a bed, as she rabbited on until dawn, dressed in couture riddled with cigarette burns, hat fixed askew, mad with boredom.

'I'm so bored I'm going to shoot myself.'

Bang. She shot herself in the foot. Time after time. She had a brilliant capacity to describe her condition. 'I think I turned the colour up too high on the TV and the knob broke.' The picture flared, blurred and compressed into a kaleidoscope of horrific images, like homelessness, that spiralled slowly into each other, as she watched speechless (some hope) through the eyepiece. Equally, when Alexander McQueen did not invite her to go with him to Givenchy as his official muse, her operatic reaction to the scandal made it impossible for her ever to turn back. Doors slammed behind her as she ran towards her doom, like Caroline Lamb, stalking the ballrooms of Mayfair, cutting her wrists in front of everyone and getting amazing attention from it.

Now she was addicted to electric shock treatment and, for a while, each time she had it she was briefly rendered functional. High and jangly, perhaps, charged, literally, with electricity, but she clattered on, rushing out, organising trips and dinners. The batteries soon wore out, and she broke down again. The bridge came after the latest power cut.

I got up and walked into the hospital. Two wide corridors stretched in each direction, with custard walls and old pink lino. A large stone staircase wrapped around a central hall, and behind a desk a large moody nurse read *Heat* magazine.

'I'm looking for the John Carruthers Ward.' My weedy public-school voice echoed through the asylum.

'This way. I'll show you,' said a voice from above. It was Posh, leaning over the balustrade.

The gigantic lady looked at her sceptically. 'You should be back in your ward.' Her voice echoed up the stairwell.

'Relax. I'm here, innit,' said Posh.

The nurse grunted and went back to her magazine. 'Follow her,' she instructed and continued reading.

'Who you here for?' asked Posh without looking round, in a thrilling adenoidal twang.

'I'm looking for my friend Isabella.'

'Oh yeah? Well, you've come to the right place.'

We climbed three floors and I followed her through some swing doors into another dirty corridor. On either side large windows revealed grim dormitories of two or three beds, lockers and a sink. A vague smell of lunch, cabbage and mince, hung in the air. Posh walked me to another Checkpoint Charlie and peeled off without a word. I didn't need to ask the new nurse for directions, because at that moment Isabella appeared at the end of the corridor on crutches.

'Oh my God, I don't believe it. Rupey, what are *you* doing here?' she shrieked.

'I'm checking in. Been feeling a bit edgy recently.'

'God, well, you've come to the right place, hasn't he, nurse? We're all very edgy here.'

She limped slowly towards me, dressed as an extra from *Les Mis*. Her hair was dyed black and cut short. She was hatless for once and her eyes were, finally, smashed plates. She loved the effect it was having on me and laughter gurgled up from inside her as we hugged.

'I'm dying for a fag. Do you want one?'

'Not really.'

'Good. Let's go to the smoking room then.'

She swung down the corridor past a table where a large clammy young man sat.

'Give me a hug,' he said in a dreary monotone.

'Oh God!' Isabella rolled her eyes. 'You'd better do it. He goes ballistic otherwise. Only once, OK? Rupey's a film star and he has to hug people all day.'

He humbly nodded and then clung to me for what seemed like an eternity. Isabella began to laugh.

'OK, that's enough, you two,' she said and tried to prise us apart but the boy held on tight.

'Oh God!' giggled Isabella. 'Nurse! Ray won't let go of Rupey.'

'Yes I will,' said Ray sheepishly as the nurse strode purposefully towards us from her post. She looked fairly steely and even I shrank back. Maybe she would hose us down, but no such luck.

'Be good, now, Ray,' she reasoned, instead. 'I'm sure they'll let you go with them, if you Be-Have. Won't you, Isabella?'

'God, yuh.' For the first time I could see the head girl in her. 'Come on, Ray,' she said. We limped on with our new friend shuffling behind.

'Can I have another hug?'

Issie turned and looked at me, eyes glittering with merriment. 'Darling, I know. It's Bedlam.'

I don't know what they had filled her up with but she was like the Merry Widow that afternoon, jangly and intense, a mad grinning puppet.

We settled down in a room with a few armchairs and a TV. On the floor was a gigantic ashtray full of cigarette ends next to a bowl of fruit. Isabella quickly lit up.

'Rupey, could you get me some drugs?' she asked gaily, through a cloud of smoke.

'Not really. Why?'

'I've got to kill myself before the end of this week.' She might have been talking about a planned visit to Peter Jones.

'Couldn't you hold off for a bit?' I asked.

'I don't think so, no. And as you see, one can't even throw oneself out of the windows here.'

They were covered with chickenwire. She honked with laughter, watching my confusion like a parrot, her face cocked to one side, making strange clicking noises through her nostrils.

'Would you like a coffee? Only Ness, I'm afraid.'

Posh stalked in and sat down. She handed Issie two packets of cigarettes.

'God, thanks. I'm just making some coffee. Want some?'

'Could you pay me now? I'm right out of cash,' demanded Posh.

Isabella seemed mesmerised by this ice queen, now decked out in après-ski with a headband and gigantic dark glasses covered in fingerprints. Issie's nervous hands were like two sand crabs with black claws, crawling from their holes. They scuttled through her bag and extracted a fifty-pound note, which Posh immediately snatched and snapped into her own purse.

'I haven't got any change,' she said, meeting Isabella's adoring gaze with a challenging glare. Isabella looked wistfully for a moment as another fifty disappeared. Then she laughed. The one she did when she caught someone out. The quacks of a duck taking off. Wha-wha-wha!

'This is Yaz. Wha-wha-wha.' We shook hands. 'Yaz is my assistant. Aren't you, darling?'

'Yeah.'

'I saw you in the park,' I said.

'I saw you.'

'It's good that you can come and go like that.'

'She can't!' accused Yaz flatly, pointing at Isabella like a robot.

'I'm the worst case they've ever had, Rupey,' nodded Isabella modestly.

'She can go out because she's not that mad. She's really together, aren't you, Yaz?'

'Oh yeah,' replied Yaz lazily, and they giggled like evil schoolgirls, lighting up new cigarettes from the stumps of their burning butts.

'She's got her own company and everything,' continued Issie, as smoke belched from their collective funnels.

'Oh really?' I asked politely.

'Tell him what it's called.'

'Yeah. Creepy Crawly Productions,' said Yaz.

'See?' marvelled Issie. 'I could *never* do that.'

'Yeah. I'm making three albums, and I'm producing them myself.' Silence.

'Through Creepy Crawly?' I ventured. I knew how to play along.

'Exactly,' said Isabella.

The two ladies looked at me intensely, parrots again, watching every muscle in my face to see how all this madness was hitting me. We were in *One Flew Over the Cuckoo's Nest* – the NHS version.

'God, that's fantastic! How great,' I breezed enthusiastically, and the girls relaxed. Yaz stretched out in her chair, all arms and legs, blowing out a huge stream of smoke. Isabella's hands, endlessly crawling, now searched for a bottle of scent, Fracas, and dabbed it on her neck as she listened incredulously.

'Yeah, I got a fashion line as well. Creepy Crawly Couture, and then there's Creepy Crawly Interiors. I'm putting the money aside for when I get out.'

'Three albums!' repeated Issie religiously.

Now another man came in. He was small and tubby and dishevelled, with mad eyes and a Jack Nicholson grin.

'Hug,' warned Ray.

'Fuck off, you pathetic retard!' sneered this city slicker, throwing himself into a chair and fixing me with a wide-eyed grin of utter madness. 'Rupert fucking Everett, I presume,' he drawled. Issie and Yaz giggled flirtatiously and squirmed in their seats.

'This is Patrick. He's been here the longest,' explained Isabella.

'How long?'

'How long?' he boomed, slapping his thigh.

They had all been given the same giggle pill, I concluded, because, with the exception of Ray, they seemed to be constantly on the verge of helpless laughter.

'Very long.'

They all screamed with joy.

The girls made coffee, and passed sugar and milk around. Ray hugged me a few times, satiating my pathetic actor's ego. Even the criminally insane responded to my animal magnetism.

The sinking sun threw amber shafts across the old lino floor. Smoke billowed and swirled through its rays. I had fallen into an etching by Hogarth. Isabella sat carefully next to a shadow so that one side of her face was shrouded, its eye merely glinting through the fog, the other staring wildly. Soon I was forgotten. These lunatics were engrossed in one another, laughing and talking, smoking cigarettes back to back, as they began to debate some sore point previously scored in group – they were fascinated by one another's dilemmas – but Isabella suddenly turned her gaze on me.

'I don't know what I'm doing here.'

'How you feeling?' asked Yaz with thinly disguised boredom.

'They don't know what to do with me, these people,' said Issie, picking up an orange from the bowl on the floor and gesturing loftily at the room. 'I don't know what to do with myself. I find it hard to survive for the next five minutes. I feel like this fucking orange. A pancake in a wheelchair. A mouth on a seat. A broken record.'

Nobody said a word.

'A pancake?' asked Patrick. 'You're mad.'

'I know. But you don't understand. There's something worse than madness. I have lost intellectual curiosity. I don't understand why no one will help me to die. I have succeeded in failing to kill myself.'

More silence.

'Jesus will help you,' said Ray.

'Oh Christ, here we go,' snarled Patrick. 'Do you want him to come in here and give you one?' He mimicked Ray in an insulting baby voice.

'Don't, Patrick!' warned Creepy Crawly.

'You shouldn't talk about Jesus like that,' shouted Ray, standing up. The girls leant back in their chairs, watching and smoking.

'You're a fucking poof,' snapped Patrick. 'All poofs want Jesus to give them one. It's a fact.'

Ray lunged, knocking over a table covered in coffee cups, his great big flabby hands clasped around the various chins of his tormentor. The two girls watched, their bodies tense. In a minute they would fly squawking to the rafters, crashing around the room, and hurl themselves at the windows. Panic was in the air. Lightning might strike at any moment as all these dark clouds, bruised and electrified, converged on one another.

A male orderly appeared out of nowhere and threw himself into the smog, and Nurse could be seen through the windows, cantering down the hallway. The two men were untangled from one another and thrown unceremoniously into their chairs. There was a frozen moment, as everyone caught their breath, and I thought I was going to faint or puke or both, but then the tea party sailed on as if nothing had happened. The girls cleared up the mess, chatting and hooting, and I felt as if I had aged twenty years.

I walked Isabella back down the corridor towards her dorm. We kissed and I left, the years falling off as I approached the exit. I waved at Patrick through the window of the recreation room. He leered back. As I got to the hall I heard a stifled giggle from the other end of the corridor. I turned. Far away now, through endless shards of dusty light, Isabella and Yaz watched me from the door of their room, arms around each other's waists. The sun shone through their hair, throwing weird amber haloes around their heads. They were saints illuminated by madness. Yaz whispered in Isabella's ear. Issie looked at me and laughed; then they turned and went back into their room.

All the hairs were standing up on my entire body. Even my pubes.

CHAPTER TWENTY-TWO

The Deserter

You never know when it's the last goodbye. For me and Isabella it was in the back of a Bombay taxi. I was taking the night flight to London after a harrowing freebie trip conjured up by Issie as the guests of Dulux Paints, India. Only she could have found such an incongruous bedfellow. It all looked simple enough. Some dinners, a press conference and the Dulux fashion show. There was wind of a consultancy post for Issie. That wind turned into a barely perceptible breeze as she left the fashion show halfway through, remarking that if we were going to have to sit through the whole of the Dulux colour chart in saris, we would not only be there all night but be dead in the morning from pneumonia. It was an outdoor event on a cold night.

'Well, that would solve a lot of problems!' I said and she guffawed. You could always joke about serious things with Issie.

'Well, I'm not going to die of boredom,' she said and off she stormed.

The bigwigs of Dulux eyed us coldly as she squeezed past the decidedly B-list front row before clambering onto the catwalk, those feet she claimed would never walk again teetering on Manolos in a spirited trot towards the exit, leaving Kentaro, her wonderful assistant, and me to watch in horror as she nearly collided with a dancing troupe of nautch girls who were advancing down the runway towards her in all the colours of the Dulux rainbow.

The trip was, of course, a disaster. We were late for every dinner and always left early. Issie rolled her eyes as the latest emulsion was discussed in depth. Another collapsed pipe dream that fuelled her constant fear of bankruptcy and the vivid fantasy she had of ending her life on the street. We argued one night at dinner about her sabotaging her mission and Issie stormed off to her room. I followed guiltily a few minutes later to find her sitting in the bath. Like the Queen during the war, she always bathed in six inches of water. It was one of her only economies. She looked like a pathetic little child sitting there as I apologised and we made up.

'You do get rather huffy sometimes!' I reasoned.

'That's what they used to call me at school. Huffy,' she replied as tears rolled out of those huge eyes and she blew her nose noisily into a drenched Kleenex.

But soon she was snorting with laughter, clambering into a gold McQueen dress, doing her lips and fixing a stuffed parrot onto her head, all at once, laughing drinking and smoking, just how she liked it. The wobbly caravan was back on the road, and she careered off into the night to a party given by Francesca Thyssen, leaving me to deal with the lemon-lipped ladies of paint.

Bombay was as hot as Delhi had been cold-hot but Huffy was on tremendous form. We commandeered one of those tiny beetle-like taxis and its driver's eyes could be seen in the rear-view mirror in a look of muted shock. Isabella and Kentaro were quite a sight.

'God. Look at those eyes! They're giving me a hard-on!' drawled Issie.

'Oh thank you,' the driver replied politely.

It was so hot that we decided to cool down in a run-down Art Deco cinema where the new James Bond film was playing in Hindi.

Issie was thrilled by the dark theatre, with its balconies and dilapidated frescoes, and the sea of upturned faces, all male, transfixed by Judi Dench.

'All you can see is shiny hair and eyeballs! I love it!' But she couldn't sit still for more than five minutes, so we left Kentaro watching the film and sat in the foyer smoking and chatting.

The strange thing was that for someone who was suicidal, she was constantly dazzled by life and the world was equally dazzled by her. I came back from the loo to find her holding forth in her frankly rude Indian accent to a group of giggling usherettes, handing out cigarettes and trying to persuade the girls that I was a big star.

'You must have seen *Another Country*? No? Well, you've got to see it!'

Of course all they could see was her, a veiled black widow belching smoke from a red gash. She may have loved the glittering salons of the rich and the gowns of her monstrous protégées, but she was just as happy, or unhappy, in the crumbling Victorian railway station that afternoon where we rested on a bench, listening to the announcements and watching thousands of Indians late for their trains. But then she looked at her feet, which was always a bad sign, a prelude to the fugues of despair.

'The doctors say I'm never going to walk again. They've never seen anything like it,' she announced dramatically for the thousandth time.

'But Issie,' I replied, 'we've just pretended we were local girls running for a train to the suburbs!'

'Yes, but that was acting!'

'No, darling, this is acting!'

She looked at me and took my hands. She knew I would never understand. There is an unbridgeable gap between the depressed and the rest of the world. There was no explaining although Isabella had a brilliant turn of phrase to describe her state.

'Look, Rupey, there's all this movement around us but I'm just a mouth on a seat.'

I laughed and groaned inwardly. 'Issie, you're not just a mouth on a seat! We're having a good time. Honestly, sometimes I don't know what to do with you.'

'Nobody does. I don't know what to do with myself. I don't know how to survive the next five minutes. I feel like a ghost. A pancake in a wheelchair.'

'But you're not in a wheelchair!' I reasoned.

She ignored me. 'I'm a broken record.'

'Well, that's true.'

She had a Kleenex in her hands. I knew what was coming next.

'Rupey, see this Kleenex. That's me.' She threw it to the ground and it bounced off in the breeze. 'See? Nothing! Just a Kleenex!'

She surveyed me, sombre, face to one side, big eyes, a parrot again. You didn't know whether to laugh or cry and she enjoyed the confusion.

That evening was the last night of the freebie. I was leaving at midnight and the next day she would be back on the high seas, sailing on to the next port, a friend's family in Gujerat, and then who knew. She was driving herself towards the homelessness she feared so much. We sat in the hotel, looking out of a huge window at the new India under construction in front of us. Skyscrapers bathed in tungsten were being built late into the night by half-naked untouchables. The old India was gone. Soon it would be a giant shopping mall.

For some reason I had a book of war poems with me. Issie loved them. She identified with their stories of doomed youth and death in the trenches. I read one called 'The Deserter' by Gilbert Frankau:

> 'I'm sorry I done it, Major.'
> We bandaged the livid face;
> And led him out, ere the wan sun rose,
> To die his death of disgrace.
>
> The bolt-heads locked to the cartridge;
> The rifles steadied to rest,

As cold stock nestled at colder cheek
And foresight lined on the breast.

'Fire!' called the Sergeant-Major.
The muzzles flamed as he spoke:
And the shameless soul of a nameless man
Went up in the cordite smoke.

We were silent for a while as the full impact of the poem fell on us like a thick fog. Isabella was shell-shocked from a life in the trenches of fashion. She had tried to desert, but for her the firing squad was the rest of us trying to keep her alive. And I was deserting her. Somewhere I knew that I couldn't face her for much longer. It was too depressing to watch her doggedly elbow her way towards her doom.

So there we were in the taxi to the airport.

'I hate saying goodbye. I always feel I'm being abandoned,' she said.

'You've got Kentaro,' I reasoned. He stood beside her, bearded in a miniskirt.

We hugged, and I watched her waving through the back window of the cab until they had disappeared into the Indian night.

CHAPTER TWENTY-THREE

The Last Day of Hats

Isabella's funeral took place in Gloucester Cathedral where she had been married only a few years earlier. Outside the cathedral André Leon Talley stood in a gigantic billowing cape that flapped as the wind got underneath it and soared into the air, almost lifting poor André from the ground as he perused himself in the wing mirror of his people carrier.

The coffin arrived in a horse-drawn hearse. The black horses wore black plumes between their ears and were encrusted with diamonds fixed on at the very last minute by Philip Treacy and a team of mourners. The coffin itself was made of wicker and looked like a giant picnic basket. On top of it lay Isabella's favourite hat, a death ship with black sails and feather flags attached to the tops of its masts. In the choir of the cathedral, the coffin was placed on a velvet dais. These feathers blew in some imperceptible draught, giving the boat a ghostly feeling of movement, as though it was actually crashing through the foam of lilies upon which it sat, with Isabella aboard, towards the other shore, the undiscovered bourne where hopefully God wouldn't give her such a hard time as the *Sunday Times* and the rest of us had.

Isabella's girlfriends, dressed to the nines for the send-off, veiled, corseted and gloved in black, marvellously framed by the ancient pews of the choir, were like medieval princesses or the phantom ladies of the barge that appeared on Windermere to transport King Arthur to Avalon. A boy sang Purcell's 'When I Am Laid In Earth', accompanied by the organ. His voice echoed through the church. 'Remember me,' he implored as the coffin was carried out and it sounded as if she was calling us from space.

The effect of it all, the sadness, the faded grandeur, the society beauties, the death boat and the music, turned the funeral into one of the great moments. It was the end of something. For a brief spellbinding moment, Isabella's aesthetic came alive and was complete. Someone should have shot it for *Vogue*.

PART FIVE

CHAPTER TWENTY-FOUR

Nude Sunday in Berlin

Isabella's ghost is like the image that an electric bulb – too closely scrutinised – brands across the optic nerve. One closes one's eyes or turns out the light and it appears multiplied. For a while it is inescapable, but tonight – quite suddenly – she has gone.

It is a snowy night in Berlin. I am sitting in the dark, looking out as a gathering storm flutters then swirls and finally tumbles in silence across the large window. A rented room, a cheap hotel, a foreign tongue (or two) – and the past simply falls away.

My room is large and high, with moulded ceilings and old lumpy wallpaper, calcified by endless coats of paint – the latest one being a kind of half-hearted emerald green. Carved rudely into the side of this quite handsome room is a tiny bathroom with walls of cracked white tiles, a hipbath and an ashtray fixed to the wall by the loo. Sitting on that loo smoking a cigarette is one of life's guilty pleasures, watching the dust particles float past the open door, through which can be seen, dominating the bedroom, an ugly old bed like a gigantic wooden tomb. At its head the curved walnut gravestone lacks only the name of its dead occupant (me) engraved across the middle. At its foot

the wooden board is high as a garden fence. Attached to either side
are matching night tables, small towers with cupboards, shelves and
tiny drawers (for storing false teeth and curlers) and a little swivelling
mirror on the top.

Of the same overweight family as this bed are an ungainly armoire
and a clumpy chest of drawers, all vast and ugly, in two tones of
walnut – in short, an early twentieth-century suite of luxury bedroom
furniture and the last will and testament of some solid, dowdy, middle-
class couple who died on it years ago. One can imagine seeing it in the
windows of Landauer's department store – described by Christopher
Isherwood in his Berlin novels, or winking in the background of all
those baffling bits of film leading up to the war where jerky sped-up
shoppers are stopped by Hitler Youth with leaflets from entering the
soot-caked doors of shops owned by Jews. Somehow, miraculously,
these relics are still here. They have withstood all the clean-outs, the
conversions, the direct hits and the derelict decades endured by this
room. The proprietor of this wonky place has shown me pictures of
these barges and their moorings – taken here – dated 1927.

Double sets of windows run along one side of the entire room.
There's a dusty no man's land in between them, a cemetery for bluebottles. They lie flat on their backs, legs in the air, knocked senseless
and then dead from endlessly crashing against the panes. I watch
them in my daydreams (my time in this hotel room has a different
rhythm from the rest of my chaotic life; I can sit here for hours,
watching the dust, listening to the various creaks and contractions, the
gurgles of the old pipes, the shrill banter of the chambermaids hoovering next door), and it occurs to me that we have more in common
than I had hitherto imagined – me and the dead bluebottles, and
even the ghosts of the ugly bed for that matter – because in our way
we have all been knocked senseless, banging our heads against life's
invisible and incomprehensible walls. But *remarque* – as the French
say: at least the flies have a magnificent glass casket worthy of Lenin
or Snow White. Their winding sheets are the smog-stained net curtains that hang from the old metal rails in the ceiling and sound like

toy trains when they are drawn. They billow theatrically when the windows are open and convert the daylight into a chalky gloom, a big white mist before which we are all – the living and the dead – fleeting black shadows passing for the night, check-out time negotiable in some cases.

On summer evenings – those pale German nights – with the windows open and the curtains waving gently in the breeze, you don't have to close your eyes to be transported through time. Who slept in this bed as the bombs rained down? Some tiny old couple, baffled by the times, woken suddenly by the sirens howling on the Kurfürstendamm. Like them, the whole house shivers and gasps as the bombs scream and explode, nearer and nearer, and they grope their way through the pitch black to the cellar. All this terror has been ingested somehow, held within the walls of the room, in the doors of the armoire and the dusty corners of the clunky chest of drawers.

On summer nights and even more in winter (now), as snow falls silently outside the dark room, I find myself in that semi-conscious state veering towards sleep, the hard edges of reality softening and bending towards the jumbled vista of dreamscape, my hopes and fears leaping to the stage to take on their dramatic roles. I hear the terrible sound of running feet, of raised voices suddenly silenced, of banging doors and overturned tables, of whispers in the corridor and the stifled scream of someone being dragged past the door.

In the house where I grew up there was a small piece from the floor of Hitler's bunker. Just a nugget of concrete, really, studded with a few pieces of brown and gold mosaic, it sat in a display cabinet in our drawing room, incongruously surrounded by little glasses, china dogs and figurines. When the conversation drifted towards war, as it inevitably did, I would sit in front of that nugget and wonder what it all meant. Hitler didn't particularly interest me, he was too ugly, but the idea of a bunker, an underground maze of tunnels and secret chambers, accessible only through a hatch in the ground, was tremendously exciting, and the word Berlin stuck in my little brain, a trip switch that transported me into a secret fantasy world of explosions, darkness and uniforms. I didn't have to consult a clairvoyant to know the future. It was already written as I crawled around those forests of polished shoes and stockinged ankles in my romper suit, looking up through the clouds of cigar smoke, at the squawking heads of the grown-ups waving in the branches high above, during that sepia-tinted English country childhood long ago.

'Tony pulled it off the floor of Hitler's bunker with his bare hands – were you in Berlin after the war?'

Shortly after the wall came down, I was in Berlin with Pink Floyd, acting in a few filmed sections for their mammoth production of *The Wall*. While we were rehearsing one afternoon on what was then No Man's Land, but is now the Sony Building (same difference), the ground suddenly gave way under the weight of our stage and we discovered a maze of underground passages. We had fallen into a bunker. After the initial excitement died down, I set off to explore with a flashlight and a very camp Jewish princess in teetering heels who was working on the concert and whom I knew from London. Inside the darkness was so thick it was almost solid. The gloomy shaft of daylight through which we had fallen disappeared as we delved further and further into the past. The beam of the flashlight and the princess's shrieks bounced against walls that still contained all the desperation and fear of war, and upon which soldiers waiting to die had painted murals of victory. The cliffs of Dover under a forest of flapping swastikas. English peasants with their arms raised in surrender. Their ghostly faces squinted at us – they hadn't seen light for fifty years – and we stared back, speechless. It was the strangest feeling, like diving through a submarine cave into a bottomless underground sea of sorrow.

'Girlfriend, let's get out of here!' said the princess, and we ran stumbling towards the light as if our lives depended on it.

Berlin lives under a vast unshed tear. There is a statue in the Tiergarten of a girl on tiptoes looking towards the Brandenburg Gate, through which ran the wall that divided East from West. She is straining to see someone on the other side, her lover perhaps, whom she will never meet again. She stands near the memorial to the Russian dead. (There is no memorial to dead Germans.)

The Tiergarten is a dark frozen mass in winter and a seductive tangle of waving leaves and winding paths in summer. On hot afternoons nude queens play Frisbee on the wide lawns while Turkish families sit around their campfires, and Eastern bloc Bertas with shaved vaginas sprawl on rugs under the brief spells of sun, reading magazines. At some point they all pack their bags and saunter towards the Biergarten on the edge of the park where people sit at long trestle tables drinking giant glasses of amber beer under the trees. Lovers row on the lake. Children scream. The clatter of plates and the chattering crowd cross-fade from day to night. Coloured lights twinkle in the branches, the band plays one last song, and the kitchens close. Under the blanket of night the fairies and goblins arrive; skinheads and dealers, bent cops and politicos, lean against lamps and flit through the shadows, their cigarettes glowing like fireflies in the distant copses on the Midsummer Night's Dream.

My room is at the Hotel Bogota in Schlüterstrasse, just off the Kurfürstendamm. It is a large white building, quite old, actually, and steeped in history, but effaced by thick layers of post-war pebbledash. A bright orange awning, more New York than Berlin, reaches into the street over a threadbare red carpet. Inside, the Bogota is a throwback to the West Berlin of the seventies. Groups from East Germany surge through the foyer. Breathtaking students eat the delicious homemade jam and black bread in the dining room at breakfast, where an old grandfather clock chimes every quarter of an hour. English ladies on war tours rub shoulders with leather queens on a skinhead convention.

It is my favourite hotel in the world, but don't get your hopes up. Mine is the only room filled with that clunky old furniture from the twenties, and it was painted emerald green in my honour. (I don't know what that says. A similar thing happened at the London hotel I frequented for many years. I returned one day and they had painted my room black. Either I have made some spiritual progress or else my Irish roots are showing through.) At any rate the rest of the rooms each have four or five single beds, banana walls and no bathroom. The loo is down the hall, which I love. Guests march towards it in their dressing gowns with their wash bags under their arms. Just like the old days. The floors creak with history under their slippers, and Gregorian chants can be vaguely heard piped through the building. The Bogota is a rabbit warren of custard-coloured corridors and hallways laid with tattered, red, swirly-patterned carpets that remind me of a West End theatre. Sometimes, late at night, returning flushed from another evening in the mazes and secret rooms of the Berlin night, one comes across a sleeping form – a Bratislavan student, perhaps, who has fallen on the way to their room – snoring gently.

The Bogota used to share its walls with a bedraggled old hookers' bar, which I loved. It was low-lit with stained velvet banquettes and stained jolly ladies of the night. In bustiers and fishnets, *les girls* stood outside in the summer months, under a blinking neon sign, right next to the steps of the hotel. Until last year. One of them, Denise, grew pot at home, and always gave me a little bag. In the warm evenings they leant against the wall by the door, under the red light, smoking and chatting. 'Baby! You wanna see Denise?"

Now the 'Piano Bar' has become a kitchen design centre, another deathly tendril from the rest of Europe that will one day turn Berlin into everywhere else. Soon, I suppose, the Bogota will change with the prevailing weather into another of the dreary Four Seasons.

Last week I took Bruce Weber to see Helmut Newton's grave.

In the cemetery at Schöneberg death was tucked in for the winter under blankets of autumn leaves. The cold air and the hard earth reminded one – much more than in the summer for some reason, when death is pretty – that beneath our feet were rows of frozen remains lying on frozen lace cushions in the frozen clay.

*

'I still can't believe he's dead,' someone had said the night before Helmut's funeral.

'Completely dead,' June, his widow, replied firmly. 'Helmut is completely dead.' And she knocked back a glass of German schnapps (Steinhäger).

All the mourners were sitting in the Newtons' favourite bar, Diener's. Deeply drunk on Steinhäger and beer, served to us by Rolf the ancient barman, we were luxuriating in memory and loss. Here, tonight, with Helmut hanging above us in the ether, as if by a thread, we were delicately, magically, attached to the past, to a Berlin lost and irretrievable. Nothing much had changed in Diener's since 1939. We sat clustered around little tables lit by dripping candles in bottles, and Lizletts, the old owner, looked at June solemnly.

'She hasn't left this house since the end of the war,' whispered June.

And it was true. She hadn't.

It was raining on the day, as the cortège left the hotel in a caravan of flashing police cars and motorbikes. Berlin had done Helmut proud. Chancellor Schröder was part of the entourage, and so was the city's whizz-kid gay mayor. Traffic was stopped as we sped by. It was strange to think of Helmut fleeing Berlin all those years before. Now she had him back, feet first, in a motorcade. Instead of June, Helmut's new bedfellow would be another exiled Berliner, Marlene Dietrich, who lived in the grave next door.

'Don't worry, I can squeeze in,' said June, her sense of humour always intact.

Paparazzi surged around the group as we disembarked. In the middle of the graveyard was a little chapel into which we all crammed ourselves, and then June, in a black trouser suit, a beret and coils of black pearls around her neck, sang a lament by Schubert. She was suddenly a little girl, and everyone's heart melted.

'On every tree that blossoms in the grove,' she chirped, 'On every stone I see where'er I rove, Thine is my heart. Thine is my heart.'

Higher and higher she sang. Soon the windows might shatter, but

no matter, it was brilliant, spine-chilling and deeply moving. By the
end, even the Chancellor was in tears. We left the chapel for the
grave, a small flock of crows in our flapping black weeds. Roger
Moore, Joan Juliet Buck, Michael Chow, Wendy Stark. Some of us
would never meet again. That's what death does to the living. Our
unifying thread had snapped.

'Come on, Rupert!' said June. (She had asked me to help her read
some Shakespeare, and I was thrilled.) We stood in front of the grave
as the rain stopped and the sun came out.

'Newton weather,' she whispered, before launching into *King Lear*.

Now, two years later, Bruce clears away the leaves, and looks at the
picture on the headstone of Helmut taken by June. The two foremost
photographers of the twentieth century regard one another from
across the grave. Bruce, alive, is surrounded by a swarm of assistants;
Helmut is dust, with only Marlene to hold the everlasting light meter.

Leaving the cemetery, we pass a stone angel perched on a gravestone with a cigarette in its mouth. God bless Berlin. Smoking is
actually encouraged in Germany. But not for much longer. In eleva-
tors and telephone booths, by the sides of toilets and in your cinema
seat, you are more than likely to find an ashtray. The curling smoke
drifts between you and the screen at the Zoo Palast, it makes the candles glow at Adnan's restaurant, and you can hardly see through it at
Bergheim, my favourite club. As for the lowlife nightlife, you can't get
in without a fag in your mouth.

Of all the Berlin ghosts, my favourite is Christopher Isherwood.
Before the war he lived near Nollendorfplatz, and while Bruce is
taking pictures of some uppity dancer from France, imported spe-
cially, I take Nan Bush, his long-time girlfriend and business
manager, to see the house. His books on Berlin were a turning point
in my life, and he is often on my mind as I pass the Metropol into
Motzstrasse. Everything has changed and nothing has changed. Late
at night, if you close your eyes, you can still hear the ghostly whistles
of young men calling from the smoggy streets to their girls in the vast

flats above, where lights twinkle and the tomblike walnut beds are turned down for the night. Streets of houses, 'like monumental safes crammed with the tarnished valuables and second-hand furniture of a bankrupt middle class', have not changed much despite the fissures of war and the pebbledash veneer. Berlin is still bankrupt, but thank God for it. There is something a poor city has that a rich one can never achieve. One day she will be the centre of a unified Europe. If we last that long. She will crystallise into the same wedding cake that is London, Paris and Rome.

But for the time being – this March afternoon – she sits under a chalky sky full of snow, slightly shabby in dirty beige and grey. The street lights are already on, even though it is not dark, but the night swoops in at this time of year. Any minute now the Wagnerian clouds are going to give birth to the promised blizzard and there is an odd thickness in the air, a feeling of urgency. People rush about their business and the street is almost deserted as Nan and I amble along chatting, looking in junk shops and stopping at a coffee shop over the road from the plaque marking Isherwood's Berlin home. The odd flake of snow floats through the air and Nan chats about fabulous things like Scavullo and life on Fire Island in the seventies.

People worship Bruce Weber, but I adore Nan. She is like a character from a Beatrix Potter story, a little field mouse in trousers with a ponytail and twinkly eyes. She has a tiny voice that can barely be heard and she comes from the same school of delivery as Andy Warhol. That is to say that her tones are expressionless and half-hearted, and yet like Andy Warhol she manages to convey enormous character, warmth and humour within the catchphrases ('Aww gee' for Andy and 'It's so crazy' for Nan).

She sometimes seems to be in a dream but she might easily be going through the day's invoices rather than staring at a parallel universe because actually she is one of the toughest women in the toughest business. As Bruce's business manager, she has built her man's considerable talent into the juggernaut brand it has become by the sheer force of her ambiguous character. The circus of Bruce Weber consists

of assistants, managers, stylists, make-up artists, hairdressers, printers
and even a pet model agent. A family of retrievers completes Bruce's
entourage, and their animal psychic is never far from the scene. This
caravan moves with military precision from season to season, from one
of their fabulous homes to another, Florida in winter, Manhattan in
summer. They are forever on the Dixie trail. Here today, Paris tomorrow: fifteen people, five cars, $20,000 worth of film, models (and their
fathers, if they are under age) flown in from all corners of the earth –
this whole magical kingdom is conjured up by this tiny woman with
the voice that no one can hear. She has given every fibre of her being
to it and it has quite possibly worn her out.

'It's just so crazy,' is all she will admit in that tiny voice. 'Bruce
wants two elephants by eleven o'clock.'

I leave her in an antique shop slowly browsing under the distrustful scrutiny of the large lady proprietor, promising to meet her and
Bruce later for dinner, but I nearly don't make it, due to a curious
wardrobe malfunction.

On my way home I pop into one of my favourite bars for a drink
before dinner. Unbeknown to me it is Nude Sunday and as soon as I
open the door I am presented with a bin liner by a venomous skull in
the hatch.

'Put your clothes in here,' he orders.

Slightly cowed, with people arriving behind me, I do as I'm told,
even if there's nothing I actually want to do less after an afternoon in
the freezing cold than go to a nude party before dinner. But it seems
a bit uncool to quibble, and I am shunted into a kind of production
line, like a chicken, by the bony head, his bony hands shooting
through the hatch and waving me – with my bag – into a sort of
holding pen where a chubby queen is losing her balance, bending
over to undo her shoes. She's looking daggers at a skeletal skinhead
who is crashing about drunk.

I begin to undress and pack my kit in the bin liner, feeling fatalis-
tic. Another couple of men come in with their bin liners and now it's
a really tight squeeze, all elbows and bottoms in the air – but not in a

good way. A red light flashes on and off over the skull's head; he presses a buzzer with a long finger, and the door to the outside world opens and closes and then opens again, exposing us to the glare of the street, the bemused glances of the passers-by, and, more importantly, the animal urge to bolt semi-nude for the outside world. But such is the hold one man can have over another that the bony queen has got me down to my boots and now I am shunted through a thick leather curtain into the club itself.

Clutching my bin liner to my chest, I set off across the bar through the smoky gloom where a variety of fairies are perched here and there, chatting and smoking or looking vacant – like cats – staring at another dimension while tugging at their neighbour's teats. There is a staircase down to a hellish underworld and the coat check is at the back of the place near the toilets where a line of naked men – each one carrying their worldly belongings, like immigrants, or worse, but don't let's go there – waiting to get a wristband and a ticket in return for their clothes. The coat-check man has seen better days and wears thick glasses that magnify his eyes to the size of an owl's. He moves slowly, tying each bag, stapling it with his stapler, then sellotaping a raffle ticket to it, before putting it on the shelf next to all the other bags. He is so ordinary as to seem macabre, framed by the door, with the long, narrow room behind him crammed with body bags on shelves, lit by a naked bulb, his magnified eyes blinking under a balding pate. I nearly decide to turn back – I often do – but soon I am given my wristband and my raffle ticket. It is number 342. I make a mental note, and then saunter to the bar to get a drink.

Actually it feels quite stunning to be naked. There are no defences left. The communists should have declared permanent nudity rather than revolution, because everyone is the same; not even the proudest beauty can withstand the test of total scrutiny. There is always some wobble or curve or lumpy vein exposed. All the personality endowed by clothes, money and position is simply stripped away, and the result is a palpable release of tension here tonight. Even the man who has laid the gigantic tool of his trade on the bar stool next to him is panting and winking like a chummy old Labrador. He has a pace-maker. It is just the kind of mixed crowd I love – Golden Gays and autumn leaves and one soiled Adonis, a weird beauty hell-bent on slavery. A couple of men in gas masks are deep in conversation, leaning on the pinball machine. Their compressed voices are coming out through the ends of long tubes attached to their masks, which sit like trunks on the flashing glass surface.

I sit on a stool at the bar, order a gin and tonic, and settle down to watch some porno on the TV. The red light blinks and in no time the place is full. I would class it as a fair to middling evening. Certainly no one here to dress up for. Pretty soon I am feeling the energy of some-one's eyes boring into the back of my head and turn to see an elephant of a man standing a little way off. He has a giant stomach overflowing two long thin piano legs. He is looking at me intently and I look away but it's too late. One glance is enough for a voracious, dan-gerously drunk fairy. He flops from his stool like a porpoise splashing into the waves, and swims through the crowd to resurface, spluttering, on the stool next to me. He has a shaved head, large watery eyes and a ping-pong bat in his hand.

'Johnny Cochrane Patrick. I met you with Joan Golfer.' He has a high breathy voice and offers a fleshy hand.

'She's dead,' is all I can think of to say.

'I know!' he moans, eyeballs briefly disappearing. 'I miss her every day. Such energy! She loved you.'

'Did she?'

'Oh yes. By the way, loved the book.'

I strain every nerve on my face to look pleasantly surprised. 'Oh, thanks.'

'I simply *adored* the chapter on Roddy McDowall. What was he like?'

'Very nice, really.'

'Really?'

The great big eyes are close to mine now, beckoning for more details. I study my drink. I am not going to enlarge.

'I loved what you said about his cock,' he coaxes.

'Oh, good.'

'Fancy having a look downstairs?'

'Not right now. Thanks.'

'You're quite frosty, aren't you? Joan said you were!'

There doesn't seem to be any point in denying it. 'Yes. Very.'

Pause. He scrutinises me closely for some moments, then gets up and suddenly thwacks me hard on the bum with the ping-pong bat.

'Ow!' I scream.

'Yah!' He laughs as if he knows something that I don't. 'Don't worry. Your secret's safe with me.'

He swims back off into the bar, his head moving above the crowd like a lady trying to keep her perm dry in a choppy sea. I last see him disappearing downstairs into the dungeon, gripping the handrail for dear life.

I decide to call it a day. I go back to the myopic queen and give him my raffle ticket. He gives me a bag. I open it.

'These aren't mine!'

The world stands still. A line of about five men has formed behind me. Two of them are from Lancashire and are quite drunk, talking loudly.

What?' asked the myopic queen.

I repeat myself – slightly louder.

He studies my ticket and the ticket on the bag. 'This is yours,' he insists.

'No. It isn't.'

'That poor bugger lost his ticket,' says one of the Lancashire bears.

Now everybody is looking at me. Like Eve in the Garden of Eden, I suddenly feel my nudity and try to make myself as small as possible, which is not easy at six foot four. Only one thing *is* getting as small as possible and the myopic queen regards it disdainfully before pushing me to one side as he starts to give the others their bags. When the two bears get to the head of the queue, I shrink into the shadows but they recognise me anyway.

'It's that guy from the TV. What's your name?' one of them bellows.

Luckily I am still in possession of my wits. 'Jeremy. Jeremy Irons.'

After a few good-humoured jokes about lending me their under-wear, they say how cheap and easy it is to get to Berlin – and I joke back that it's quite easy to be cheap as well – and they say, 'That's true,' taking their clothes, and now there's nobody left so I become completely hysterical. It's a bad move because the myopic queen freezes over with indignation.

'You're going to have to wait till the end of the night.'

'I can't. I have to work.'

'You should have thinking of this when you are coming!'

'But I didn't give me the wrong ticket. You did.'

'What you want me do? Take down alls bags and looking for?'

'Yes.'

'Ach!' he says simply and turns away.

I am cowed again, and go back to the bar and sit there fuming for twenty minutes until I spy the English queen staggering up from the underworld. I can't face another conversation about Joan Golfer so I go to the bar and ask for the manager. The venomous skull appears. I explain the situation – sotto voce. He has long thin lips and a suppressed smile plays across them like a cardiogram. I want to slap him. He returns with me to the coat check, where the myopic queen starts to shout in German and stab at the air with his finger. His glasses have steamed up. He takes them off, revealing two large wet jellied eggs, which look at me blindly. I feel slightly reassured and so I barge my way through the door into the coat-check room.

'We have got to go through all the bags,' I scream.

I am trying to remain calm but there's very little point. I have already lost all dignity. The myopic queen puts her glasses back on and looks to the skull for approval. Germans don't like having their routine changed and I can tell I am about to be here until the end of the night. There are three hundred bags, after all.

The skull sighs. 'We look.'

MQ begins to grab bags from the shelves, throwing them to the ground, undoing the knots he has so painstakingly tied, pulling the clothes out and waving them at me. They look weird, like dead people's clothes, dirty and tragic. None of them are mine. He shoves them back indiscriminately, but I don't care. Each queen for herself at this stage. Now I am on all fours, clambering over the piles of bags, ripping them open and looking inside. Occasionally I look over my shoulder and see a couple of fairies standing there on the other side of the hatch, looking at my naked arse, happily waving their raffle tickets, laughing as I flounder in this sea of plastic. Finally the English queen arrives.

'God. Poor you, darling,' he says, leaning over the hatch as he is given his bag. 'Have you tried rimming yourself?'

'Fuck off. I'm not in the mood for jokes,' I snap.

He begins to talk in a flawless German to the manager.

'Good idea. Is your phone in there?' asks the skull.

'Yes.'

'So let's ring it,' huffs the English queen. 'What's your number?'

I tell him. He dials. We all listen. Nothing.

Why did I get that new ringtone? It is nothing more than the chirrup of a little cricket. How am I going to hear it above the din of the bar?

He tries again. Nothing again.

He tries once more and this time I hear it. Brrrup brrrup brrrup brrrup brrrup brrrup. It's coming from an unmarked bag on the floor. I lunge for it, and there they are – my clothes, my wallet, my shoes. I have rarely felt so elated and I cradle them, glaring at the others manically, hoping that this little episode is going to be quickly forgotten. It has been too revealing in more ways than one. But no one seems to want to elongate the moment. The myopic queen sniffs regally and picks her way through the debris, trying to create some order. The skull disappears with the English queen, and I fall over myself, dressing too fast. I want to get out of this place and never come back.

At the door the skull is back in his hatch – on the telephone – and as I tumble from the inferno I can hear him laughing. Doubtless he is recounting to some other skull, in some other hatch, in some other special-needs fetish club, the hysterical scoop of the evening.

While I have been imprisoned naked, a blizzard has raged over Berlin and the whole city is covered in a thick sparkling blanket of snow. It is still falling. Bright around the street lights, thick as wedding cakes on all the cars; balanced delicately two inches high on every branch and twig, unsullied by footprints and tyres, drifting silently from the pink night sky onto the deserted street. Light spills from the windows of the sex shops. Faceless mannequins in full leather look out blindly. It is unbelievably beautiful and I walk all the way to the restaurant, feeling the warmth of my poor clothes as if they were long-lost friends. My nudity hides within them, seeking out the familiar corners and swearing never to desert them again. I am reborn, like Scrooge at the end of A *Christmas Carol*.

Adnan is my favourite restaurant in Berlin. It is a long high cream room with tables in rows, crowded with overdressed women glittering in the candlelight, served by waiters in linen aprons, and cajoled and flirted with by the owner: the Turkish giant Adnan, who has hands as big as your head – and we all know what that means – and hair like Anna Wintour. One wall of the entire restaurant is glass, so the interior glows tonight like a Christmas card, or an upmarket crib framed by the dark snowy night.

Bruce's party is still going. It is a Last Supper of fashion. Bruce sits in the middle, a psychedelic rabbi in a rainbow shawl and a skullcap, surrounded by disciples, beautiful, vacant models, make-up artists and hairdressers, the holders of the light meter, the reflector, the nuncios from the magazine. Nan and the agent sit together at the end. Which one is Judas, I wonder? Maybe it's me.

I sit down next to Nan and tell her the story of my night. She listens with a faraway smile, but eyes twinkling.

'That's so crazy,' is all she says but I know she thinks it's funny.

CHAPTER TWENTY-FIVE

Mr Geoffrey

Situated on 44th Street between Eighth Avenue and Broadway, the Shubert Theatre is an ugly theatre on an unprepossessing block. Sardi's is across the road, and none of it lives up to the old songs. One simply cannot imagine Lillian Hellman or Noël Coward stalking across this urban sprawl, or reading their rave reviews at midnight under the wonky scrutiny of Sardi's famous caricatures. New York covers its tracks like no other city, and the past can be glimpsed only through the taxi window crossing the tumbledown bridges. Otherwise it is a city enslaved to the moment, which is why old people always look like the homeless here. They are not. They are the past. The stage door of the theatre is located around the corner in Shubert Alley. It is made of gold, like the entrance to a vault. Above it, across the whole flank of the building, is a gigantic poster of *me* (and the others).

Directly inside, partitioned off in a cardboard cubicle, is Rose, the stage doorkeeper and also the black widow of a TV career that died in the seventies. Rose used to be the star of a daytime soap. She is a formidable show-business creature with jet-black hair scraped into a ponytail, dressed for a jazz class – all in black – with conical breasts. She is a no-nonsense hag and we fall out on day one.

'Are you gonna sign in?' she asks with ever increasing sharpness every time I come through the stage door.

'Signing in doesn't rhyme with Broadway star. I'm here, aren't I?'

'You gotta sign in.'

'What is the point of being in the theatre if you have to sign in?'

'I don't know but you gotta sign in.'

'Well, I refuse. So have me fired.'

Rose shakes with fury and I stomp through a door into the tomb-like gloom of the backstage area.

I am performing eight times a week for six long months in Noël Coward's *Blithe Spirit*. I last appeared in this play at Ampleforth, the Catholic seminary where I was originally bitten by the acting bug (among other things). In that production, I played the vampish Elvira, the role originally played by the divine Kay Kendall. (Who?) I stole the show. And the costumes. Now thirty-five short – or long: I can't decide which, so elastic seems time – years later, I have graduated to male parts. Tonight I am playing the thankless lead, Charles Condomine, a writer of crime novels who – for the purposes of researching a book – invites a batty clairvoyant to hold a seance in his house during which, by mistake, she conjures up his dead ex-wife. Charles's theatrical role is to feed the three women in the show. The funniest lines are said by Madame Arcati, the clairvoyant, originally played by Dame Margaret Rutherford and now by Angela Lansbury – whose entrance round sometimes extends for five whole minutes while the rest of us stand around extending our ghastly smiles into malicious grimaces of welcome and she beams star quality across the footlights, ostensibly at us, but really at her public, nodding modestly and waving them on with subtle movements of encouragement and various *oeillades*.

The Broadway public are the most enthusiastic theatregoers in the world. In fact they are the only thing left in this shell of a city that reminds one of the America one fell in love with. They are warm,

wacky, generous, cigar-smoking, wig-wearing, facelifted, golf-play-
ing, caddy-driving, old-school out-of-towners. They arrive in coaches
and wait in droves at the stage door after the show. They are pep-
pered with actual New Yorkers, actors, directors, various queens,
their mothers and other fag hags, and together make up the most
generous reception in the world. Even I receive an entrance round –
nothing in length to that of La Bedknobs, but a round nonetheless.
At the Shubert Theatre.

It is quiet and arctic backstage, just the drone of the air-conditioning
system and the noise of a faraway Hoover. As in *All About Eve*, Angela
Lansbury's dressing room is by the side of the stage. The Broadway star
can dive right from the make-up chair into the audience – in fifteen seconds. I knock on the door. Angela sits in a coral silk dressing gown,
wearing a rust-coloured Princess Leia wig and panda eye make-up, in a
tiny pink room with a pink sofa and no natural light. In the corner
stands a gangly blonde dresser who doubles as her assistant. She is also
the stalker and general weird expert on all concerning *la vie en*
Lansbury. Angela is doing her lips in the mirror. She pecks at my reflection in the glass and goes on with her work. She speaks English or
American, depending on her mood or who she's talking to. With her
fans she's Jessica Fletcher. With me she's Miss Marple.

'Good house tonight?'

'Rather good.'

'Julie's in. Drinks in my dressing room after, and then we'll go for
a nibble.'

I should be in heaven. A nibble with Julie Andrews. But I'm not.
I am a dead weight, sitting around all day, dreading the moment
when I have to come into work. I have never felt so drained and it's
only week five.

'I've just seen a picture of your latest facelift,' teases Angela, waving
a gossip rag that features a double-page before and after spread.

'Don't.'

An editor I vexed has launched a viral attack, sending out a
bloated mugshot of my so-called botched facelift.

'Well, at least they're talking about you!'

Angela is charming and reserved, with a flint-sharp ambition under the cape and galoshes. She has the eyes of an owl and the tenacity of a mountain goat. She is old from the old school. Outwardly very friendly, ultimately detached. (She is what I would call a Frosty Two. Really nice and chatty and interested ... but frosty. If you are Frosty Four, for example, you are not even nice or chatty or interested. Actually, Four can be the easiest to deal with.) Old-fashioned descriptions suit her best. She is a good sport. A lady. But she is also eighty-three years old, and as any seasoned Broadway star knows, she must divide her energies judiciously. Most of hers goes into her performance. Then her fans.

Troops of pasty, wild-eyed freaks gather in lines outside her door after each show, proffering autograph books with shaky hands. They want their pound of flesh, however self-effacing they are. She receives them like a headmistress preparing for bed, in her doorway, clutching their hands but pushing them firmly out at the same time. On stage she takes no prisoners, grabbing all the reviews and a Tony, leaving the rest of us slightly dazed and confused in her undertow, but I don't mind. She is a fascinating creation and I have loved her since *Gaslight*.

I leave Angela's dressing room with a bit more spring in my step and surge onto the stage. The Shubert is a musical theatre so the stage is wide enough for thirty chorus boys to high-kick in a row. *Blithe Spirit* is a drawing-room comedy, normally staged in an intimate house where the spectator can observe the whole cast in one glance. Our production is a tennis match where the dialogue is lobbed between characters on opposite sides of the stage. Timing a laugh across this wide space has all the precision of throwing a sausage up Oxford Street. The circle is far away and wide. The stalls are deep. We must scream the show eight times a week. Any subtlety we may have discovered in the roles during rehearsals – and some of us didn't – is quickly ironed out by the sheer size of the house, and soon we are all belting out Noël Coward as if we are Ethel Merman.

The theatre is quiet and empty now, and as cold as the grave. In that medium's half-light – of wonky sconces and a dusty chandelier – the two circles and the stalls look like a big gaping mouth with two dangerous jaws bristling with rows of faded coral teeth into which I spit a few quaint British vocal exercises, flapping my arms like a penguin, chanting g-g-g-g-g-g-d-d-d-d-d-d-g-g-g-g-g-g-d-d-d-d-d-d, and wishing I could be transported into the past and come off stage to find myself in *A Chorus Line*, which opened here in 1974. My dressing room is the old chorus boys' room. It's been closed for years. My six-degrees-of-separation from that amazing musical is that I had a three-night stand with a boy from the show in the summer of 1978. I have hardly given him a second thought since that week, until getting this job. Now I think about him all the time, and I can't even remember his name. But as I begin to get my bearings in the modern city, trying to come to terms with all the change, I see him everywhere. He is the ghost leaning at all the street corners this freezing February in 2009, in a New York City that has disappeared without trace.

One. Singular. Sensation is the defining anthem of New York in the seventies. I belt it out and the past echoes faintly back from the empty boxes and balconies, but the Broadway of Michael Bennett, *A Chorus Line*'s creator (one of my show-business pin-ups), is quite simply another world. In his day you could nip up to 42nd Street for a blow job during the coffee break at rehearsals. Now you can just get fucked up the arse by Mickey Mouse Incorporated.

My crazy bird dancer has blond curly hair, matching brows and lashes, blue eyes and big pink lips. He is the all-American boy, corn-fed but catty. I meet him late one night on Second Avenue. He is wearing satin hot pants and football socks. He has a vial of that cocaine you get only in the seventies, and rockets go off in my head after the first hit, liberally piled onto an attached spatula in the relative shade of a bush. He has been dancing and fucking his way across the city – still up in that pre-dawn magenta light of another blistering day, cruising the park on Second Avenue. I am on my way back to Catherine Oxenberg's flat in Tudor City. He lives in a gangsterish walk-up in the East Village. We go there. Tangled and spent, we sleep all day, and hit the street again, on point, fresh as cucumber, at that magic hour when the light begins to soften, and the reds and greens of the stop signs glow fiercely in the battle for the night. I walk with him through Union Square into Hell's Kitchen. People are already sitting on the stoops, smoking and talking and waving at him as he pirouettes and soft-shoe shuffles towards Broadway.

'How come everybody knows you?' I ask.

'That's New York,' he says, tapping to a final halt at the stage door of the Shubert and kissing me goodbye.

He never asks me to the show, but on the night before I leave I buy a ticket and sit high up in the rafters – miles away – and watch entranced at the amazing story of thirty different versions of him, chorus boys and girls stripped like soldiers of their individuality and suppressed into a unified chorus line just in time for opening night. One. Singular. Sensation. If only I could know, right now, that I will be on that stage myself one day and that everything *will* happen – or won't, but that's life for you, and I don't, and I leave the theatre dejected and crushed, wandering into Time Square, doubting that I will ever amount to anything.

I have converted the old chorus boys' room into a fabulous black penthouse. Compared to all the other dressing rooms in the theatre, which are poky, toiletless and windowless, one on top of the other, mine is completely private and includes two rooms, a loo, a shower and a terrace. *And* a separate exit from the theatre, down a fire escape via the scene dock of another theatre – the Broadmoor – and even hitting a different block. (Jeremy Irons is currently torturing the public there. But not for much longer.) The only downside is that the staircase from the stage is steep and two storeys high. It becomes harder and harder to climb as the run goes on.

Standing at the ironing board in the chorus boys' room, looking at his watch because I am two and a half minutes later than usual, is the person who is going to get me through the next six months. He is called Mr Geoffrey. He is an old-school theatrical dresser – tending towards musicals – that invaluable cog in the theatrical machine who can often knock some sense into a stampeding diva when lawsuits, lovers and a treasured director have failed. An hysterical sobbing star may have convinced the management that she can't go on and desperately needs a rest and is thinking vaguely of suicide, but she still has to stagger to the dressing room and meet the steely gaze of her dresser, that curious creature, often an ex-artiste of sorts herself, but one who has been forced to commit her creative pretensions to an early grave, sacrificing everything to get some tipsy star onto the stage each night. She doesn't put up with any nonsense.

'I don't want to hear that crap!' Mr Geoffrey says now, as I crawl up that steep chorus boys' staircase, wailing.

'God! Mr Geoffrey, I don't know what's wrong with me. I've got *no* energy. I didn't sleep a wink again last night.'

'Don't burn out on me! Don't. OK? I am not dressing that flat-footed freak.' (My understudy.)

'Not even once? Could you get me a glass of champagne, please, darling?'

'Not even once. So don't even go there.'

Mr Geoffrey must be cruel to be kind, but kind he is. He has brought in his iPod, which is crammed with every show tune ever recorded. We kick off the previews with 'A Chorus Line' – my current obsession – and soon I have cheered up and am lashing on the slap while Mr Geoffrey sings along and the evening cranks up.

A theatre runs like clockwork on the day of a show. Everything happens at exactly the same time. First Erin arrives from Wigs with a wicker basket full of decapitated heads. A civilian may be forgiven for thinking that Erin has just murdered Angela, but in fact she is just making her rounds, and here she is, at 7.05, to stick a furry centipede called a front piece to my forehead. Erin is a red-headed giantess in hot pants. She is big and ballsy, in high boots and boob tubes, as if she has just climbed off a float at some carnival. She is having a turbulent affair with a dancer Mr Geoffrey knows. Mr Geoffrey thinks he has another girl. Gossip is the glue that keeps a company together, and my dresser and I survey the lives of the entire crew every night from our nest, sharing and dissecting the titbits we pick up in the field downstairs. Now we catch each other's eyes as Erin re-enacts last night's date. Mr Geoffrey shakes his head.

'He hasn't even asked me to his first night. Is that normal?'

'Perfectly normal. You can't go anyway. Who's going to put on my wig?'

'All I'm saying is I love you and you deserve more,' reasons Mr Geoffrey.

These angels know that one of their jobs is to cajole me into a good mood from my swamp of self-involved despondency, and little by little they nudge me into a reasonable humour, like two parents with a spoilt child who won't get on his potty. I attempt to convince them that I am on the edge of collapse. Now it's their turn to look at each other in the mirror.

'Come on, baby,' says Erin, rubbing my shoulders. 'You can do it.'

'If those – I was going to say girls, but clearly they aren't – discuss the menopause once more before Act One, I will seriously pass out.'

A gaggle of ladies and me congregate in the wings each night just before the show. Led by Jayne, the lady who plays my wife, all manner of lady issues are discussed, most of which I find fascinating. However, I'm not sure if I want to know who among the stage crew is still having their period, male or female. I've got to carry the show!

'How can I go on stage being bubbly and effervescent when all I can think of are these undead vaginas wandering round in the gloom behind me? It's too frightening.' I am in high spirits now.

'Just ask them not to talk about it,' laughs Erin.

'Already Mr Geoffrey has had to put me in thermals because various people insist that the stage is kept at sub-zero temperatures – which God knows must be eating into our profits. I won't mention any names and I hope I am not unsympathetic ...'

'Wait a minute,' interrupts Erin. 'Are you saying you're not sympathetic?'

'No, I'm saying I am.'

'But you're not,' says Erin.

Uh-oh! Home truth moment. I get busy with my make-up.

'You nearly made Jayne cry the other night. There.'

'Ow!'

She gives one final tug at my wig, picks up her box of tricks and moves on.

'You haven't been very nice to Jayne, it's true,' confirms Geoffrey a few minutes later.

I haven't. She drives me mad. Actually she is the best thing in the show, but I just want to slap her.

'Let's see what Madonna thinks.' Mr Geoffrey rolls his eyes and scrolls down the iPod. 'Forget everyone's menopause. *This* is putting you in the terrible mood.'

'Where Do We Go from Here' is my all-time Madonna favourite. It perfectly suits my mood, and soon Madge is soaring through the chorus boys' room at full blast.

'Where do we go from here? Life isn't what we thought it would be.' I mouth the words dementedly as I apply more make-up.

'My God,' says Mr Geoffrey, 'are you doing the show kabuki tonight? Ease off on the eyebrows.'

'Really?'

'Ladies and gentlemen, the house is now open,' says the tannoy, followed by all the usual apparitions.

At seven-fifteen Bruce Clinger arrives. He is the company manager. He really *is* a throwback to the old days. He is a giant with a bald pate and a potato nose. He is extremely earnest and shy, a gangly youth imprisoned in a large middle-aged body. He may have started off as a dancer because his huge feet in their beautifully polished shoes often find themselves in fifth position. He speaks Broadway, another echo of lost New York. He is a Jewish show queen who started in the seventies and worked his way up. He speaks humbly and carefully, pitched high and slightly adenoidal, and there are still reminders in his voice of a stubborn Hungarian grandmother who refused to learn English. I adore him. He weathers my mood swings with humour and patience. We have come through Signing-In Gate and Alcohol Gate. I have a glass of champagne in the interval. I always have. Apparently it's illegal and the theatre is going to be closed down, but we have reached a compromise. Paper cups.

Tonight I am spitting with fury at our producers. I think they are cheating me.

'Bruce, I want to see all the return sheets, please. I just don't understand why we are not making more money.'

'Oh gosh,' gasps Bruce. 'I didn't know there was a problem. I'll toyck to the office about it.'

I swivel in my chair towards him. 'I have a percentage, you know,' I say grandly.

Bruce steps on his feet and wrings his hands. 'Oh gosh. I'm really sorry you're upset.'

'Yes I am. Plus my back is *agony*. I could hardly get up off that fucking sofa yesterday in Act One.' Etc.

He is funny and shortly we are laughing. In my egocentric madness I am soon convinced he is falling in love with me and, like one of those old drunken stage hags on the skids who have to suck the lifeblood from anything on three legs to survive, I decide to make him a project. Mr Geoffrey says I must have projects to get me through the run.

'I've decided to make Bruce fall in love with me,' I say one matinée afternoon.

'It may not be as easy as you think,' snips Mr Geoffrey, arranging some flowers. He is still angry with me for stepping on his hand.

Madonna joins in the conversation from the speakers. 'Where do we go from here?'

'You said I had to have projects.'

'Not that kind.'

A couple of days ago I stand on Mr Geoffrey's hand during the quick change and he has a meltdown, even accusing me of being drunk. I am quite shocked.

'This is my livelihood,' he screams, nursing the poor hand in front of my face. 'How will I work if I can't use my hands?'

'I'm terribly sorry, Mr Geoffrey.'

I am mortified, although at the same time I think to myself: this is all a bit *Les Mis*, with the hand and the livelihood, but anyway a wise mistress says nothing.

The next day Mr Geoffrey is in the room ironing as usual, when I come up the stairs. He is white. I am quite nervous myself.

'Sit down,' he says before I even get through the door.

I obey.

'Rupert, I am so sorry that I went off on you last night.' He puts his hand in front of his mouth and looks at me with those silly wide Polish blue eyes and then bursts into tears. 'I don't know what happened. I guess I'm just tired.'

'Oh thank God, Mr Geoffrey. I thought you were never going to forgive me.'

'Of course I'm going to forgive you.'

We hug and sob and are discovered thus by Bruce.

'I hope I'm not interrupting anything.'

'That's fine, Bruce. Come in.'

'You remember you were asking about percentages.' Bruce is wringing his hands again.

'Oh, yes,' I reply loftily, regretting that outburst of the other day.

'Well, God, you know, I don't know how to put this, but you don't *have* a percentage.' He looks terrified, his mouth fixed in a terrible smile.

'I don't?'

'You don't.'

'Oh, how very discouraging.'

'I'm sorry,' sighs Bruce, but he gives me my per diems instead.

On preview nights Michael Blakemore our director clambers up to the chorus boys' room, slightly breathless. He is eighty-one years old with a bad knee and the climb is steep. Michael is a wise owl of a director with a magnificent head of white hair. He has sat through rehearsals hardly moving a muscle, observing us through ringed eyes – solemn and all-seeing, occasionally hooting the odd direction, consulting his French's acting edition of the play for Coward's original stage directions. Now he can be spotted during the previews in the stalls – a solitary figure with a plastic bag – in a different seat each night. In real life I am myopic but for some reason as soon as I get on stage I develop X-ray vision and I can always spot him, sitting rigid, a homeless person in a trance wedged into the animated crowd.

His face is completely inscrutable, even when Angela neatly cuts three-quarters of the play during an early preview and finds herself saying the lines of the last act during the first scene. It threatens to be a short evening but there isn't a trace of emotion on Michael's face as we turn the ship about and clumsily tack our way back to the beginning of the play. He is a great director with the strangest method. He does nothing. He watches and waits for the actors to discover themselves, nudging us gently into a performance with a raised finger and an ambivalent phrase ('I'm not sure whether I would do that'), so that the process seems effortless and our own invention.

During an early set-to in the rehearsal room, he suggests that I simply drop the glass I am holding and freeze when I see the ghost of my ex-wife, while of course I want to have a full-blown fit. I loftily announce that I am not prepared to simply be everybody's feed.

'Well, what do you want to be, then? An epileptic?' he asks, fixing me with his owlish eyes, the slightest hint of an upward inflection in his expressive voice. (He is from Australia and speaks in a divine dialect, now extinct, shared with other Antipodeans of his generation and profession – Coral Browne, Peter Finch – in which the cheerful twang of New South Wales is channelled into the frosty clip-clop of Received Pronunciation.)

'What do you want to *do*?' he asks again.

'I want to steal the show,' I shriek maniacally.

'I don't know how happy Angela will be with that,' he replies, laughing. 'Remember Coward played this role. He knew how to look after himself. Don't worry. You'll be terrific. But if you want to have a fit, it's fine with me.'

It transpires that he was in the first play I ever saw (aged six), playing Badger in *The Wind in the Willows*. He is telling a story about it one day – how the eighty-year-old actor playing Mole falls from the stage into the orchestra pit during a matinée but is back on stage that night – and a brain cell burps from the hidden depths and suddenly I remember everything, the river bank, the girl with long hair singing, Toad Hall, and an alarming battle with some weasels. From now on I call him Badger.

On the night before he returns to London he comes to the dressing room to say goodbye.

'Look after him,' he instructs Mr Geoffrey.

I am almost in tears. He has become my father in this uncertain time and with his departure the prison sentence of the run is suddenly a harsh reality. 'I want to go home too,' I whine.

'It'll go by in a flash,' says Badger.

'I rather wish I hadn't settled on quite such an energetic performance.'

'Well, you wanted to steal the show.' We hug and I watch him lumber down the endless stairs. At the bottom he turns. 'You did, you know.'

'Did what?'

'Steal the show. Speak soon.'

And he turns away, waving, while I collapse on the floor sobbing.

'Save your acting for the show,' says Mr Geoffrey, yanking at my bow tie and brushing me down.

Over the road from the theatre is Sardi's, the most famous restaurant in New York. The faces of bygone Broadway stars, caricatures with vast heads and noses balanced upon hopeless matchstick physiques, cover the walls above faded velvet banquettes where groups of ancient Americans congregate before a matinée, dressed for *Rosemary's Baby*. The waiters are a mafia – often as ancient as their

clientele – and have perfected the art of passive aggression. They listlessly serve specialities that include Sardi's wilted salad – comprising
a sliced gherkin like a hepatoid cat's tongue over a gigantic slice of
tomato surrounded by dangerous-looking drops of pus. New York
should really be renamed the big tomato.

The golden days at Sardi's are over, but this year, the year I get old,
it suits me perfectly. I sit at the same table every day. I make friends
with all the sour-faced waiters. Like me, they have been embittered,
and need only a little tickle to cheer them up. I know I've won over
the hardest case of all with my special needs charm when I place an
order and he looks at me for a second.

'I wouldn't have that if I was you.'

'Why, thank you, Charlie. I'll take your advice,' I reply.

From then on he winks every time he walks by.

Some days I can hardly face going into the theatre so I cut into
Sardi's and head straight for the bar where I order a vodka martini
with a twist. I settle on a stool in the window and observe the comings
and goings over the road at the Shubert.

Many of our audience members have been fans of Angela's since
Gaslight. They are fork-lifted from buses in knots of Zimmer frames
and walking sticks. They are absolutely charming and are going to
love the show. I think theatre should be banned for the under-sixties.

Our poster, as high as the theatre itself, covers the side wall on
Shubert Alley. We are all looking into the crystal ball, but I don't
need to be a clairvoyant to know that this job is not going to be the
stepping stone back to the West Coast as I had planned it to be. I
didn't even get a Tony nomination. As if reading my gloomy
thoughts, Charlie joins me at the window.

'You gotta be a fool to be in this business,' he says.

'Mine or yours, Charlie?'

'Both. Too much bending over.' Charlie rubs his back, winking.

'Certainly *not* backwards, in your case,' I reply.

And there we leave it. My own caricature now hangs in Sardi's.
That's something.

CHAPTER TWENTY-SIX

Tasha

Tonight the lights are all out on Broadway because Natasha Richardson is dead. She falls on a ski slope in Canada, gets up, goes back to her hotel, has a headache and then goes into a coma. Brain-dead, she is flown back to New York, while her family rush from all corners of the world to her bedside. Finally gathered, the decision is made to turn off her life support system. Her organs are removed – someone is looking through her forget-me-not eyes right now – and she is pronounced dead in the late afternoon three days after the accident. Tonight her mother Vanessa, and her two sisters, Joely and Katharine, lead a vigil in Shubert Alley as the lights are turned out and everybody pauses for thought.

I watch this spectacle on the television in my dressing room, getting ready for the play. On the little screen Vanessa, Joely and Katharine are bundled up against the cold just yards away from where I'm sitting. Mr Geoffrey is ironing in the background. The cartoon voice of the Eyewitness News presenter talks about shock and death and bewilderment, and the tannoy announces show time. Life has taken a virtual turn. I am watching on TV something that is actually happening on the other side of the wall, to people I have known very well, and, for a second, time literally stands still.

Last Tuesday I am running out of the theatre and, in that little vestibule between the stage door and the interior, I find Natasha with an older lady in tow, in the middle of a spirited confrontation with Rose and the no-neck redneck who operates as a bouncer at the stage door after the show. Natasha's voice is raised and she is stabbing at the bouncer with her finger. Her friend confirms everything Natasha is saying, like a back-up singer in little bursts between Natasha's belted-out melodies. Rose, who knows who Natasha is but is trapped inside her cubicle, two hands on the glass, looks desperately round for help. It's a small space, a lot of people coming in and out, and a hungry public are crammed against the stage door, ready with their cameras flashing each time the golden gate is opened. Natasha has been made to stand in line by the loathsome bouncer.

'No Richardson here.' He frowns, checking his list. The name rings no bells and he shakes his head.

She has told him she is my friend, but he doesn't care. Someone in the crowd says, 'Hey! That's Na-tah-sha Richardson.'

'No Richardson here,' he chants, waving his clipboard.

'Tasha,' I say.

She turns to me, eyes wide, half laughing, half crying, a coiled spring. 'Rupsy, there you are!'

We hug and she is trembling like a leaf.

'What's happened?'

'You'll never believe it.'

I take her out of the throng to the staircase that leads underneath the stage. Her friend comes with her. Natasha explains and dabs her eyes with the corner of a tissue.

'He just shouted out Richardson! Richardson! Like a piece of meat.'

The bouncer himself appears, with some guests for one of the cast. 'There he is!' accuses Tasha.

He turns around. 'I gotta have names. It don't matter who the party is,' he declares, red-faced and blunt.

'But I'm a friend of the leading actor.'

'I don't know that,' says the pig, evenly.

'Yes you do. I told you.'

Now Mr Geoffrey appears, with Rose behind. Gale Natasha has swept us all up into a hurricane and everybody stops and turns.

'What's going on?' asks Mr Geoffrey nervously, and I swirl into action like a cyclone. I am incapable, in such electric surroundings, of anything else.

'This arsehole refused to let my friend come into the theatre.'

'I did not refuse. I just need names and then I need to check the names.'

'Oh, did you need to check Peter O'Toole last night? Did you make him tell you his name? What are you afraid of? This dangerous crowd?' As if by magic the stage door opens and a hundred jolly old ladies wave and blow kisses. The door slams shut again. 'I don't think so.'

'I don't need to listen to this,' shouts the pig.

'No, you don't. Leave.'

'Calma, calma,' tries Rose, while Mr Geoffrey hustles the bouncer back to his post outside the theatre.

Now Natasha laughs. She puts her hand to her chest, changes gear and ploughs right on. 'Sorry, darling. Anyway, you were great. Michael Blakemore said he had no idea you were such a good comedian. I said, we all know that! But what about that sofa?'

'I know.'

'It's awful. What are you up to?'

'I'm just running out for dinner. Robert's here. Did you know?' Robert is her ex-husband and one of my closest friends.

'No. I didn't.'

'Are you going in to see Angela?'

'Yes.'

I guide her there.

'We *must* meet up,' we say in unison, laughing and hugging. I knock on Angela's door and pass the two ladies into the room.

I blow a kiss and escape.

A week later.

'*Blithe Spirit* was the last play she saw,' Vanessa says in a strange musical voice, as if she is trying to work something out.

'Yes. Isn't that odd?' I reply.

She turns to me, those blue-diamond eyes dead with disappointment. 'Very.'

She leads me and Robert by the hand towards the open casket, in which Natasha lies, cocooned in white satin on a lacy pillow for eternity, in virginal white with rust-coloured make-up on her gaunt lifeless cheeks. Vanessa, like a seasoned undertaker, or an actress who has mastered a difficult prop, neatly lifts the bottom half of the casket lid to reveal a blue woollen blanket covering Tasha's legs.

'She loved this,' mouths the matriarch, stroking the body and kissing the hands of her dead daughter.

We must have terrified faces, because she looks up at Robert, with a classic Vanessa half-smile – biting her lip, boring into him with her burning eyes.

'You can kiss her,' she says.

'I will,' says Robert, but he doesn't. He touches her hands instead. They are beautiful. I never really noticed them when she was alive. Her long sensitive fingers are crossed over her belly and for a moment they seem to be rising and falling as she breathes. One hallucinates when confronted with death. We all look down into the coffin, searching for life, but it only whispers round the rigid features in the thousand memories of the living. Every past action has a new colour now, matched against the intractable black of death. It is quite overwhelming and makes me giddy.

As if sharing this sentiment, Vanessa briefly grips the side of the coffin with the same expressive hands and fingers as her daughter.

For a moment she looks as if she is going to fall but she gathers herself and sets off towards the other room.

'Come and see her!' she chants, arms wide, to the group hanging back.

Robert and I stand on either side of the coffin, lost in thought, searching the face for some recognisable trace, but death has sucked all the character away. It's unimaginable that Tasha's great big china-blue eyes are seeing for someone else right now. Her lashes lie against her cheek and tremble slightly at the hum of the outside world, the traffic, the brakes, horns and wailing sirens that she will never hear again. I look up at Robert. He changed his entire life for this woman.

Natasha and Robert get married during a cold grey weekend in February and we are all staying at the Wyndham just behind the Plaza, a shivering group of refugees from each corner of the globe. The Wyndham is a tall thin hotel favoured by writers and theatre folk, the last of the great theatrical B and Bs. Jessica Tandy and Hugh Cronin have a permanent suite there. Maria St Just supervises (terrorises) New York productions of Tennessee Williams's plays from Suite 43. It is dusty and overdecorated with vast swooshing curtains lined with plastic, complicated wallpapers (peeling) and lampshades dripping with tassles. Each room or suite has its own theme, and the lift trembles and groans up the building, driven by a series of sweet doddery lift boys. Somebody once said that to spend a night at the Wyndham is like waking up inside your grandmother's knickers. This fantastical hotel is perhaps not the best place from which to make a new start in life.

The evening before the wedding we have drinks in Robert's suite. The curtain is hanging off the rail in one corner and the tightly packed, blue-squiggle wallpaper has a damp patch over the bed. Natasha and her girlfriends briefly entertain us before leaving for their hen night, while we go for a grim bachelors' dinner at Elaine's. It is a drunken affair in that dismal eatery and nobody quite knows what's going on, but we all know something is. As it happens, last night the couple had a blinding fight and – unbeknown to the rest of us – are thinking of calling the whole thing off. But for the time being, Elaine hobbles about like the little clairvoyant from *Poltergeist*. Robert is a coiled spring and we have an early night but are nonetheless worn out by jet lag on the morning of the ceremony.

I am at breakfast downstairs in a nearby diner with Tony Richardson, Natasha's father, his best friend Jeremy Fry the inventor, and Annabelle Brooks, the beautiful gazelle who finally manages to snare my evasive friend Damian (Chapter 8) into marriage. She is everyone's mutual friend at the table. She used to go out with Jeremy's son Cosmo, and met Tony at a dinner party years ago where she caught fire, lighting a cigarette from a candelabra. A whole table of young county folk screamed with laughter that night – no one more than Annabelle, who didn't realise she was in flames until somebody doused her with Perrier. Dripping and smoking like a peat field, she turned back to her dinner companion and continued with the conversation they had been having. Tony falls in love. Annabelle is his kind of girl.

'Have you written your speech, Tony?' she asks now.

'A gloomy peace this morning with it brings, the sun for sorrow will not show his head . . . You know the rest.'

Tony recites from *Romeo and Juliet* in the voice that many people have tried – and failed – to impersonate. It is a famous voice: gloomy, deliberate, slightly breathless and utterly compelling. The winter sun shines on his face through the window. He looks ancient in it, as though he is made of dust, the crumbling statue of a Roman emperor. Any minute now a strong wind will blow him away. But not just yet.

He is still a strange magic character, like a magnet. Some things (us) cling to him. Other people can't get away fast enough. He is a director on set and off, quietly manipulating the present company – be they civilians or pros – into confrontations and reconciliations, prodding them with a well-placed niggle, an innocent enquiry, so that lunches and dinners become explosive theatrical events. Everyone loses their heads around Tony, and are drawn – against their wishes sometimes – into the fantastical dramas he weaves, a twentieth-century Prospero. This latest one, the compact between Robert and Natasha, has not been of his making, and right up until today he has doggedly aired his reservations.

'I don't see why they can't just keep on as usual,' he says for the thousandth time.

'But they're in love,' pleads Annabelle.

'Don't be ridiculous. I'm not saying they shouldn't be together. Just not marriage. It never works.'

'You're always telling me and Annabelle to get married,' I remind him.

'That's completely different. You and Annabella need one another.' At which point, looking fiercely at me through his eagle's eyes, he begins to chuckle. 'Oh, Roopsi Doopsie! What are we going to do with you? You're such a floozie.'

'I think they make a good couple, T,' says Jeremy Fry.

'You don't know what you're talking about, J. Look at you. Imagine if you got married to Medieval Garb, how sorry we'd all be?'

(Medieval Garb is Jeremy's boyfriend, a rather flighty opera director, who has long been the butt of Tony's humour. According to legend, he once came down to breakfast in a kimono and someone described it as Medieval Garb. The name stuck. He has since become the director of the Paris Opera.)

Jeremy sits next to Tony on the banquette. If Tony is white and gaunt, then Jeremy's face is the shape and colour of a beetroot. They are both craggy eccentric geniuses although Jeremy is at present flummoxed by his new invention – 'a revolving wheelchair', according to Tony. 'Have you ever heard of anything more ridiculous?'

Tony has been overlooked by Hollywood and reduced to TV movies. He is too clever for the new managerial LA. They have casually written off his vast talent.

Today they are both dressed scruffily – they never take luggage on a trip. They address one another by their initials. Like T, J is a dangerous enemy, particularly when drunk, but a great friend. (He will be sitting by Tony's bed the night he dies.)

The service itself takes place in the apartment of John Gregory Dunne and Joan Didion. In the photo, Robert – one of the best-looking men we all know – seems slightly chubby. (This is his last year of drinking.) Natasha looks beautiful but strained. The service is agnostic, ministered by a jolly dresser. There is no music and we all stand uncertainly, marooned on the slippery parquet of the Dunnes' drawing room, balancing delicious nibbles and high flutes of champagne, unsure what to do next. We are a group of marvellous eccentrics, yes, but not the youthful crowd one expects to see at a wedding. At a wedding everyone is looking forward. There is no past. Here everyone is looking over their shoulder, except for one guest who has mislaid his false teeth. Life has already crashed against this crowd – including the newlyweds – and the whole thing feels more like the Thanksgiving party of everyone's shrink than a wedding. The walls of the Dunnes' house are shiny grey, the colour of ghosts, and half the faces in the pictures are dead. Maria St Just, John Gregory Dunne, Tony and Jeremy and, of course, the bride herself.

The wedding breakfast – or late lunch – takes place in a dark restaurant with raw brick walls on the Upper East Side, where the theme tune from *The Godfather* plays endlessly. Tony doesn't recite the end of *Romeo and Juliet*. He gives a beautiful speech, talking about how he knew Robert's father and loved him. This means a lot to Robert who, I think, loves Tony more than Tasha.

Adding to the transitory nature of the event, everyone is leaving directly for the airport after the lunch, so we all have our bags. Annabelle and I are going back to LA. (I am making a film with an orang-utan in the morning.) Tony and Jeremy are leaving for Africa tonight, embarking on one of their legendary trips. No luggage and no medication for Tony, who is terribly unwell. He knows this. No one else does. Not even Robert and Natasha, who are going on their honeymoon in the morning.

Tony directs the party from a chair, forcing me and Vanessa to make headscarves out of napkins and sing 'How Do You Solve a Problem Like Maria'. It's a jolly pub wedding out of Dickens. My final image is of Robert and Natasha against the brick wall of the restaurant, laughing, smoking and drinking – as Vanessa and I bring the house down, and Tony watches like a wizard, knowing everything.

On the way to the airport, I have never felt so lost in my life.

Robert and I move from the coffin. It's another magnet and we pull ourselves away from it, while others succumb and are slowly enveloped by its field, edging closer and closer, while we struggle back to the living and join Tasha's half-sister Katharine and her mother Grizelda for a stiff drink. Tasha's head can be seen now, far away in a pool of light, rising out of the casket at the other end of the room. Now Vanessa and Uma Thurman are leaning over her. Vanessa holds Uma back like a heroine in a nineteenth-century melodrama. It is a theatrical wake for theatricals. We have played scenes like this in rep and on the West End stage. Some of us are better at it than others, but it is a brilliant way to deal with the tragedy. It's nearly show time for me so I say goodbye and leave.

Outside, the paparazzi have intensified, and a lady with a micro phone runs after me down the icy street.

'Can you talk to CNN?'

Natasha is flying to heaven on the red carpet. She is more famous today than she has ever been. Too late as usual! I walk over to Broadway across the frozen park in a strange, twisting mood, at once elated and regretful. Dirty snow is piled by the sides of the icy pathways. The lake is frozen. The city towers over the treetops, a galaxy of windows sparkling with life, while the dead whistle round the naked branches in the park below. They are wagging their fingers.

*

Tasha and I gave one another a wide berth while she was alive. We knew each other well, but despite many connections and similarities we didn't get along. Perhaps we were more alike than we cared to admit. Both of us dreamt, after all, of entirely different careers for ourselves than the ones that we ultimately achieved. (She wanted to be Vivien Leigh and I wanted to be Montgomery Clift.) Both of us had a sharp tongue concerning others, oversensitivity about ourselves, equal doses of practicality and hysteria, and a stumped vulnerability on the various crossroads of our private lives. Both of us tried endlessly to remodel ourselves – physically and psychologically – for those elusive conventional careers. The fact is, we were both better character actors than love interests. We both passed through periods of excess. They just didn't coincide.

By the time I reach Columbus Circus I have plunged into a terrible depression but it's too late. Suddenly I see the fiasco at the stage door in a new light. Tasha was holding out an olive branch, and it all went wrong. It's quite an effort, after all, to come and see someone in a show. Why didn't I ask her to dinner that night after the play? It *was* strange that the last show she saw was mine and a play about death. She could have been in it, actually, and still be here.

Life's too short to bear a grudge. But I did.

CHAPTER TWENTY-SEVEN

Death Threats

I am crossing Eighth Avenue on the afternoon Michael Jackson dies. You don't need to see it on the TV or read about it in the news. It is passed mouth to mouth along the street, like a cold.

'No shit,' says a Puerto Rican boy with cornrows. He turns to me – a complete stranger. 'Michael Jackson's dead!'

'You're kidding?'

My heart races as we cross the street. Coming towards us like a wave, the crowd on the other side have already been hit with the news. In the middle of the road a big fat girl bursts into tears. She stands there as the lights change and the traffic swarms around her. 'Michael!' she wails. Somebody guides her to the other side.

It is matinée day in theatre land. There are queues around the block, and they are falling over with the news like skittles or playing cards, passing the tragedy down the line to the poor person at the end who screams it to the street. I rush into the theatre.

'Have you heard?' asks Rose, glued to her transistor TV set.

'Yes,' I reply.

'I can't believe it!' she stammers. We are friends now, Rose and I.

In the dressing room Mr Geoffrey is ironing in front of the TV and crying – very *Cage aux Folles* – but this is no time for jokes. Life carries on mechanically, one eye trained on the TV, where the tribute biographies are already running. Again and again we hear the 911 phone call, set against footage of the ambulance arriving at the hospital, the aerial shot of the house, the tour rehearsals, all the highlights and lowlights of Michael's incredible life. Sitting with Bubbles, going to court in pyjamas, dancing cartwheels on stage as a little boy, sitting in the branches of a tree aged forty, giving the fatal interview to the vile Mr Bashir. (I wonder how he is sleeping tonight.) The images of Michael's face, one superimposed upon another, from the beautiful black youth to the chalk-white child-catcher, are a kind of postmodern *Dorian Gray*, a portrait of the Afro-American struggle that has turned from *The Slave* into *The Scream*. Weaving through the scandal, the same image returns. A little black boy singing and dancing cartwheels.

Connie (my PR) has organised for me to do an interview with the *Daily Mirror* in London. I have been putting it off but finally the date is set with their US showbiz correspondent for an early dinner before the show.

The journalist is a fabulous Fleet Street slapper, middle-aged, from Middlesex, living in Manhattan. She has big round Liza Minnelli eyes and of course we talk a lot about Michael Jackson. She has just got back from LA where she was sent as soon as the news broke, and where she managed to get the cellphone number of Michael's bodyguard (the famous 911 call), and she was driving around LA on the day of the death, trying to talk to him, while all the other hacks were following the same fabulous lead.

'Very *Wacky Races*,' I say and she laughs.

I have nothing against journalists. We're all trying to make a living, after all, and the pressure on writers is enormous. Being an occasional journalist myself, I am sympathetic to the struggle. Getting an interview out of a cagey celebrity – who is unwilling to enjoy or see the fact that he or she is either a cunt or a sex maniac or broke or on drugs or whatever – can be like getting blood out of a stone. From our point of view – the people who need to promote – these monsters are surely some of the hazards we must cheerfully embrace, and generally I try to give my best. Plus I adore the ingenuity of some of the sleuthing. This lady actually slips into Michael's wake, just three rows away from the golden coffin. I am impressed.

We talk about other things of course during the interview, but one thing is absolutely clear and we return to it many times. We both adore Michael and are miserable that he has died.

Imagine my surprise and horror, then, when Connie calls me up at about six o'clock one morning.

'Darling, London calling. What's going on? Have you gone mad?'

'What time is it?'

'Darling, the press are going crazy after what you said about Michael Jackson.'

Now I wake up. 'What did I say?'

'I'll read it to you.'

I groan. I hate Connie reading. It takes for ever. She clears her throat.

'This is the headline, darling. It's quite bad actually. "Why Michael Jackson deserved to die."'

'Whaaat?'

'Yes! I don't know what to do.'

She reads me the entire interview and I nearly faint. Everything I have said has been completely reorganised. It is unbelievable.

'Did you call Michael a freak?' asks Connie.

'Yes. Of course. He is. But I didn't say it rudely. She understood precisely my tone.'

'Did you say he deserved to die?'

'No. I *said*—'

'Darling, you don't have to scream at me. I'm only your poor PR. I spoke to the editor and she said it's all on the tape.'

Very artfully, this hag – or one of her swamp bitch colleagues – has strung my actual words into something completely contrary to the spirit of our discussion. I am apoplectic with rage. I immediately ring the editor of the *Mirror* – who is a friend – I have, after all, been a 3 a.m. girl in my time. He promises to look into it and says that he will print whatever I want to say, but the damage is done. Connie tries to field the press but one explosive interview in the *Inverness Herald* turns global if the wind is in the wrong direction, and pretty soon I am the lead story on Perez Hilton. Mr Geoffrey isn't talking to me. (Again.) I feel miserable. On the other hand the ingenuity of the press is impressive. Having more or less engineered Michael's death by their relentless smears, they must now change their tune in order not to look guilty. They need to find other people to shovel the shit for them. I am today's scapegoat.

The first death threat arrives at the theatre a few days later. At first I suspect Mr Geoffrey, but I can see that he is as surprised as I am to read it. Its message is simple and to the point.

'You are going to die. Make peace with your God.'

Actually, I am rather chuffed. A death threat? *Moi?* The idea of being gunned down during a performance of *Blithe Spirit* is of course thrilling. On the other hand when the second one comes I wonder if I should call Interpol.

'Not Interpol, you silly fairy. You are locked in the sixties!' snips Mr Geoffrey, swishing from the room.

And then I think, fuck it. I can't be bothered. Blogsville seethes with hatred, and actually I feel quite deflated because I loved Michael Jackson. Luckily nobody remembers anything these days, and my killers think better of murdering me, but I will not talk to the *Daily Mirror* again. They have become too slutty. Even for me.

It is the last Sunday of July, and one of the first beautiful days. Spring has been wet and cold and a strange tropical summer has settled on New York. It has rained ceaselessly, and the city swelters in a sticky mist. But today there is a light breeze and a clear blue sky as I leave my key under the mat, listen out for one last subway train rattling beneath the street and set off for the Shubert Theatre one last time.

As Angela said last week at our farewell lunch, 'You see. You did it. You thought you would never make it but you did. You gave a hundred per cent in every show.'

I should really take a full page in *Variety* for the quote.

We are waiting in the wings for the last time in our usual huddle. The hum of the audience becomes denser and denser on the other side of the curtain as various announcements call them to prayer and suddenly it's exciting again. Please take your seats. The performance is about to begin.

'For the last time!' we all chant in a chorus.

The whole event is about to tumble into oblivion. A play exists only in the moment, remembered in conversation and a few faded photographs, but when the curtain comes down for the last time, a play is dead. In show business we die again and again and again. Everything suddenly has a new intensity. Jayne, my wife in the play, picks up her bunch of flowers to take on stage. We hug. I have exhausted her, driven her mad, but it's all in the past now. I climb the scaffold to my little perch above the stage for the last time and get ready for my Act One walkdown. I have a great entrance in this show. I surge onto the stage from a large sweeping staircase to rapturous applause (sort of). Up here I can survey the whole machine in action. Stagehands whisper into their headsets. The front of house manager comes through the pass door with the all clear. Standing on the other side of the stage, waiting to go on, Dr and Mrs Bradman greet me in mime. Simon Jones bows elaborately. Tooly curtseys. We are all ready.

The lights and the chatter fade to a buzz and black. The curtain goes up and Jayne strides into the light with her flowers. Her voice sounds heightened and disembodied from here – like an old recording – thrown as it is into the vast auditorium, while in the gloom of the backstage area Mr Geoffrey prowls about, organising the clothes for my first (and last) quick change, and Ara gets on with her knitting.

One last glass of champagne at the back of the stage with Christine, my dead wife. It has become our little tradition. We have sat here day after day, huddled against the back of the set, whispering and laughing, and we have come to know each other very well. We have given one another careful notes, suggestions – 'Do you have to clear your throat before every joke?' – and aired ancient grievances – 'Are you ever going to forgive me for not learning my lines?'

Christine has delicious butterscotch throat lozenges and we both have one. She is an extraordinary show creature – unrecognisable as herself. As Elvira she is a Hollywood goddess from the fifties, a night-club hostess from paradise – with a peroxide wig and Marilyn make-up. In real life I have hardly ever seen her since rehearsals. (One day a German housewife waves at me from across the street. She is pulling a case on wheels, and I wave blankly back. It is Christine. We walk towards the theatre – strangers almost in our civvies.) We meet each night behind the stage, strapped up, covered in glue and slap. Christine comes from musicals so knows all the tricks of the trade. Tonight she looks about eighteen as she surveys me through those gigantic lashes for one last home truth, and I answer back through painted lips.

We are not ourselves and so have revealed everything to each other in these stolen moments before Act Two. We each found the other bossy – my word – and controlling – her word, during rehearsals, but we adore each other by the end of the run and she is the only one – apart from Mr G – with whom one can have a constructive and insightful bitch about the rest of the cast. She is also a conspiracy theorist and, looking back on this season of Obamania on Broadway, everything she says about 'that man' in our secret moments has more or less come true.

'Never again,' we both say at least three nights a week of the Broadway experience, but we say it with that rueful smile that knows. Until the next time.

During the final interval I sit in my empty dressing room with Mr Geoffrey. He is packing one last bag. I am smoking a joint. We are in high spirits but we know that it is quite likely we will never meet again – or even if we do it won't be the same.

'Listen, babe, I'm going to shoot right off after the show,' he explains as he folds.

'Me too. We're not going to say goodbye now, are we?'

'No, but in case we don't catch each other later . . .'

And we both burst into tears.

Before the last act we congregate on the stage, exhausted. Angela lies on the sofa. I sit on the end. Christine and Jayne are perched on an armchair. I wiggle Angela's foot for the last time.

'How are you, Angela?'

'Dead. Thank God it's over,' she replies and the curtain rises.

Pretty soon I am alone on the stage, doing the final speech. The spotlights glare and a thousand faces hang on my every word. It's magic.

'I'm going a long way away,' I say and the words have a special weight. 'Somewhere you'll never find me. Goodbye, my darlings. Parting is such sweet sorrow.'

I always play it bitter-sweet and tonight it is sadder than ever. The two invisible ghosts trash the set. Curtains are torn down. The piano lid slams up and down. Books fly from the shelves and – our own special effect – the tree outside the big bay window crashes into the room. I duck off stage and the whole cast is standing in the wings screaming while the audience applaud and whistle and someone even calls, 'Encore!'

'You gotta be kidding,' laughs Angela.

We fix the glittering smiles on our faces for the last standing ovation. In the waves of applause all the rancour of the last few months evaporates and we all smile fondly at one another. The curtain falls for the last time and it is over. Almost immediately the crew begin dismantling the set. Another show will be on the stage next week.

There are drinks upstairs so no one says goodbye.

The chorus boys' dressing room is bare now. Mr Geoffrey is nowhere to be seen. My bags are in the car. I sit in front of the mirror and cross off the last date on the calendar I painted in make-up on my first day.

'Are you coming to the party?' calls Erin from the bottom of the stairs.

'In a minute,' I shout back.

'One. Singular. Sensation,' I whisper to myself in the mirror. I take one last look around the room.

Then I steal down the fire escape and through that maze of passages to the stage door of another theatre on another street where the car is waiting to take me to the airport.

It is a creamy and beautiful dusk. The streets are packed. Restaurants overflow onto the sidewalks. Taxis screech to a halt as the lights change and crowds advance like armies from either side of the wide avenues. It is New York at its best. The river twinkles below as I drive over the rusty old Triboro Bridge. Manhattan gleams like a mirage on the other side of the water.

I may not have thrown double sixes in the Monopoly game. I didn't get rave reviews. I have not been flooded with offers and won't be going out to the coast like Eve Harrington. But maybe I achieved something better. I never flaked out. My cellphone is in my hand. I chuck it out of the window. Ciao, Manhattan!

EPILOGUE

CHAPTER TWENTY-EIGHT

The Grim Reaper in Wiltshire

Crouched by the brook in the water meadow of our hidden valley, enclosed within a labyrinth of high brick walls, it looks suddenly like the house of death. That's the first thought that strikes me when I come through the gate at the top of the garden. A hush falls over a house when the grim reaper approaches. Tonight he is coming across the gloaming, on the crimson fingertips of the sun, gilding the edges of the house as it drags the day behind the ridge. The moon is already a vague smudge and all the scents of summer explode with the oncoming night. A window opens.

'Is that you, darling? I'm just bringing Daddy downstairs.'

Coming through the back door – the same noisy latch – it has become an old people's house in the six short months since my last visit. There is an abandoned wheelchair outside in the garage and a faint smell of disinfectant; the loo in the hall has arms while our pièce de résistance, which has shocked many a guest, is a chairlift, which tonight brings my dad – like Katharine Hepburn in *Suddenly Last Summer* – crashing through the ceiling into the study from his bedroom above. It's a great entrance, and my father beams with pleasure as he is transferred from the lift via the wheelchair to his magic armchair, which rises and falls like a slow-motion ejector seat at the touch of a button. Daddy can no longer walk.

We have tea. Death comes in with the familiar noise of the trolley clattering through the hall.

My father listens to my mother's quiz with his ear cocked, laughs occasionally, but says little. My mother wants to know all the details, who was where and what they all said and 'What an awful bore that you didn't get a Tony.'

'What did I do?' asks Daddy, confused.

'A Tony, Daddy. It's an award. Not *you!*'

Mummy and I laugh and Daddy says, 'Slow down.'

'Forget an actual Tony. What about a nomination?'

I am always trying to bring my mother down to earth concerning my career, although there's little point. As far as she's concerned, I am the most famous and successful actor in the world and that's that. That I don't accept this written-in-stone *fact* is something to do with self-hatred and all other newfangled weirdnesses we young go on about.

As in all good plays, the conversation at tea never stops, one person's line drifts seamlessly into the next, with the appropriate pauses for laughter. My mother is lively and funny and happy to bring some high spirits into the room where otherwise there is only the grim reaper and the news for company.

'Shall we have some news?' suggests my father casually for the tenth time today.

'But you've just had it, darling,' my mother quips, pouring us all more tea.

'Oh, really?' he asks with deep interest.

'Yes, really. You're going to bore me soon if you just watch the news non-stop. It'll make you gaga.'

'Thank you,' he sings, reaching slowly with shaking fingers for a crumpet.

*

Summer wanes, observed by my father in his chair under a rug from his favourite spot in the garden. The first falling leaves are reflected in the one dark glass of his spectacles. It's the only movement on a face lost in contemplation.

Soon it is too cold to sit outside and he comes into the house for the last time. As the big autumn winds howl across the plain, stripping the trees bare, shaking the windows and doors, my father turns with the whole globe towards the frozen slumber of winter. His breath shortens with the days. He calmly observes the world like an old dog in his electric armchair by day or his electric bed by night – all operated by Mummy with a dial – watching the news from various different positions. The news is one of the rocks to which he clings, reminding him briefly of himself. Life reduces to a pinpoint, like the follow-spot on a face at the end of a play fading to black. In the last glimmer of light some things remain. Daddy still loves women and drink although his methods of flirtation have become confused.

'How's your drinking problem?' he asks his favourite girlfriend who comes to lunch one day.

'Fine, thank you very much. How's yours?' that lady snaps back, quick as a whip.

'Not very good. I'm being bullied if you must know.'

Drinking – another of the rocks – has become a preoccupation, the last rebellion.

'Can I have some more beer, please?' he asks in a sing-song schoolboy voice.

'No, darling. You're only having one nowadays, remember?'

Pause.

'Oh dear. Am I?'

My brother comes up with the idea of mixing his Speckled Hen light ale with alcohol-free beer. It works. For a while. At first he can't believe his luck. Four beers at lunch!

'I should really be more drunk by now, you know,' he confides to me secretly one day.

'Well, how marvellous that you're not, don't you think?'

'I'm not sure. I rather like it, you know.'

Sometimes he stares like a cat at a parallel universe, standing on its edge.

'Yes, vu-rry,' he says, answering some complicated philosophical question.

'Very what, Daddy?'

'I forget. What *was* it?'

Sometimes he watches something closely and in detail. Sometimes he searches your face for a clue. Often he nods off. Occasionally he is on form. Sex is a subject that is always sure to get both my parents laughing, coming as they do from a generation unequipped for discussion about such personal issues – 'not happy-clappy like you'. I can have them both in hysterics with a couple of well-aimed questions. On homosexuality, for example, of which, despite her best intentions, my mother is thoroughly distrustful. She confronts my father with gales of laughter when I say, 'Daddy had tons of affairs at Stonyhurst. Didn't you, Daddy?'

'Darling, you didn't, did you?'

My father, who can't swallow properly any more and is always choking, is heaving slowly with mirth. He rolls his eyes, and starts to choke.

'Oh Mummy, really,' he snorts, getting out his large red and white hanky and blowing his nose loudly and sneezing at the same time. 'Of course we did.'

'*No!*'

He sneezes again.

'*Yes.*'

One night I ask my mother if she can remember her best sexual experience. This question, needless to say, brings the house down.

'Making you,' says my father, after the laughter subsides.

'Darling, what *do* you mean?' asks Mummy, aghast.

'Making you,' he repeats, to arpeggios of glee from his wife.

'Oh, Tony, you do make me laugh.'

She is on the move again, cantering off to the kitchen to finish dinner. The grim reaper slips back into the room.

'That's why you're so special,' Daddy says. 'Could I have some more beer?'

The cold weather arrives and the house crackles and groans with heat – for once. My mother keeps her husband moving by the sheer force of her personality. He is longing to retire to his bed, but she knows that as soon as that happens, it will be the end, and although he drives her mad, she can't let him go. They have been married, after all, for fifty years.

And so he is moved around like a valuable vase. His handlers are Steve, Marianne, Rachel and Lauren. They are saints. They arrive in the kitchen at eight in the morning where my mother is a whirling dervish in her dressing gown.

'Goodness, is that the time? I'm still undressed.'

She storms around her house like a character in a computer game, ducking through low doorways, swinging around corners and screeching up the stairs. She tiptoes only when she opens the door to my father's shrouded room each morning with her heart in her mouth. Will he still be alive?

'Just a few more minutes,' is all he needs to say for her to speed off – clomp clomp clomp – down the stairs to get his breakfast tray ready with which she miraculously appears through the floor of his room in the lift a few minutes later.

Marianne, his lovely German nurse, is a much slower character than my mother, and loves to chew the cud downstairs in the kitchen.

'Come on, everyone,' says Mummy. 'Let's not sit around, shall we?'

Marianne is full of surprises. For example, she is a nudist and has a tattoo on her bottom, which she has shown my father. Daddy has forgotten what a tattoo is.

'Marianne has drawn a map on her bottom,' he says one day at lunch.

'What on earth do you mean, Tony?' asks my mother.

'She showed it to me.'

'What?' shrieks Mummy.

'At least, I'm pretty sure she did.' Daddy can still back-pedal.

Mummy harbours a competitive streak, born years ago on the lacrosse field, encouraged now by Steve, and while she needs to have help looking after my father – she is exhausted – she hates to relinquish one hairbrushing.

I sit in the middle of this rush-hour traffic, trying to keep calm, but it is impossible. My mother is happy only when everyone is on the run, and she's right in a way. The grim reaper can't operate amid all this movement, and so the major plods on across the high pass, slowly but surely, with much elegance, considering how reduced are his circumstances. All in all, his old age has been a great success, and I can't find in myself a heavy heart. He has finally become the person he has always wanted to be.

'After all,' I reason to my mother, 'I will die alone in the actors' rest home. If I'm lucky some dresser fairy from the theatre where I have my final seizure will come to prise the amethyst ring from my bloated finger, but otherwise . . .'

'That's why I wished you'd got married,' says my mother sympathetically.

Marianne baths my father with the greatest care. She shaves him, brushes his teeth and gets him dressed. He comes down on his chair-lift at about eleven o'clock for Nescafé in the kitchen.

'Oh thank you, darling,' he says to Steve who gives him his cup – the same large white cup with worn-out hunting scenes round the sides that he has had his coffee and tea in since the sixties.

'It's Steve, Major.'

'Oh really? Oh God!'

Steve and I meet regularly in the pub at the end of our village. Walls have ears at home, and here we can discuss 'the situation' at our leisure. The situation being the handling of the two old people in our care. The Swan is another thatched throwback, poised like my father on the edge of extinction. An extortionate rent and the increasing risks involved in drunk driving are squeezing the life out of it. But for the time being it is a cosy black-beamed backwater, a low snug with a smoking fire and a German helmet hanging above it filled with flowers.

In his regular corner stands Dave Smith, the last local man, studying his nightly pint, speaking to no one, while the rest of the villagers are now professional commuters with eighteen cars each, or army officers on their way back from Tidworth or Porton Down. No one from the housing estate on the hill comes in. The Swan is too sedentary for them. They prefer the rowdier atmosphere of Amesbury where thrilling squaddies crash loo seats over one another's heads.

Steve can be found here most evenings at six-thirty and that's where we meet. My parents, brought up not to frequent bars, are nevertheless fascinated by the pub and all its travails but never dare to go there for a drink. My mother particularly thinks she knows everything that is going on within its walls, including how many pints Steve has before coming home. What she doesn't know is that Steve has fallen in love with the girl who works behind the bar and pretty soon they are having a baby. This news has been imparted to me and I am instructed to break it to them how and when I want. It doesn't go down very well, partly because Steve already has two other families further up the vale, and partly because my parents feel themselves to be the moral compass of the county, and, like the Queen, have a divine right to lofty views.

But Steve is a kind of saint, very attractive to women, and made to be a father. He is a character from Hardy, large with a cheerful, handsome face. He is extremely resourceful, loyal, funny and still knows all the country secrets that everyone else has forgotten. His latest child Lewis is born two weeks before my father's death, and the last picture I have of my dad is of him holding little Lewis in his arms. It is a strange snapshot – two creatures at either end of the spectrum, neither of them really aware that the other is there. It is uplifting and depressing at the same time. The thought of the long hard slog, getting from one end to the other, is shattering when you're in the middle. Steve's elder son Rob works behind the bar in the Swan, and listens disinterestedly as we discuss the situation. A teenager is not remotely interested in death.

On the last Tuesday of my father's life we have dinner in his room. My mother and I sit at a card table at the end of his bed. I am perched on the corner, she sits in his wheelchair. Daddy lies against the cushions with his glasses off and his hair brushed back. His eyes glitter. He's having a vision. It's us, flickering like an electric light. Perhaps he knows that it will soon snap off so he watches with all his strength. My mother and I chat at him and he beams back but something is suddenly revealed. He gasps and lifts his hands in defence, eyes wide and glassy. It passes.

'I think you had another TIA, darling,' says my mother, scrutinising him closely.

He is used to the process now. Rooms expand and contract, colours flare and fade as his faltering heart pumps blood into the far reaches of the optic nerve, slowly and weakly, but he is no longer concerned. He has given himself to the flow. It is carrying him now through eddies of consciousness, from the shallows to the depths and back again.

'Do you mind awfully if I say goodnight?' he says.

'But darling! Ru has come all the way down from London.'

He looks at me for a long moment, lips strangely pursed. 'Has he?' he finally asks in a dreamy voice.

I wiggle his big toe through the blanket.

I never see him again.

On Wednesday morning they both fall over in the downstairs loo and can't get up. The wheelchair has got stuck against the door. My father is too heavy for my mother to lift on her own and so they wait for Stevie Wonder to appear.

They are a funny sight. A woman of seventy-two sitting on the loo with a ninety-year-old man with his trousers down, lying at her feet. The walls of the small room are covered with mementoes – *Spy* and Giles cartoons; a *Playboy* calendar from the seventies; photographs of the family – me in films, my brother in helicopters, school groups, army groups. Their whole life is looking down on them.

'You've been a great support to me,' Daddy says deliberately. 'Thank you.'

The hall clock strikes the hour.

On Thursday morning with the usual clatter my mother appears over the horizon with a smoked haddock.

'I don't want it,' he says flatly.

'You've got to eat.'

My mother puts it down in front of him, whipping round the room like a force ten wind, opening curtains, fixing a napkin to his pyjamas, preparing medication, before stopping for a moment to watch him. He is sitting up with his eyes shut.

'Darling, come on. You're going to die if you don't eat.'

With that she storms back downstairs and my father dies alone with a haddock on a plate, simply and without fuss, in his cream-panelled bedroom, looking through the window at the wintry garden that he will wander from now on only as a ghost.

Coffee is at eleven o'clock as usual, and so they are sitting around my father's bed, my mother, Rachel our lovely cleaning lady, Marianne, Steve, and Colin Fox the vicar. They each have a cup and saucer. My father lies dead between them.

'He looks so peaceful,' says my poor mother, who is holding herself together remarkably well. He doesn't actually, but everyone says that. The dead look dead. Drained. His lips have sunk. His skin is ice cold. He lies on the pillow with his hair brushed and his hands over his chest and the room is an empty shell. My mother holds his finger.

'Oh dear, he used to say this finger always hurt. I'm afraid I wasn't very sympathetic.'

She cries. Grief turns her back into a young girl before my eyes, the mother who used to weep as the school train pulled out of King's Cross, a young, tender, unsure creature. I had completely forgotten about her.

A little later I creep back into his room to sit with him alone. The silence buzzes. The face of my father has sunk further. On serious issues we have never talked and we never will.

The nearest Daddy and I ever get to 'one of those chats' is a conversation in a taxi in the autumn of 2001. We are driving down Pall Mall on the way from lunch. He has had his first big fall coming back from a regimental lunch, when he hits his head on the garage floor and starts speaking backwards for a while. But he rallies – he has the most impressive will – and is soon back in the office and staying in his London flat for one night a week, hauling himself up the stairs, stopping for a breather on a plastic chair on the landing. We are sitting side by side in the taxi, comfortably silent, looking at a grey London afternoon passing by outside.

'Mummy says you and Martin have split up,' he says casually. Sudden tension.

'Yes,' is all I reply.

I don't really want to get into it. It's too late for all that. We turn the corner into St James's. My father is thoughtful for a few minutes, framed in the juddering taxi window, with all symbols of Empire falling away – St James's Palace, Berry Brothers, White's.

'Is there nothing you can do to fix it up?' he asks finally. We look at each other for a moment.

'Not really. No. I don't think there is.'

The rest of the ride goes by in silence. We get back to his flat, where I have to push him up the stairs, my hands on his bottom, and hold him up as he rummages for the keys.

The undertakers arrive. They are typical of their trade, grey and puffy-eyed, with long fingers to handle the dead. They are extremely nice.

'You might want to leave,' says the head man after the discussion is over and the time has come for Daddy to go. My mother takes the hint.

'No. I'm fine,' I reply.

They get their stretcher, disguised in a blanket, and put it on the floor by the bed. One of the undertakers takes Daddy's legs and another takes his shoulders and they expertly roll the body onto the stretcher. It flops over and for a moment the full import of death is upon me. Daddy's arm falls over his body. His face lurches to one side but it's done before it has begun. The men expertly zip him up inside and that is the last I ever see of Tony Everett.

People hate funerals. I know that I have turned that fatal corner in life – from the busy street into the churchyard, because, while I loathe weddings, I really enjoy a good passing, and the one I have enjoyed more than all the rest is my own father's. It's perfect funeral weather, bucketing down with rain. The church is packed. Colin Fox administers – even though my father was in fact a Catholic.

The world of the dead person comes together for one last sing-song, before losing itself in the crowd. Viewed from the pulpit, which I climb to read from the last volume of my autobiography – the bible according to *me* – I am tempted to sell copies in the nave because I see before me a captive audience. It's an amazing congregation of my parents' surviving friends and colleagues, of local people and my mother's family all in a row. My brother is here from Africa. He sits next to my mother in the front pew.

She is perfect once she's on stage. It is often a surprise to learn where the acting gene comes from. Hers is flawless. So is mine, although my role is easier. Hers is a great performance because inside she is falling apart. Nobody wants hysterics in this practical country world. There is no one left from my father's side of the family, and many of his acquaintance are already dead.

Nonetheless, marvellous old generals and colonels, stockbrokers and bankers with eyepatches and regimental ties, sunspots and liver spots – all the ravages of time, sun and drink – sit to attention with their mostly younger wives, pretty and resilient in the Victorian pews, as the rain pours down the windows. They are a breed verging on extinction, wartime soldiers and sailors who relinquished Sandhurst for Threadneedle Street in the sixties. The sexual revolution, the Beatles and the Stones had little influence on them. They conduct themselves according to a sexual constitution laid down during Empire. Pink tickets are the order of the day – affairs with other men's wives – to the tunes of Confrey Phillips' big band at hunt balls and Annabel's. They apply the rules of the parade ground to the Stock Exchange floor, considering insider dealing in the same light as other wartime necessities like torture. These ex-soldiers have nerves of steel in a crisis, a sang-froid their successors never learn.

'Bloody Americans,' my father always used to say. 'Panicking again.'

They are the colour of my early childhood, an extraordinary bubble in the landscape of time. They have survived magnificently in the asset-stripping world they helped to create (and then regretted), and they live in modest wealth – by today's engorged standards – in Georgian rectories and Tudor manors up and down the country. Age and experience have softened their hardline conservative edges. A lesbian daughter here, a heroin addict there, HIV in the eighties: they have learnt to adjust their views. They love dogs and gardens and holidays in India with bottles of whisky tucked into briefcases bought in Duty Free. And funerals.

They stand up now at the invitation of the organ. I wish I could say it grinds into a grandiose wall of sound and that the air throbs, but ours is an old tubercular wheezer, and so it impotently tweets the introduction, with wrong notes thrown in, but Daddy's friends make up for it. They have sung these words on parade grounds at Partition and ever since, at a hundred similar send-offs, and they stand to attention now and bellow fiercely at the coffin.

> Thine be the glory, risen conquering son,
> Endless is the victory thou o'er death hast won,

> Angels in bright raiment roll the stone away,
> Kept the folded grave clothes where thy body lay.

The service is over and the moment has come for the coffin to leave the church. It is a feeling similar to the school train leaving. This is it. The men from the funeral home – where I have gone last week to deliver Daddy's pyjamas, lovingly washed and ironed for the last time by his wife – pick up the coffin and carry it out of the church, followed by my mother, my brother and me. Two old soldiers clinking with medals hold regimental standards and we march out into the driving rain. The pallbearers hold the coffin suspended over the grave. The old soldiers stand to attention a little way off, soaked and bedraggled. They are going to catch pneumonia – so I take my umbrella over to where they are and cover them both.

'You had to be alone, even then,' reflects Connie sadly over the phone later that night.

My mother and brother stand by the grave with the vicar. The rain pours down his face, his hair is stuck on his cheeks and his bible is waterlogged. Connie and Hugh stand chanting on one side. The rain covers any tears. My heart thumps up my neck as they lower the coffin into the ground and that's that. A whole chunk of life – like the cliff of an iceberg – has just plunged into the depths. My mother's face is concentrated, my brother's blank. We leave the churchyard through the lych-gate, covered with the names of the dead in two wars, and go back to the house for the wake.

It is Christmas night 2010. For the first time since I can remember there is snow on the ground. It's a Christmas card with glitter.

'Deep and crisp and even' confirm the congregation at the midnight Mass. I am standing outside the church by my father's grave, smoking. The old stained-glass window behind the altar throws a strange spangled light on the snow, and the organ and the singing sound muffled – like a memory – through the thick flint walls of the church. A lopsided moon hangs over the spire and the stars burn fiercely in the void.

The hymn ends, replaced by the friendly voice of the vicar, Colin Fox, proclaiming the good news in that comfortable Anglican brogue – caring and slightly sung, simple and familiar to villagers up and down the British Isles who still worship tradition, if not God. In the silence after the song, the natural world goes about its business. The nearby river gurgles towards the bridge. A moorhen is woken with a splash and an indignant cry. The local barn owl hoots far away on the plain.

Inside the church the congregation begin to chant the Lord's Prayer.

My father is wearing his blue pyjamas and his old red slippers in the cold ground tonight. He has been dead for over a year.

CHAPTER TWENTY-NINE

Firefly

And so, dear reader – if you are still here – we clunk to the end of the road, straining up the last slope on the last rambling phrase, which is written in Jamaica where I am still wandering.

Today I am at Firefly Hill, the house where Noël Coward lived and died. Firefly is a living tomb, the perfect place to end a book largely about death. Uncannily, everything is more or less as the master left it. He collapsed in the bathroom early on the morning of 26 March 1973. Maybe he was looking for something inside the cupboard above the sink, his That Man talc for men, or his Collyre Alpha eyedrops. They are still there – little medicine bottles: Collyre Alpha and Mycil, ancient Q-tips and Coppertone in old tubes and jars, never moved from the rusty shelf since the day he died. The 'Room With A View' (written downstairs at the piano) is an open studio with a desk and two chairs inside a vast picture window that frames the entire north coast of Jamaica – stretching as far as the eye can see into the haze. Its jungles tip from the mountains into the azure, carved into huge bays under the constant pressure of the sea, which breaks endlessly in lace cuffs against the rocks and the

recoiling forest. You can see the roundness of the earth on the wide
verge between the sea and sky.

I am sitting at Noël's desk. He surrounds me in five faded photographs hanging lopsided on the wall. In one he must be no more
than eighteen, in a top hat and wing collar. It's the only picture of
him without a cigarette. They are masterful portraits. The twinkling
eyes, the no-nonsense regard, the accessible and yet stiff upper lip
curled towards some amusing observation, clipped and precise, like
the shutter of a camera, are brilliantly contrived. The snapshots
around the house, on the other hand, are less polished. Noël is
beached on a chaise longue, a fat tummy on piano legs, a face grown
over with oriental eyes, reaching out to the camera, unable to move.
They nicknamed him Chinese Nell in Jamaica.

The rich and famous are perched on the edges of the chairs in
which he is slumped. They all come from the same school – Liz
Taylor, Richard Burton, Charlie Chaplin – snapped, sloshed in straw
hats, smiling but anxious. Noël rallies at the sight of a lens but his
only real interest is the cigarette in his hand.

The house is approached by a steep winding lane that cuts sharply
off the old coast road, just before Port Mary. In Noël's day there
would have been a black-and-white striped signpost at the crossroads
but all that old order has gone. The lanes of Jamaica look very much
like the English countryside. On acid. The forest hangs over the
road, always encroaching. You can really feel plants living and
breathing in Jamaica, and the hedgerows crackle with life. Halfway
up the hill there has been a landslide and the lane has collapsed. A
nearby house has been snapped in half and is perched comically on
a cliff with one side hanging off.

Navigating the potholes of these terrible old roads is an art like
riding rapids. One must keep going. To hesitate is fatal. The road
passes through a small village, where young men and boys lounge
outside two makeshift bars, listening to reggae blasting from speakers
on the street. They shout 'White man' as I drive by. In a field carved
out of the forest other boys play makeshift cricket. The driveway to

Firefly snakes around the hill, overgrown with giant bamboos. They tower into arches over the drive, creaking in the wind, and the sun flickers through them. At the end of the drive – the light at the end of the tunnel – is a simple whitewashed house commanding one of the most breathtaking views in the world.

I am elated when I first discover Firefly. It happens to be – by chance – the anniversary of Noël's death, in March last year. When I get to the white marble slab and I read the date, my blood runs cold. I have just completed my season on Broadway in *Blithe Spirit* and it feels as if I am expected. I am thrilled to sit by his grave and gossip about Angela Lansbury learning the lines, Christine's Marilyn wig, and tell him how sorry I am for all my terrible behaviour while I was doing *The Vortex*, twenty-five years earlier in London.

Then – 1989 – his best friend Joyce Carey came to the show and told me that Noël had come into the auditorium during the second act. She held my hand and imparted what I presumed was Noël's message from beyond the grave. It wasn't a rave.

'You must speak up, dear,' she said with eyes wide with horror.

At the time I shrugged off the note, wondering only what could have happened to those big flapping ears of Noël's in heaven. Now years later – a writer of sorts myself – I cannot help but sympathise with him as I remember out loud doing half the play in French one night. How dismissive I was of him then in my proud madhouse. At least I gave my all in *Blithe Spirit*, though.

I am chatting away and the big black caretaker is watching me from the shadows of the giant rubber tree. He is laughing but I don't care. It feels extraordinary to be sitting there with the view, and Noël lying under the ground. I wonder what he is wearing.

I wander through the house, which smells of unopened cupboards. In the sitting room the framed pictures of Myrna Loy and Maggie Smith have faded in the sun. There are two baby grand pianos, spooning and browbeaten, unplayed for decades, hopelessly out of tune. Piles of dog-eared sheet music – every show tune imaginable – lie around an old Decca gramophone with a forty-five of 'Any Little Fish' on the turntable. In the master's studio his oil paints and brushes are still where he left them, an unfinished canvas on the easel. The paintings are everywhere, black boys walking up from the sea, a winter scene in England, a man in hot pants with a visible package. They aren't bad. But they aren't Gauguin. Old sofas and armchairs watch, blank and collapsed. The table downstairs is still laid for the famous lunch with the Queen Mother, who drove four hours from Kingston to see him. The table is laid for eternity.

But this year there seems to be a terrible sadness coming from this living tomb – surely the most unusual of all the tribute museums in the world to a dead star. The house is empty and silent, just the distant boom of the sea crashing against the reef far below. Sitting at his desk in the room with a view, I feel suddenly engulfed in a sort of locked-up misery.

I think Noël died of a broken heart. He moved into Firefly at the age of fifty in 1951, unaware that, apart from a new career in cabaret, his golden age had passed. A new era in theatre was dawning, and people found him hopelessly old-fashioned. He unwisely ranted about hippies and kitchen-sink drama in a string of articles for the *Sunday Times* in England in 1961. (He thought John Osborne a fake and was underwhelmed by the Beatles. I agree.) His war work was overlooked. After all, he spied for Britain and took enormous risks. Then, as the sexual revolution began to rage, he was torn down and scrapped like the Happy Prince. I don't think he ever recovered from the hurt and it still echoes through the house. He threw terrible tantrums, banished everyone, and melted his brain going over it all again and again in his head, puffing himself slowly to death. Knighthood came insultingly late, thanks apparently to the homophobia of the Duke of Edinburgh. Finally the wind blew the bitterness away and left an empty space. Noël Coward stopped talking.

Cole Lesley, his butler, and Graham Payne, his ex-lover (big cock, small talent), went up to see him on the evening before his death.

They were not invited to stay for dinner. In those days he ate alone. They left him at 8.30 and walked down the hill to Blue Harbour, Noël's other house, cackling in Polari, as the frogs beeped. Noël settled down on the plantation bed – still there – with a tray, to read a bit of E. Nesbit.

'Goodnight, my darlings,' he said, watching Cole and Graham disappear into the fragrant night. 'See you tomorrow.'

The old queen on the edge of the jungle turned out the light.

I have been writing here for a few days now. Occasionally the sound of a minibus grinding up the hill, nearer and nearer, breaks the silence. Minutes later six or seven fabulous hags from Broadway hobble over the brow of the hill. Sometimes upper-class couples from the UK make the pilgrimage. They are Noël Coward's last living fans – people who actually saw him in shows.

'Gee, look at Myrna Loy,' chants a Texan lady downstairs, while an English lord, face the colour of a blood orange, remembers how much his nanny loved Lilian Braithwaite.

One woman looks at me and gasps. 'Rupert? Is that *you?*'

'Yes,' I reply, still typing.

'Omygod! Geena, get over here! We saw your last performance in *Blithe Spirit.*'

More ladies appear. They all came to *Blithe Spirit*. It's a party. I am thrilled, moved and suddenly – inexplicably – Noël is absolutely there and the hairs on my arms stand up.

Night swoops in fast as the sun falls behind the mountains. I drive down through the hills behind the coast road, past small villages clustered on the edge of the jungle. The lazy smell of burning wood wraps itself around the evening breath of the forest and the day fades dramatically. People walk along the side of the road towards the car, suddenly lit by the headlights, expressionless and unreal, zombies almost. It is Saturday evening. Lights twinkle from all the tiny wooden churches of unheard-of denominations that are scattered along the winding road. They overflow with large women singing or listening to the shrieks of the loopy preachers predicting meltdown. The roadside bars – shacks, really – are the churches for men, silhouettes now in the glow of paraffin lamps and fairy lights. The music blares and the air is sweet with ganja. They stare as if one was the first arrival on the island.

'White man,' they shout.

Even a little baby, learning cricket between his father's legs in the middle of the road, converted into a family pitch, looks at me as I drive carefully past. 'White,' he whispers, smiling.

Fade to black. The End.

On the wall of Noël's studio, his last poem hangs, typed, framed and fading.

> When I have fears, as Keats had fears,
> Of the moment I'll cease to be,
> I console myself with vanished years,
> Remembered laughter, remembered tears,
> And the peace of the changing sea.